SPORTS IN AMERICA
RECREATION, BUSINESS, EDUCATION, AND CONTROVERSY

ISSN 1557-5535

SPORTS IN AMERICA
RECREATION, BUSINESS, EDUCATION, AND CONTROVERSY

Stephen Meyer

INFORMATION PLUS® REFERENCE SERIES
Formerly Published by Information Plus, Wylie, Texas

GALE
CENGAGE Learning®

Detroit • New York • San Francisco • New Haven, Conn • Waterville, Maine • London

796
Sports

Sports in America: Recreation, Business, Education, and Controversy

Stephen Meyer

Kepos Media, Inc.: Paula Kepos and Janice Jorgensen, Series Editors

Project Editors: Elizabeth Manar, Kathleen J. Edgar, Kimberley McGrath

Rights Acquisition and Management: Christine Myaskovsky, Kimberly Potvin, Edna M. Shy

Composition: Evi Abou-El-Seoud, Mary Beth Trimper

Manufacturing: Cynde Lentz

Gale
27500 Drake Rd.
Farmington Hills, MI 48331-3535

ISBN-13: 978-0-7876-5103-9 (set)
ISBN-13: 978-1-4144-8149-4

ISBN-10: 0-7876-5103-6 (set)
ISBN-10: 1-4144-8149-7

ISSN 1557-5535

This title is also available as an e-book.
ISBN-13: 978-1-4144-9632-0 (set)
ISBN-10: 1-4144-9632-X (set)
Contact your Gale sales representative for ordering information.

pub. 43.50 (58.00)

Printed in the United States of America
1 2 3 4 5 6 7 16 15 14 13 12

TABLE OF CONTENTS

CHAPTER 1

Why do people care so much about sports? This chapter defines sports and profiles the depth of Americans' passion for them. It summarizes sports participation, attendance, and viewership statistics. The chapter also briefly outlines the major team and individual sports in the United States, as well as the Olympics, and examines the relationship between these sports and the media. Finally, it touches on the connection between sports and health, as well as the sports gambling phenomenon.

CHAPTER 2

What sports do people like to play and what sports do they like to watch? Using data from a variety of sources, this chapter looks at the numbers for sports participation and attendance at sporting events, covering all the major team sports as well as newer and emerging sports, such as snowboarding. It also examines the money Americans spend on sports equipment, and which sports they spend it on.

CHAPTER 3

Given that business, sports, and the media are so intimately connected, it is sometimes difficult to determine where one ends and the other begins. This chapter delves into the financial relationship between big-time sports and television, from its roots during the early days of television to the present. It also reports on viewership numbers, advertising issues, and public image concerns.

CHAPTER 4

This chapter focuses on the major professional sports in the United States: baseball, football, basketball, and hockey, as well as soccer, which is on its way to joining the list. How did these sports rise to their current status, and where are they headed? The structure of the leagues and the often combative relationship between players and team owners are analyzed. The chapter also addresses the building of new stadiums and the controversy over using public funds to partially support these stadiums.

CHAPTER 5

Not every sports enthusiast is interested primarily in the major team sports. Many prefer, for example, the head-to-head competition of golf, tennis, auto racing, and/or boxing, which are all covered in this chapter. The chapter also discusses the leagues or structures to these sports and how they operate and how much money the top professionals compete for.

CHAPTER 6

The role of school sports is a delicate one. College and high school athletics are at once both an element of a well-rounded education and a training ground for hard-core professional competition. These dual roles often come into conflict. College sports have become big business, and as a result high schools have not escaped the influence of money. This chapter examines participation in school sports, the influence of money on the academic institutions that sponsor them, and other issues such as gender equity and the benefits of participation. The growing intensity of school sports has trickled down to youth sports as well; this chapter explores related issues, such as the risks of single-sport specialization by very young athletes.

CHAPTER 7

The Olympic Games are an idealistic attempt to bring the world together to celebrate friendly athletic competition. Even though the movement seems to have fallen short of this goal, the Olympics are wildly popular across the globe. This chapter reviews the history and business aspects of the Olympic Games, including both the Summer and Winter Olympics and the associated games for people with disabilities.

CHAPTER 8

It is no secret that physical activity is an important part of a healthy lifestyle. This chapter investigates some of the specific health benefits of sports participation, both physical and mental/behavioral. It also covers the risks that are involved in athletic pursuits, from physical ailments such as bruises and broken bones to the emotional trauma that affects children who are thrown into overly competitive environments.

CHAPTER 9

What are steroids? What are dietary supplements, and why are many of them banned in most sports? How are the governing bodies of sports fighting back? This chapter describes the variety of substances athletes use in the belief—often correct—that they will make them stronger and faster. It provides the history of performance-enhancing substances, from herbal concoctions used in the ancient Olympics through the more recent BALCO scandal and problems that have plagued Major League Baseball and professional cycling.

Americans like to bet on sports almost as much as they like to play them. Sports gambling is a huge business in the United States, and most of it is underground. From pari-mutuel betting on horse and greyhound races, to legal sports bookmaking in Nevada, to the office Super Bowl pool, to offshore Internet betting operations, this chapter surveys the scope of sports gambling in the United States. It also considers the problems sports gambling sometimes creates.

PREFACE

Sports in America: Recreation, Business, Education, and Controversy is part of the *Information Plus Reference Series*. The purpose of each volume of the series is to present the latest facts on a topic of pressing concern in modern American life. These topics include the most controversial and studied social issues of the 21st century: abortion, capital punishment, care of senior citizens, crime, education, the environment, health care, immigration, minorities, national security, social welfare, women, youth, and many more. Even though this series is written especially for high school and undergraduate students, it is an excellent resource for anyone in need of factual information on current affairs.

By presenting the facts, it is the intention of Gale, Cengage Learning to provide its readers with everything they need to reach an informed opinion on current issues. To that end, there is a particular emphasis in this series on the presentation of scientific studies, surveys, and statistics. These data are generally presented in the form of tables, charts, and other graphics placed within the text of each book. Every graphic is directly referred to and carefully explained in the text. The source of each graphic is presented within the graphic itself. The data used in these graphics are drawn from the most reputable and reliable sources, such as from the various branches of the U.S. government and from private organizations and associations. Every effort has been made to secure the most recent information available. Readers should bear in mind that many major studies take years to conduct and that additional years often pass before the data from these studies are made available to the public. Therefore, in many cases the most recent information available in 2012 is dated from 2009 or 2010. Older statistics are sometimes presented as well, if they are landmark studies or of particular interest and no more-recent information exists.

Even though statistics are a major focus of the *Information Plus Reference Series*, they are by no means its only content. Each book also presents the widely held positions and important ideas that shape how the book's subject is discussed in the United States. These positions are explained in detail and, where possible, in the words of their proponents. Some of the other material to be found in these books includes historical background, descriptions of major events related to the subject, relevant laws and court cases, and examples of how these issues play out in American life. Some books also feature primary documents or have pro and con debate sections that provide the words and opinions of prominent Americans on both sides of a controversial topic. All material is presented in an even-handed and unbiased manner; readers will never be encouraged to accept one view of an issue over another.

HOW TO USE THIS BOOK

Sports have an enormous presence in American life. Most Americans engage in sporting activities of one type or another and enjoy watching sports in person or on television. The American passion for sports has made it a major industry worth billions of dollars. It has also brought with it a host of problems. Illegal sports gambling is commonplace. Athletes at all levels have been caught using performance-enhancing drugs. Professional athletes and their teams squabble over their shares of the profits to the dismay of fans. The lure of money has also had a corrupting influence on major college sports and encouraged student athletes to quit school and turn professional at an increasingly young age. Meanwhile, less popular sports, including many women's sports, struggle for attention and funds.

Sports in America: Recreation, Business, Education, and Controversy consists of 10 chapters and three appendixes. Each chapter examines a particular aspect of sports and American society. For a summary of the information that is covered in each chapter, please see the synopses provided in the Table of Contents. Chapters generally begin with an overview of the basic facts and background information on the chapter's topic, then proceed to examine subtopics of particular interest. For example, Chapter 8: Sports and Health begins with an overview of the health benefits that are associated with physical activity. The chapter reviews government initiatives that are aimed at promoting exercise and fitness among Americans, while outlining a range of physical and psychological advantages to an active lifestyle. The chapter also explores the risks that are involved with sports and fitness participation by assessing diverse sports-related injuries and investigating their long-term impact on young athletes. An in-depth discussion of concussions follows, with a particular emphasis on the increasing awareness of the damaging effects of head injuries on professional football players. The chapter concludes with an analysis of recent youth physical fitness trends, along with an assessment of various sports and fitness programs. Readers can find their way through a chapter by looking for the section and subsection headings, which are clearly set off from the text. They can also refer to the book's extensive Index if they already know what they are looking for.

Statistical Information

The tables and figures featured throughout *Sports in America: Recreation, Business, Education, and Controversy* will be of particular use to readers in learning about this issue. These tables and figures represent an extensive collection of the most recent and important statistics on sports and their role in American society— for example, graphics cover adult attendance at sporting events, the percentage of people who gamble on sports, the number of Americans who participate in various sports, and the values and revenues of particular sports teams. Gale, Cengage Learning believes that making this information available to readers is the most important way to fulfill the goal of this book: to help readers understand the issues and controversies surrounding sports in the United States and to reach their own conclusions.

Each table or figure has a unique identifier appearing above it for ease of identification and reference. Titles for the tables and figures explain their purpose. At the end of each table or figure, the original source of the data is provided.

To help readers understand these often complicated statistics, all tables and figures are explained in the text. References in the text direct readers to the relevant statistics. Furthermore, the contents of all tables and figures are fully indexed. Please see the opening section of the Index at the back of this volume for a description of how to find tables and figures within it.

Appendixes

Besides the main body text and images, *Sports in America: Recreation, Business, Education, and Controversy* has three appendixes. The first is the Important Names and Addresses directory. Here, readers will find contact information for a number of government and private organizations that can provide further information on sports and related issues. The second appendix is the Resources section, which can also assist readers in conducting their own research. In this section the author and editors of *Sports in America: Recreation, Business, Education, and Controversy* describe some of the sources that were most useful during the compilation of this book. The final appendix is the detailed Index. It has been greatly expanded from previous editions and should make it even easier to find specific topics in this book.

ADVISORY BOARD CONTRIBUTIONS

The staff of Information Plus would like to extend its heartfelt appreciation to the Information Plus Advisory Board. This dedicated group of media professionals provides feedback on the series on an ongoing basis. Their comments allow the editorial staff who work on the project to make the series better and more user-friendly. The staff's top priority is to produce the highest-quality and most useful books possible, and the Information Plus Advisory Board's contributions to this process are invaluable.

The members of the Information Plus Advisory Board are:

- Kathleen R. Bonn, Librarian, Newbury Park High School, Newbury Park, California
- Madelyn Garner, Librarian, San Jacinto College, North Campus, Houston, Texas
- Anne Oxenrider, Media Specialist, Dundee High School, Dundee, Michigan
- Charles R. Rodgers, Director of Libraries, Pasco-Hernando Community College, Dade City, Florida
- James N. Zitzelsberger, Library Media Department Chairman, Oshkosh West High School, Oshkosh, Wisconsin

COMMENTS AND SUGGESTIONS

The editors of the *Information Plus Reference Series* welcome your feedback on *Sports in America: Recreation, Business, Education, and Controversy.* Please direct all correspondence to:

Editors
Information Plus Reference Series
27500 Drake Rd.
Farmington Hills, MI 48331-3535

CHAPTER 1

THE UNITED STATES' SPORTS OBSESSION

WHAT ARE SPORTS?

A sport is a physical activity that people engage in for recreation, usually according to a set of rules, and often in competition with each other. Such a simple definition, however, does not capture the passion many Americans feel for their favorite sports. Sports are the recreational activity of choice for a huge portion of the U.S. population, both as spectators and as participants in sporting competitions. When enthusiasts are not participating in sports, they are flocking to the nation's arenas and stadiums to watch their favorite athletes play, tuning in to see games and matches broadcast on television, listening to sports broadcasts on the radio, or following games and score updates on their computers, cell phones, and other electronic devices.

There are two broad categories of sports: professional and amateur. A professional athlete is paid to participate; an amateur athlete is one who participates without receiving compensation. The word *amateur* comes from the Latin word for "love," suggesting that an amateur athlete plays simply because he or she loves the game.

SPORTS PARTICIPATION

Sports participation is difficult to measure because there are many different levels of participation, from backyard games to organized leagues, but analysts continue to refine research methods. The most direct approach is through surveys. Each year the National Sporting Goods Association (NSGA), the trade association for sporting goods retailers, conducts an extensive nationwide survey about Americans' participation in sports. Key results of the survey are shown in Table 1.1. More Americans played basketball than any other team sport in 2010. The NSGA estimates that 26.9 million people aged seven years and older played basketball more than once that year. Other popular team sports included soccer (13.5 million participants), baseball (12.5 million), softball (10.8 million),

volleyball (10.6 million), and tackle football (9.3 million). Of the team sports featured in Table 1.1, basketball showed the most dramatic growth in participation from 2008, increasing by 10.1%. In contrast, softball saw the most dramatic decrease in participation, dropping by 8.4%.

Americans love to participate in individual sports as well. The NSGA estimates that 39 million Americans went bowling in 2010, making it the most popular of all competitive sports nationally. The Sporting Goods Manufacturers Association (SGMA), another industry group that carefully tracks sports participation, also identifies bowling as the most popular competitive sport and estimates the number of participants even higher, at about 55.9 million Americans in 2010, according to its *2011 SGMA Sports, Fitness, & Recreational Activities Topline Participation Report* (2011). According to SGMA estimates, this number represented an increase of 7.6% since 2000, when 51.9 million Americans went bowling at least once.

As Table 1.1 shows, the NSGA indicates that 21.9 million Americans over the age of seven years went golfing more than once in 2010. Tennis was also popular in 2010, with 12.3 million Americans getting out on the courts at least a few times. Figure 1.1 reveals shifts in sports participation trends between 2008 and 2010. Even though participation rates in individual and team sports dipped slightly during this span, a greater percentage of respondents were involved in fitness sports in 2010 compared to 2008. Racquet sports, outdoor sports, and water sports also experienced slight dips, whereas winter sports enjoyed a relatively substantial increase in participation between 2008 and 2010. Figure 1.2 offers a glimpse into various levels of athletic participation according to age group and type of activity.

Another way to gauge interest in sports is by examining how much money people spend on equipment. According to the NSGA, consumer spending on sporting goods rose slightly between 2009 and 2010, from just

TABLE 1.1

Sports participation, by total participation, 2010

[Participated more than once (in millions). Seven (7) years of age and older.]

Sport	Total	Percent change*
Exercise walking	95.8	2.6%
Exercising with equipment	55.3	−3.4%
Swimming	51.9	3.4%
Camping (vacation/overnight)	44.7	−12.0%
Bicycle riding	39.8	4.3%
Bowling	39.0	−13.3%
Aerobic exercising	38.5	16.3%
Hiking	37.7	10.9%
Workout at club	36.3	−5.3%
Running/jogging	35.5	10.3%
Fishing	33.8	2.8%
Weight lifting	31.5	−8.8%
Basketball	26.9	10.1%
Billiards/pool	24.0	14.8%
Golf	21.9	−2.0%
Yoga	20.2	28.1%
Boating, motor/power	20.0	−16.2%
Target shooting (net)	19.8	0.3%
Hunting with firearms	16.3	−13.5%
Soccer	13.5	−0.3%
Table tennis	12.8	−3.7%
Baseball	12.5	8.9%
Tennis	12.3	13.2%
Backpack/wilderness camp	11.1	−9.3%
Softball	10.8	−8.4%
Volleyball	10.6	−1.0%
Dart throwing	10.5	−14.1%
Football (tackle)	9.3	4.8%
Skateboarding	7.7	−8.5%
In-line roller skating	7.5	−5.4%
Scooter riding	7.4	−9.4%
Skiing (alpine)	7.4	5.6%
Mountain biking (off road)	7.2	−13.5%
Archery (target)	6.5	−8.3%
Paintball games	6.1	−2.7%
Snowboarding	6.1	−1.2%
Kayaking	5.6	14.8%
Target shooting—air gun	5.3	2.4%
Hunting w/bow & arrow	5.2	−16.7%
Water skiing	5.2	0.6%
Gymnastics	4.8	23.5%
Hockey (ice)	3.3	7.9%
Muzzleloading	3.1	−19.6%
Wrestling	2.9	−0.9%
Skiing (cross country)	2.0	19.5%

*Percent change is from 2008.

SOURCE: "2010 Participation—Ranked by Total Participation," in *Research: Sports Participation*, National Sporting Goods Association, 2011, http://www.nsga.org/files/public/2010_Participation_Ranked_by_Total_Participation_4Web_100521.pdf (accessed May 31, 2011)

over $24.4 billion to slightly under $24.6 billion. (See Table 1.2.) However, this figure still represented a noticeable drop from 2007, when Americans spent a total of $25.1 billion on sports equipment. Figure 1.3 also indicates an overall increase in consumer spending on sporting goods between 2009 and 2010.

SPORTS ATTENDANCE

Besides participation, another measure of interest in sports is the number of people who attend games in person. Sports attendance in the United States is dominated by the four major team sports: baseball, football, basketball, and hockey. In professional team sports, attendance is affected by two main factors: the size of the market in which the team plays and the team's current success. Big-city teams and winning teams typically draw bigger crowds than small-town teams and losing teams.

The overall state of the national economy can also take a toll on attendance at major league sporting events. For example, Aaron Gleeman reports in "MLB-Wide Attendance Declines for a Third Straight Season" (NBC Sports, October 4, 2010) that regular-season attendance for all 30 Major League Baseball (MLB) teams fell from a record 79.5 million in 2007 to 73.1 million in 2010, a decline of 8%. The National Basketball Association (NBA) also experienced a decline in attendance during the same period. In "Trouble Ahead? Looming Labor Battle Could Blunt NBA's Boom" (*USA Today*, May 31, 2011), Michael McCarthy reveals that the NBA's regular-season attendance figures fell 2% between the 2006–07 season, when a record 21.8 million fans attended NBA games, and the 2010–11 season, when attendance was 21.3 million. However, McCarthy notes that NBA attendance during the 2010–11 season actually rose 1%, compared to the 2009–10 season. According to ESPN, in "NFL Attendance—2010" (2011, http://espn.go.com/nfl/attendance/_/year/2010/sort/homeTotal), regular-season attendance at National Football League (NFL) games fell from a record 17.4 million in 2007 to 17 million in 2010, a drop of 2%. Of the four major American sports leagues, only the National Hockey League (NHL) saw a modest increase in attendance during this span. In "NHL Attendance Report—2010–11" (2011, http://espn.go.com/nhl/attendance), ESPN indicates that regular-season attendance for professional hockey games grew from 20.8 million during the 2006–07 season to 20.9 million during the 2010–11 season, an increase of 0.3%.

PROFESSIONAL SPORTS

Professional sports is a multibillion-dollar industry in the United States. Indeed, American athletes are among the highest-paid athletes in the world. As Table 1.3 shows, between 2010 and 2011 the three wealthiest athletes—Tiger Woods (1975–), Kobe Bryant (1978–), and LeBron James (1984–)—all came from the United States. Furthermore, five of the 10 richest sports figures in the world were American. In "The World's Highest Paid Athletes" (*Forbes*, May 31, 2011), Kurt Badenhausen reveals that athlete earnings include a wide range of income streams, including product endorsements, appearance fees, and licensing deals.

Team Sports

The four biggest professional sports leagues in North America are the MLB, the NFL, the NBA, and the NHL. Plunkett Research estimates in "Introduction to the Sports Industry" (2011, http://www.plunkettresearch.com/Sports%20recreation%20leisure%20market%20research/industry%

FIGURE 1.1

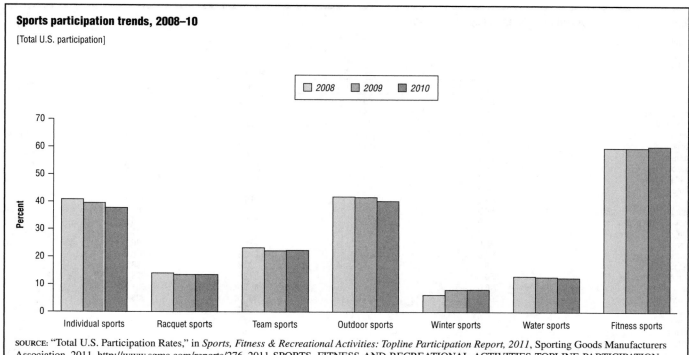

Sports participation trends, 2008–10

[Total U.S. participation]

SOURCE: "Total U.S. Participation Rates," in *Sports, Fitness & Recreational Activities: Topline Participation Report, 2011*, Sporting Goods Manufacturers Association, 2011, http://www.sgma.com/reports/276_2011-SPORTS,-FITNESS-AND-RECREATIONAL-ACTIVITIES-TOPLINE-PARTICIPATION-REPORT----NEW-RELEASE (accessed July 7, 2011)

FIGURE 1.2

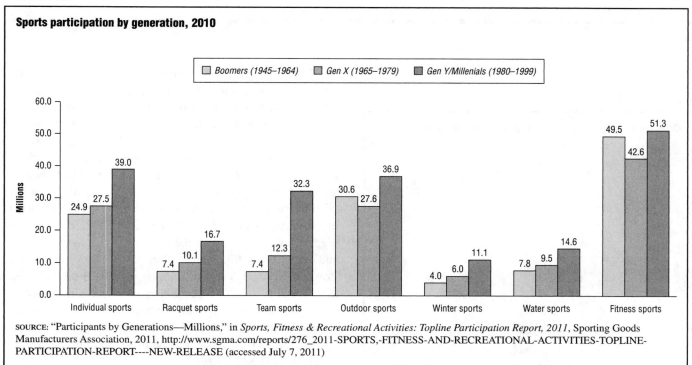

Sports participation by generation, 2010

SOURCE: "Participants by Generations—Millions," in *Sports, Fitness & Recreational Activities: Topline Participation Report, 2011*, Sporting Goods Manufacturers Association, 2011, http://www.sgma.com/reports/276_2011-SPORTS,-FITNESS-AND-RECREATIONAL-ACTIVITIES-TOPLINE-PARTICIPATION-REPORT----NEW-RELEASE (accessed July 7, 2011)

20overview) that in 2011 these four leagues combined were generating roughly $23 billion in annual revenues.

Baseball has long been considered "America's national pastime." According to the MLB, in "Standings" (2011, http://mlb.mlb.com/mlb/standings/index.jsp), the MLB consists of 30 teams that are divided into the 14-team American League and the 16-team National League. Each league is in turn divided into three divisions. The MLB season consists of 162 games, running roughly from early April through late September, followed by playoffs and the World Series.

TABLE 1.2

Consumer sports equipment purchases, by sport, 2006–10

[In millions of dollars]

			Forecast		
	2010	**2009**	**2008**	**2007**	**2006**
Archery	383.0	379.4	394.4	395.9	$396.2
Baseball & softball	378.0	374.1	395.8	401.4	388.3
Basketball	241.0	239.0	252.7	265.1	295.8
Billiards and indoor games	300.0	312.0	396.0	531.1	574.0
Bowling	155.0	154.9	170.3	176.2	181.5
Camping	1,526.0	1,496.4	1,460.7	1,452.6	1,526.3
Exercise	5,354.0	5,301.0	5,328.4	5,500.2	5,238.5
Fishing tackle	1,861.0	1,859.1	2,067.4	2,247.0	2,217.7
Football	86.0	85.4	91.5	95.9	97.0
Golf	2,864.0	2,835.8	3,495.4	3,721.5	3,668.6
Helmets, sport protective	156.0	153.3	171.1	165.0	142.0
Hockey & ice skates	173.0	169.2	157.2	146.2	142.2
Hunting and firearms	5,165.0	5,199.1	4,548.1	3,941.5	3,731.8
Lacrosse	33.0	32.2	31.9	30.7	32.5
Optics	1,091.0	1,069.7	1,023.8	1,018.8	1,013.9
Racquetball	28.0	28.1	30.8	33.6	38.4
Skin diving & scuba	350.0	342.8	372.6	376.4	369.0
Snow skiing	516.0	502.3	481.5	531.0	501.0
Snowboarding	294.0	291.2	301.3	325.0	314.0
Soccer balls	75.0	73.3	72.1	76.8	74.3
Tennis	364.0	368.0	386.5	439.7	417.9
Volleyball & badminton	33.0	32.9	32.6	31.8	30.8
Water skis	na*	40.0	48.8	53.1	47.4
Wheel sports	379.0	382.7	397.1	433.5	422.1
Athletic team goods sales	2,591.0	2,565.5	2,617.9	2,671.3	2,618.9
Total equipment	**$24,568.0**	**$24,421.0**	**$24,861.9**	**25,061.3**	**$24,497.0**

*Not available.

SOURCE: "Consumer Sports Equipment Purchases by Sport," in *Research: Consumer Purchases/Sporting Goods Market*, National Sporting Goods Association, 2011, http://www.nsga.org/files/public/ConsumerSportsEquipmentPurchasesbySport.pdf (accessed May 31, 2011)

FIGURE 1.3

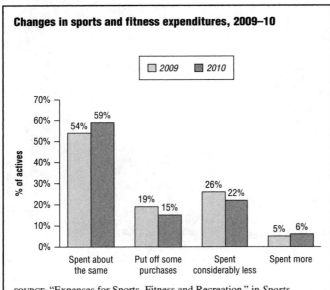

Changes in sports and fitness expenditures, 2009–10

SOURCE: "Expenses for Sports, Fitness and Recreation," in *Sports, Fitness & Recreational Activities: Topline Participation Report, 2011*, Sporting Goods Manufacturers Association, 2011, http://www.sgma .com/reports/276_2011-SPORTS,-FITNESS-AND-RECREATIONAL-ACTIVITIES-TOPLINE-PARTICIPATION-REPORT----NEW-RELEASE (accessed July 7, 2011)

The premier professional football league in the United States is the NFL. There are 32 teams in the NFL (2011, http://www.nfl.com/teams) that are divided into two conferences: the National Football Conference (NFC) and the American Football Conference (AFC). The NFC and the AFC are each divided into four divisions. NFL teams play a 16-game season, which begins around Labor Day in September. It ends with a single-elimination playoff series, culminating in the Super Bowl in late January or early February. The Super Bowl is the biggest sporting event in the country in terms of viewing audience. According to the Nielsen Company, in "Super Bowl XLV Most Viewed Telecast in U.S. Broadcast History" (February 7, 2011, http://blog.nielsen.com/nielsenwire/ media_entertainment/super-bowl-xlv-most-viewed-telecast-in-broadcast-history/), in 2011 over 111 million viewers watched Super Bowl XLV, making it the most-watched television program in U.S. history.

The NBA (2011, http://www.nba.com/home/teams/) consists of 30 teams that are split into the Eastern Conference and the Western Conference, each with three divisions. The NBA season begins in early November and lasts for 82 regular-season games. The regular season is followed by the NBA playoffs, which begin in April. Unlike football and

TABLE 1.3

Top-10 highest-paid athletes in the world, 2010–11

Athlete	Sport	2010–11 earnings*	Nationality
Tiger Woods	Golf	$75.0 million	United States
Kobe Bryant	Basketball	$53.0 million	United States
LeBron James	Basketball	$48.0 million	United States
Roger Federer	Tennis	$47.0 million	Switzerland
Phil Mickelson	Golf	$46.5 million	United States
David Beckham	Soccer	$40.0 million	United Kingdom
Cristiano Ronaldo	Soccer	$38.0 million	Portugal
Alex Rodriguez	Baseball	$35.0 million	United States
Michael Schumacher	Auto racing	$34.0 million	Germany
Lionel Messi	Soccer	$32.3 million	Argentina

*Through May 1, 2011. Earnings include salaries and bonuses, prize winnings, appearance and licensing fees, and endorsement revenues.

SOURCE: Adapted from Kurt Badenhausen, "The World's Highest Paid Athletes," *Forbes*, May 31, 2011, http://blogs.forbes.com/kurtbadenhausen/2011/05/31/the-worlds-highest-paid-athletes/ (accessed June 16, 2011)

baseball, basketball has a women's professional league, the Women's National Basketball Association (WNBA, http://www.wnba.com/). Financed by the NBA, the women's league consists of 12 teams, six in the Eastern Conference and six in the Western Conference. They play a 34-game regular season, after which the top-four teams in each conference compete in the championship playoffs. Unlike any of the major men's professional sports, however, the WNBA does not generate substantial revenues. Indeed, Michael Buteau reports in "WNBA Owners Make History, Not Profits" (*Bloomberg Businessweek*, September 16, 2010) that none of the WNBA teams turned a profit during the league's first 14 years of existence.

The top professional hockey league in North America, the NHL (2011, http://www.nhl.com/ice/teams.htm?nav-tms-main), consists of 30 teams that are divided into the Eastern Conference and the Western Conference. These conferences are in turn broken into three divisions. The NHL regular season, like that of the NBA, is 82 games long. It culminates with the Stanley Cup playoffs, which ultimately determine the NHL champion. The league's popularity suffered a blow when the entire 2004–05 season was canceled due to a labor strike, but the NHL steadily rebuilt its fan base in the ensuing half decade. In "Best-Ever Business Year Highlighted by Record Revenue" (April 13, 2011, http://www.nhl.com/ice/news.htm?id=559630), the NHL notes that it achieved record revenues of over $2.9 billion for the 2010–11 season.

Even though hockey remains the only league to have experienced a labor dispute that resulted in cancellation of an entire season, each of these sports is occasionally subject to disputes that threaten their continuity and that sometimes result in cancellation of part of a season. Labor disagreements in professional sports often pit the league, which represents the interests of the team owners, against the players, who are represented by a labor union.

In 2011 the NFL and the NBA saw long-standing collective bargaining agreements between owners and players expire. In the midst of the ensuing labor disputes, both leagues imposed lockouts, which prevented players from using team facilities and prohibited financial transactions such as trades and free agent signings. As of September 2011, the players and owners in the NFL had resolved their differences, whereas the NBA remained under intense negotiations. The NBA league season remained highly uncertain as of early September 2011.

Detailed information on professional team sports is provided in Chapter 4.

Individual Sports

Team sports get most of the media attention in the United States, but professional sports that feature individual competitors are also of considerable interest.

The premier golf tour in the United States and in the world is the PGA Tour (2011, http://www.pgatour.com/r/schedule/), which in 2011 consisted of 46 events offering roughly $300 million in total prize money. The PGA Tour organization also runs a developmental tour called the Nationwide Tour and a tour for senior players called the Champions Tour. There are several other prominent regional professional golf tours based in other countries. Women's professional golf has a similar structure. The most prominent women's tour is the LPGA Tour, which is operated by the Ladies Professional Golf Association. There are also several other regional women's tours around the world.

Men's professional tennis is coordinated primarily by two organizations: the International Tennis Federation (ITF), which coordinates the four international events that make up the Grand Slam of tennis (the Australian Open, the French Open, the Wimbledon Championships, and the U.S. Open), the Davis Cup competition, and Olympic tennis; and the Association of Tennis Professionals (ATP), which operates the worldwide ATP tour. The ATP World Tour is divided into three tiers: ATP World Tour Masters 1000, ATP World Tour 500, and ATP World Tour 250. The 2011 ATP World Tour (2011, http://www.atpworldtour.com/Tournaments/Event-Calendar.aspx) included 63 tournaments all over the world. Women's professional tennis is organized by the Women's Tennis Association (WTA), which runs the premier women's tour. In 2005 Sony Ericsson signed a six-year, $88 million agreement to become the official sponsor of the tour's worldwide title events; in 2010 this deal was extended an additional two years. According to the WTA, in "2011 WTA Tournament Calendar" (2011, http://www.wtatennis.com/page/Calendar/0,,12781,00.html), the 2011 WTA Tour included 57 events in 32 countries and paid more than $87 million in total prize money.

Auto racing enjoyed a huge surge in popularity in the United States beginning in the mid-1990s. The most important racing circuit for stock cars—which resemble ordinary cars externally—is the National Association for Stock Car Auto Racing (NASCAR). NASCAR (2011, http://www.nascar.com/) oversees three major racing series annually: the Sprint Cup Series, the Nationwide Series, and the Camping World Truck Series.

The other major type of race car is the open-wheeled racer. The main open-wheeled racing circuit in the United States is the Indy Racing League (IndyCar). The 2011 IndyCar Series (2011, http://www.indycar.com/) featured 17 races between March and October. Even though most IndyCar races take place in the United States, the league also sponsors events in Canada, Brazil, and Japan. A second prominent open-wheeled race series, the Champ Car Series, was merged into the Indy Racing League in 2008.

Boxing is unique among professional sports in that it has no single commission that regulates or monitors it nationwide. A number of organizations sanction professional boxing matches, including the International Boxing Federation (http://www.ibf-usba-boxing.com/), the World Boxing Association (http://www.wbaonline.com/), the World Boxing Council (http://www.wbcboxing.com/), and the World Boxing Organization (http://www.wbo-int.com/). Each follows its own set of regulations, employs its own officials, and acknowledges its own champions. A fighter can be recognized as a champion by more than one organization simultaneously. Professional boxing in the United States has been plagued by corruption over the years, including tainted judging and fixed fights. Nevertheless, devoted fans tune in regularly to watch boxing on pay cable networks, and gamblers wager millions on the outcomes of boxing contests, injecting huge sums of money into the industry.

SPORTS AND THE MEDIA

For American sports enthusiasts, it is hard to separate sports from the media industry that covers professional and elite amateur events. Leagues, teams, promoters, organizations, and schools make money through lucrative media contracts that give television networks and cable outlets the rights to broadcast sporting events. For a full discussion of the intersection of sports and media, see Chapter 3.

The History of Sports on Television

The history of sports on television began with the 1939 broadcast of a college baseball game between Columbia and Princeton Universities. Five years later the *Gillette Cavalcade of Sports* televised by the National Broadcasting Company (NBC) became the first network-wide television sports show. When single-company sponsorship became too expensive during the mid-1960s, sports programming developed a new model in which different companies bought advertising spots throughout the program.

Since then, the amount of sports programming and the amount of money in televised sports has continued to grow. According to the Museum of Broadcast Communications, in "Sports and Television" (2011, http://www.museum.tv/archives/etv/S/htmlS/sportsandte/sportsandte.htm), Stanley J. Baran states that in 1970 the networks paid $50 million for the rights to broadcast NFL games, $18 million for MLB games, and $2 million for NBA games. By 1985 these totals had grown to $450 million, $160 million, and $45 million, respectively. During the 1980s the addition of cable television outlets extended the reach of televised sports even further. However, television ratings for the four major team sports generally declined during the 1990s as competition for the same audience arose from other viewing options.

Major Sports on Television

During the 1950s baseball was the most popular televised sport. Since then, however, it has lost a large share of its audience to other sports, particularly football. Even though television ratings for World Series broadcasts declined for several years, they rebounded after 2002, but sank again after peaking in 2004. The article "World Series Ratings Tie All-Time Low" (Associated Press, November 2, 2010) indicates that the 2010 World Series between the Texas Rangers and the San Francisco Giants garnered an average rating of only 8.4 (meaning 8.4% of all households were tuned in), tying the record low that was established by the 2008 World Series between the Tampa Bay Rays and the Philadelphia Phillies. The MLB currently has television broadcast contracts lasting until 2013 with Fox, ESPN, and TBS.

Well before the close of the 20th century, football had supplanted baseball as the reigning king of televised sports. The Nielsen Company notes in "Super Bowl XLV Most Viewed Telecast in U.S. Broadcast History" that five of the six most-watched television programs of all time were Super Bowl games. The NFL signed a new round of television deals in April 2005, the most lucrative being a $1.1 billion contract resulting in the move of *Monday Night Football* from the American Broadcasting Company (ABC) to ESPN beginning in 2006. (See Table 1.4.) Annually, the NFL receives over $2.9 billion in additional revenues from NBC, Fox, CBS, and DirecTV Satellite for various subsets of the NFL schedule.

Regular-season NBA basketball has never drawn as big a viewing audience as the NFL has—probably because there are so many more games—but viewership expands significantly during the playoffs. Even though the NHL attracts fewer viewers than the other major sports, it saw a steady resurgence of popularity in the years following the 2004–05 strike. Robert Seidman notes in "2011 Stanley Cup Final Scores at Retail, Online and on TV" (June 20, 2011, http://tvbythenumbers.zap2it .com/2011/06/20/2011-stanley-cup-final-scores-at-retail-online-and-on-tv/96106/) that during the 2010–11 Stanley Cup Finals, 18.3 million North American viewers tuned in to watch the decisive game seven between the Boston Bruins and the Vancouver Canucks, a record for a single NHL contest. NASCAR also enjoyed a surge in its television audience during the early 21st century, including an increased female audience and broader viewership in the Pacific Northwest and other regions of the country that had not traditionally followed auto racing.

AMATEUR SPORTS
College Sports

Most college sports take place under the auspices of the National Collegiate Athletic Association (NCAA). The NCAA (2011, http://www.ncaa.org/wps/wcm/connect/ ncaa/NCAA/About+The+NCAA/index.html?pageDesign= Printer+Friendly+General+Content+Layout) describes itself as "a voluntary organization through which the nation's colleges and universities govern their athletics programs. It is comprised of institutions, conferences, organizations and individuals committed to the best interests, education and athletics participation of student-athletes."

In *Composition & Sport Sponsorship of the NCAA* (2011, http://www.ncaa.org/wps/portal/ncaahome?WCM _GLOBAL_CONTEXT=/ncaa/NCAA/About+The+NCAA/ Membership/membership_breakdown.html), the NCAA counts a membership of 1,315 colleges, college athletic conferences, and other organizations and individuals. The NCAA is divided into Divisions I, II, and III based on size, athletic budget, and related variables. Division I is further divided into three subdivisions: Division I Football Bowl Subdivision (FBS, formerly Division I-A), Division I Football Championship Subdivision (formerly Division I-AA), and the remaining Division I institutions that do not sponsor a football team (sometimes referred to informally as Division I-AAA). Within the NCAA many major sports colleges are grouped into conferences, which function like the divisions and leagues in professional sports.

According to Erin Zgonc of the NCAA, in *1981–82– 2009–10 NCAA Sports Sponsorship and Participation Rates Report* (November 2010, http://www.ncaapublications .com/productdownloads/PR2011.pdf), 430,301 student-athletes participated in championship sports at NCAA member schools during the 2009–10 school year. The average NCAA institution had about 406 athletes—232 men and 174 women. Women's teams, however, actually outnumbered men's teams. Among men, the sport with the greatest number of teams during the 2009–10 school year was basketball. However, in terms of number of players, football was the leader, with more than 66,000 participants. Among women, soccer and outdoor track and field had the most participants during the 2009–10 school year, but more colleges had women's basketball teams than had either women's soccer or track and field teams.

For most of the 20th century, men's college teams and athletes far outnumbered women's teams and athletes, and more money went into men's sports. However, the gap has been closing, largely because of the passage in 1972 of Title IX, a law mandating gender equality in federally funded education programs. Under Title IX, girls' sports

TABLE 1.4

Latest NFL TV contracts, by network or satellite provider

ESPN
Monday night
• 8 years, 2006–13
• $1.1 billion per year
• No Super Bowls

NBC
Sunday night
• Originally 2006–11, extended through 2013
• $603 million per year
• Super Bowls in 2009 and 2012

Fox
Sunday afternoon NFC
• Originally 2006–11, extended through 2013
• $720 million per year
• Super Bowls in 2008, 2011, and 2014

CBS
Sunday afternoon AFC
• Originally 2006–11, extended through 2013
• $620 million per year
• Super Bowls in 2010 and 2013

DirecTV Satellite
Sunday ticket
• Originally 2006–10, extended through 2014
• $1 billion per year
• No Super Bowls

NFL = National Football League. NFC = National Football Conference. AFC = American Football Conference.

SOURCE: Created by Stephen Meyer for Gale, 2011

are to be funded at the same rate as sports programs for boys. Since Title IX's mandatory compliance date of 1978, women's collegiate sports have experienced explosive growth.

Much to the discomfort of some in the academic world, college sports have become big business in the United States. Spending on sports programs has been rising at a faster rate than overall institutional spending across the NCAA. Even though college sports generate substantial revenue, this revenue does not cover the cost of running the entire athletic program at the vast majority of schools, largely because only a few sports—mostly football and men's basketball programs—are actually profitable. Daniel L. Fulks of the NCAA notes in *2004–10 Revenues and Expenses of NCAA Division I Intercollegiate Athletics Programs Report* (August 2011, http://www.ncaapublications.com/productdownloads/2010Rev Exp.pdf) that Division I-FBS athletic programs had median (average) total revenues of $35.3 million and expenses of $46.7 million in 2010. Football and basketball accounted for a huge share of both revenues and expenses. Coaches' salaries often account for a substantial portion of these expenses. According to the article "Salary Analysis of 2010 Football Bowl Subdivision Coaches" (*USA Today*, December 26, 2010), of the 120 head coaches of Division I-FBS football teams, 59 earned annual salaries in excess of $1 million in 2010.

High School Sports

The National Federation of State High School Associations (NFHS) conducts a detailed survey of high school sports participation each year. In *2009–10 High School Athletics Participation Survey* (2011, http://www.nfhs.org/WorkArea/linkit.aspx?LinkIdentifier=id&ItemID=4198), the NFHS indicates that 7.6 million students participated in high school sports during the 2009–10 school year. This total was a record high. Participation among boys was 4.5 million and among girls was 3.2 million. The top states by student-athlete participation during the 2009–10 school year were Texas (780,721), California (771,465), New York (379,677), Illinois (344,257), and Ohio (334,797).

For years, football has been the most popular high school sport for boys. According to the NFHS, 1.1 million boys played high school football during the 2009–10 school year. Outdoor track and field was the second-most popular sport for high school boys, with 572,123 participants, and basketball was third, with 540,207 participants. Among girls, outdoor track and field was the most popular sport, with 469,117 participants, followed by basketball (439,550) and volleyball (403,985).

BENEFITS TO STUDENT-ATHLETES. In "Equality in Sports Participation Benefits All, Says Expert" (April 17, 2008, http://www.america.gov/st/educ-english/2008/April/200804171153161CJsamohT0.6185572.html), Jeffrey

Thomas interviewed the sociologist Beckett Broh of Wittenberg University, who noted several benefits of sports participation among high school students. According to Broh, student-athletes perform well academically but also "benefit developmentally in terms of building self-confidence and self-esteem and the ability to problem-solve; they develop socially in that they build relationships with students and teachers and parents that can act as resources for them in terms of their academics." Broh's research indicated further advantages for girls. Female athletes were found to be less likely to get pregnant outside of marriage, more likely to graduate from college, and more likely to achieve a higher income in their professional life than girls who did not participate in school athletics.

IMPACT OF ECONOMIC RECESSION ON HIGH SCHOOL SPORTS. Even though the economic recession officially lasted from late 2007 to mid-2009, the nation was still struggling to recover in 2011. At the local level school districts nationwide were experiencing serious cuts in their state funding, which presented serious problems for many high school sports programs. To deal with severe budget shortfalls, many school districts implemented "pay to play" programs, which require students to pay additional fees to participate in competitive sports. For example, Scott Hayes reports in "Schools in Financial Burdens Ask Athletes to Pay Up" (*Dayton [OH] Daily News*, July 2, 2011) that before the 2011–12 school year, the city of Lebanon, Ohio, raised its high school athletics fee to $250 per sport, an increase of 614% over the previous year's fee of $35 per sport. Steve Poitinger, the Lebanon track coach, was concerned that this high fee might discourage many new students from participating in athletics. "Your stars, the kids who are always getting their names in the paper, they'll still play," Poitinger said. "But the kids who I approach in October to see if they'd be interested in giving track and field a try? That's going to be a harder sell at $250 than it was at $35."

The Olympics

The concept behind the Olympic movement is to bring the world together through sports in the spirit of common understanding and noble competition. The Olympic Games are based on an athletic festival that took place in ancient Greece from about 776 BC until AD 393. The Olympics were revived in their modern form in 1896. The Summer Olympics take place every four years. According to the International Olympic Committee (IOC; 2011, http://www.olympic.org/london-2012-summer-olympics), roughly 10,500 athletes are expected to compete in 26 sports at the 2012 summer games in London, England. Organizers estimate that the London games will attract approximately 180,000 spectators per day.

The Winter Olympics also take place every four years, halfway between the summer games. The winter games are smaller than the summer games. The IOC (2011, http://www.olympic.org/vancouver-2010-winter-olympics) notes that the 2010 Winter Olympics in Vancouver, Canada, featured 2,566 athletes from 82 countries and attracted 3 billion television viewers from around the world.

The founder of the modern Olympics was the French historian and educator Pierre de Coubertin (1862–1937). Coubertin believed that war could be averted if nations participated together in friendly athletic competition. His ideas have not proved true, but the Olympic movement has thrived regardless. The inaugural Olympic Games of the modern era took place in 1896 in Athens, Greece, where 241 athletes from 14 countries competed in what was the largest international sporting event in history at the time.

The winter games arose initially as an outgrowth of the summer games. A handful of winter sports were included in early versions of the Olympics. The Winter Olympics finally became its own event in 1924. Until 1992 the winter games took place the same year as the summer games; beginning in 1994 they have been held in the years halfway between the Summer Olympics.

Politics have frequently disrupted, or even canceled, the Olympics. The 1916 games were canceled because of World War I (1914–1918), and World War II (1939–1945) caused the cancellation of the 1940 and 1944 Olympics. Boycotts have also diminished the scope of the games. In 1972 the militant Palestinian group Black September abducted and murdered 11 members of the Israeli Olympic team during the summer games in Munich, West Germany. The U.S. team, along with 64 other Western nations, boycotted the 1980 Olympics in Moscow in protest of the Soviet invasion of Afghanistan. In 1984 the Soviet Union and 14 of its allies boycotted the Olympics in Los Angeles, California, ostensibly because of security concerns but more realistically as a response to the Moscow boycott. Scandals related to doping (such as the BALCO affair described in detail in Chapter 9) and bribery (including the implication of the organizing committee for the 2002 winter games in Salt Lake City, Utah) have also marred the idealistic image of international cooperation and amateur athleticism on which the Olympics were founded.

The IOC is the worldwide governing body for the Olympics. Each participating country has its own national Olympic committee (NOC), whose role is to support that nation's Olympic team and to coordinate bids by cities within the country to host the Olympics. The U.S. Olympic Committee, headquartered in Colorado Springs, Colorado, is the NOC in the United States.

Individual sports are governed worldwide by international federations, which make the rules for the events within their portfolio. On the national level, there are corresponding organizations called national governing bodies (NGBs). Some of the NGBs in the United States include USA Gymnastics, USA Swimming, and USA Track and Field. These organizations are in charge of choosing which athletes will represent the United States in that sport. In the host country the Olympic Games are planned by an organizing committee for the Olympic Games, which takes care of the logistical preparations for the Olympics.

The Olympics generates billions of dollars through a handful of marketing programs. The biggest source of money is television broadcast revenue. Other sources include corporate sponsorships, ticket sales, and sales of licensed merchandise. Chapter 7 contains detailed information about Olympic revenue. It also includes descriptions of other Olympic-style meets, such as the Special Olympics, Paralympics, and Deaflympics.

SPORTS AND HEALTH

Participation in sports yields great health benefits. Many health benefits of physical activity have been well documented. Physical activity builds and maintains bones and muscles, reduces fat, reduces blood pressure, and decreases the risk of obesity and heart attacks. There is also substantial evidence that physical activity improves mental health and may help fend off depression. A number of studies, including a massive 2001 survey conducted by researchers at the University of Florida (http://news.ufl.edu/2001/03/07/body-image/), link sports participation with a better self-image and a healthier attitude toward one's own body.

A number of studies over the years have shown that sports participation by youth reduces the likelihood of engaging in risky behavior. For example, Genevra Pittman indicates in "Young Athletes Use Fewer Drugs, but More Alcohol" (Reuters, May 30, 2011) that, according to data compiled by the National Institute on Drug Abuse, teens who competed in athletics were less likely to smoke cigarettes or use marijuana than teens who did not participate in sports. According to Pittman, between 25% and 29% of teen athletes surveyed had smoked cigarettes in the past month, and between 15% and 17% had smoked marijuana. By comparison, 38% of teens who did not exercise had smoked cigarettes and 23% had smoked marijuana. At the same time, however, teen athletes were more likely to drink alcohol than nonathletes, by a margin of 57% to 45%. Pittman reports that researchers traced this rise in alcohol use among athletes to a number of factors, including peer pressure exacerbated by a team environment and the pervasiveness of advertising for alcoholic beverages during sports media broadcasts.

There are other risks that are associated with sports. Children who are placed under severe pressure to succeed by parents, coaches, and other adults are at risk of psychological damage. The stress of ultracompetitive sports participation leads to high rates of burnout among young athletes. Pressure to perform also puts children and youth at elevated risk of physical injury, as demands are put on young bodies not yet developed enough to withstand the strain. In "Sports and Recreational Safety" (February 2011, http://www.safekids.org/), Safe Kids USA evaluates the relationship between sports and injuries in children. Citing data from the National Institutes of Health, Safe Kids USA reports that 38 million children aged 14 years and younger participate in athletics each year. Of these, 3.5 million seek treatment for sports-related injuries. Furthermore, roughly 60% of sports-related injuries occur during practices. Excessive training at an early age can also exert a long-term negative impact on a young athlete's physical health. The American Academy of Pediatrics reports in "Overuse Syndromes" (June 8, 2011, http://www.healthychildren.org/English/health-issues/injuries-emergencies/sports-injuries/pages/Overuse-Syndromes.aspx) that continued overworking of certain areas of the body can lead to bursitis, tendonitis, and other chronic problems.

Chapter 8 explores both the health benefits and health risks of athletic participation.

Doping

The use of prohibited substances to give an athlete an unfair advantage over other competitors is called doping. Doping has been around almost as long as sports have. Historical writings suggest that athletes were using concoctions made of herbs or psychoactive mushrooms to give themselves a competitive edge as early as the ancient Olympics.

The modern era of doping began in 1935, when injectable testosterone was first developed by scientists in Nazi Germany. Testosterone is a male hormone that occurs naturally in the body. Boosting its levels in the blood is thought to increase strength and aggressiveness.

Several decades later anabolic steroids (chemical variants of testosterone) were developed. John Benjamin Ziegler (1917–2000), the team physician for the U.S. weightlifting squad, learned about steroids from his Soviet counterparts, and soon steroids were in wide use in the United States. By the late 1960s the IOC had compiled a list of officially banned substances, but it had no effective way to monitor steroid use.

Steroids soon spread to professional football and other sports requiring extreme strength and bulk. Professional and Olympic sports eventually developed into a kind of cat-and-mouse game between developers of performance-enhancing drugs and the governing bodies of sports that prohibited their use. The latter would invent a way to detect the latest drugs, only to discover that the former had invented a new method for avoiding detection. The issue of doping in elite athletics still remains.

One of the biggest doping scandals to date, the BALCO scandal, has been unfolding since 2003. BALCO, the Bay Area Laboratory Co-Operative, was a California-based drug distributor. The scandal erupted during the summer of 2003, when Trevor Graham (1962?–), a disgruntled track coach, provided authorities with a syringe containing a previously unknown steroid called THG. Authorities raided BALCO facilities and uncovered not only large amounts of steroids but also documents implicating a number of high-profile athletes and trainers in football, baseball, and track and field. The scandal continued to follow the baseball superstar Barry Bonds (1964–) during the 2007 season as he approached the all-time home-run record long held by Hank Aaron (1934–). Fan reaction to the prospect of Bonds holding the record was decidedly mixed, as suspicion lingered that Bonds had made his way toward this landmark with the aid of illicit substances. Even though Bonds repeatedly denied using steroids, he was eventually accused of lying to a grand jury and put on trial for perjury. In "Barry Bonds Convicted of Obstructing Justice" (Reuters, April 13, 2011), Laird Harrison reports that in April 2011 a jury convicted Bonds on one charge of obstruction of justice; however, the jury remained deadlocked on the perjury accusations. By the summer of 2011 another former baseball great, Roger Clemens (1962–), faced similar charges concerning his own alleged steroid abuse.

Professional cycling has also been hit hard by steroid scandals. Floyd Landis (1975–), a 2006 Tour de France champion, tested positive for steroids, raising questions about the legitimacy of his victory. Then, just when the Tour needed to display its cleanliness the most, several more top Tour contenders failed drug tests in 2007, throwing the sport into chaos. In September 2007 Landis was stripped of his 2006 Tour title. Three years later, in 2010, Landis publicly admitted that he had used a host of steroids during his career, including human growth hormone, testosterone, and erythropoietin. Bonnie D. Ford notes in "Landis Admits Doping, Accuses Lance" (ESPN, May 21, 2010) that Landis also revealed the names of numerous other cyclists who had supposedly used performance-enhancing drugs, notable among them Lance Armstrong (1971–). In "The Case against Lance Armstrong" (*Sports Illustrated*, January 24, 2011), Selena Roberts and David Epstein reveal that as of 2011 Armstrong was under investigation for his alleged involvement in an extensive blood-doping network. Roberts and Epstein cite evidence that Armstrong had tested positive for abnormally high steroid levels on three occasions during the mid-1990s.

Even in the post-BALCO era, baseball continued to reel from revelations of steroid use among its top players.

Alex Rodriguez (1975–) of the New York Yankees admitted in 2009 to having used steroids in 2003 after reports of positive drug tests surfaced. In addition, the Los Angeles Dodgers superstar Manny Ramirez (1972–) served a 50-game suspension in 2009 after violating the MLB's drug policy. In April 2011, after testing positive again as a new member of the Tampa Bay Rays, Ramirez abruptly retired from baseball rather than serve a mandatory 100-game suspension.

Steroid use has been linked to many potentially serious health problems, including liver and kidney tumors, high blood pressure, elevated cholesterol, severe acne, and in men, shrunken testicles. In 2009 the professional wrestler Edward Fatu (1973–2009) died of a heart attack at the age of 36. Soraya Roberts reports in "Former WWE Wrestler Edward 'Umaga' Fatu Dies of Heart Attack" (*New York Daily News*, December 5, 2009) that Fatu had been caught purchasing a number of banned drugs from an online pharmacy, including the growth hormone somatropin, as recently as 2007. Steroid use is also associated with emotional disturbances, including violent mood swings commonly known as "'roid rage." In 2007, when the professional wrestler Chris Benoit (1967–2007) killed his wife and son before committing suicide, a toxicology report revealed that he had 10 times the normal amount of testosterone in his system. Speculation ran rampant that 'roid rage was to blame. However, the medical examiner determined that there was no indication that steroids played a role.

Besides steroids, athletes turned to a number of other substances to gain an advantage before each was banned from sports. These include erythropoietin, a hormone that increases oxygen in the blood, which was at the center of a 1998 doping scandal in cycling; androstenedione, which stimulates testosterone production and was made famous by the home-run leader Mark McGwire (1963–); and ephedra, an herbal stimulant that has been used in Chinese medicine for centuries.

Chapter 9 includes more detailed information on the variety of anabolic steroids and other performance-enhancing substances that have been used over the years.

SPORTS AND GAMBLING

For millions of sports fans, the pleasure of watching a sporting event is enhanced by betting on its outcome. Even though gambling on sports (not including horse- and greyhound racing) is technically legal only in Nevada, Americans nevertheless find ways to engage in sports wagering in huge numbers, whether through small-scale office pools or via offshore Internet gambling sites of questionable legality.

Legal Sports Betting

In Nevada legal sports betting is practiced through legitimate bookmaking operations, which are often affiliated with and located in a casino. Bookmakers set the line (margin) of victory that is required to win the bet for each game. Football is the biggest betting draw among the major team sports, followed by basketball and baseball. Gambling on horse racing, dog racing, and jai alai (a handball-like sport that is popular in Florida) uses what is called the pari-mutuel system. In this type of betting, all the wagers go into a single pool, which is then split among the winners, with management taking a small share off the top.

Illegal Sports Betting

Even though both Nevada sports books and pari-mutuel gambling are lucrative industries, revenues from legal sports gambling represent just the tip of the sports betting iceberg. Legal gambling in the United States is utterly dwarfed by illegal gambling. The American Gaming Association estimates in the fact sheet "Sports Wagering" (2011, http://www.americangaming.org/industry-resources/research/fact-sheets/sports-wagering) that Nevada sports books account for less than 1% of all sports gambling nationwide in a typical year. Of the estimated $380 billion spent on sports betting in 2010, only $2.8 billion was wagered legally in Nevada.

The newest frontier for sports gambling is the Internet. Even after passage of the Unlawful Internet Gambling Enforcement Act (UIGEA) in 2006, online betting remains a billion-dollar business in the United States. In *Online Gambling Five Years after UIGEA* (May 2011, http://www.americangaming.org/files/aga/uploads/docs/whitepapers/final_online_gambling_white_paper_5-18-11.pdf), David O. Stewart reports that, in spite of legal prohibitions, Americans are still spending roughly $4 billion on illegal Internet gambling every year. By comparison, legal online gambling generates approximately $30 billion per year worldwide.

CHAPTER 2
SPORTS PARTICIPATION AND ATTENDANCE

For when the One Great Scorer comes
To write against your name,
He marks—not that you won or lost—
But how you played the game.

—American sportswriter Grantland Rice, "Alumnus Football,"
Only the Brave, and Other Poems (1941)

People have been playing games in one form or another ever since the first time a pair of humans decided to start grappling for fun rather than for food. The number and variety of sports in which people have participated through the ages is impossible to calculate. In North America, Native Americans were playing lacrosse and many other organized sports before Europeans settled permanently on the continent. In addition, one need only think of gladiators doing battle at the Colosseum in ancient Rome to realize that people have been gathering to watch other people play sports for centuries as well. The following is a summary of sports participation and sports attendance in the United States, drawing information from government and industry publications.

SPORTS PARTICIPATION

There is no shortage of data available on sports participation in the United States. Participation is measured by market research firms, coordinating bodies of individual sports, and government agencies, among others. Table 2.1 offers some insight into sports participation levels among various age groups and household incomes.

Sports participation is nevertheless a difficult thing to measure, and nobody has yet figured out how to measure it with complete accuracy. People who go for a casual walk or swim at the beach may not think of themselves as engaging in a sport, but those interested in selling walking shoes or studying the health benefits of physical activity might disagree.

There is also the matter of defining the word *participation*—does it mean a person plays the sport once per year, once per month, or only those who play almost every day? Besides determining who qualifies as a sports participant, the reliability of self-reported data presents additional problems. For example, can an individual accurately report that he played touch football with his friends 12 months ago rather than 15 months ago? Distortion is inevitable, especially with regard to recreational activities that participants tend to engage in less frequently, such as scuba diving. Furthermore, there is a tendency when responding to this kind of survey to want to receive credit for having participated in a sport, especially a glamorous one such as rock climbing, even if the respondent has not undertaken the activity in several years.

Sporting Goods Manufacturers Association Survey

Each year, the Sporting Goods Manufacturers Association (SGMA) publishes reports on various aspects of sports participation in the United States based on extensive survey data. The SGMA's annual *Sports, Fitness, & Recreational Activities: Topline Participation Report, 2011* (2011) outlines major trends in every category of sports participation. The 2011 *Topline Participation Report* contains data from 38,742 online surveys that were conducted between January and February 2011.

TEAM SPORTS. Table 2.2 shows the total number of people participating by sport in select years between 2000 and 2010. Throughout this period basketball was consistently the most popular team sport. Approximately 26.3 million Americans aged six years and older reported that they played basketball at least once in 2010, compared to the 24 million people who reported playing basketball in 2009, an increase of 9.6%. Football (22 million, including tackle, touch, and flag), baseball (14.6 million), and outdoor soccer (14.1 million) were the other team sports with the most participants in 2010.

TABLE 2.1

Participation in selected sports activities, by sex, age group, and income level, 2008

[In thousands (267,586,000), except rank]

Activity	All persons Number	Sex Male	Sex Female	Age 7–11 years	Age 12–17 years	Age 18–24 years	Age 25–34 years	Age 35–44 years	Age 45–54 years	Age 55–64 years	Age 65 and over	Household income Under 15,000	15,000–24,999	25,000–34,999	35,000–49,999	50,000–74,999	75,000–99,999	100,000 and over
Series I sports																		
Total	267,586	130,281	137,304	19,439	25,116	29,348	37,808	40,807	43,821	32,985	38,261	25,974	25,236	27,414	35,463	57,246	38,092	58,162
Number participated in—																		
Aerobic exercising[a]	36,177	10,519	25,657	1,458	2,324	4,330	8,814	6,727	6,439	3,230	2,854	2,030	2,792	2,872	3,875	7,904	5,691	11,014
Backpacking[b]	12,968	7,383	5,585	1,248	2,272	1,859	2,836	2,047	1,875	556	276	1,037	906	1,107	2,291	2,645	2,553	2,430
Baseball	15,166	12,338	2,828	4,004	3,264	2,045	2,208	1,487	992	647	519	1,245	990	882	2,142	3,747	2,358	3,802
Basketball	29,696	20,578	9,118	5,262	8,026	4,629	4,801	3,360	2,307	923	389	2,722	1,554	2,376	4,216	7,075	4,393	7,360
Bicycle riding[a]	44,707	25,294	19,413	8,976	9,076	3,794	5,366	6,858	5,870	3,006	1,761	2,830	2,689	2,908	4,837	10,978	7,068	13,396
Billiards/pool	31,680	19,655	12,025	1,563	2,752	5,478	8,483	5,950	4,609	1,882	964	2,547	2,514	3,536	3,700	6,815	4,305	8,263
Bowling	49,522	24,691	24,831	6,482	7,706	7,995	9,602	8,400	5,413	2,166	1,758	3,457	2,747	4,575	6,238	11,099	8,600	12,806
Camping[c]	49,359	25,897	23,463	5,979	6,758	5,742	8,766	7,945	8,195	3,591	2,384	3,410	3,173	4,088	7,160	12,364	9,829	9,336
Exercise walking[a]	96,613	37,337	59277	3,839	5,826	8,948	14,958	16,433	19,539	13,622	13,448	8,136	8,520	8,579	12,353	21,453	13,824	23,750
Exercising with equipment[b]	62,982	29,688	33,295	1,246	4,364	8,812	12,830	11,549	10,818	6,802	6,561	3,314	4,166	5,567	7,418	13,856	9,898	18,763
Fishing (net)	42,161	28,440	13,722	4,126	4,659	4,396	7,304	7,564	7,054	4,193	2,865	3,480	3,514	4,627	6,472	9,936	6,399	7,733
Fishing—fresh water	37,798	25,347	12,452	3,847	4,452	4,156	6,783	6,756	5,984	3,523	2,297	3,325	3,022	4,376	5,989	8,893	5,637	6,556
Fishing—salt water	9,357	7,197	2,160	517	660	687	1,466	1,972	1,751	1,298	1,005	345	755	576	1,094	2,237	1,827	2,520
Football—tackle	10,477	9,391	1,086	1,939	3,569	2,047	1,372	617	378	228	328	1,133	623	909	1,401	2,760	1,611	2,040
Golf	25,620	19,927	5,692	1,379	1,468	2,420	5,104	4,708	4,621	3,240	2,679	514	968	2,077	2,418	5,280	4,788	9,575
Hiking	38,027	19,098	18,927	3,089	3,736	3,668	8,362	6,584	6,846	3,673	2,067	3,000	2,252	3,372	5,067	8,456	5,929	9,949
Running/jogging[a]	35,904	18,670	17,233	2,834	6,062	6,508	8,784	5,625	4,146	1,459	485	1,992	1,682	3,057	4,824	7,496	5,979	10,874
Soccer	15,492	9,015	6,477	5,050	4,234	1,701	2,271	1,161	787	201	86	1,420	632	1,103	2,022	3,245	2,392	4,677
Softball	12,843	6,613	6,230	1,805	2,442	1,869	3,065	1,763	1,077	649	172	1,334	572	1,311	1,630	2,914	1,942	3,139
Swimming[a]	63,507	30,152	33,354	10,010	10,522	6,769	9,956	9,426	8,527	4,496	3,799	3,685	3,899	4,449	7,983	15,079	9,993	18,419
Tennis	12,646	6,290	6,356	1,349	2,193	2,053	2,307	1,928	1,540	816	459	425	432	508	1,288	2,893	2,405	4,695
Volleyball	12,155	5,052	7,103	1,453	3,682	1,766	1,897	1,525	1,247	399	186	539	488	995	1,886	2,411	2,318	3,517
Weightlifting	37,504	24,015	13,488	370	4,191	6,240	9,848	6,973	5,842	2,574	1,465	1,515	2,470	3,243	4,631	7,896	6,345	11,403
Yoga	16,018	3,145	12,873	452	953	2,844	4,128	2,956	2,386	1,238	1,062	1,329	1,208	1,315	1,655	3,527	2,088	4,895
Series II sports																		
Total	267,586	130,281	137,304	19,439	25,116	29,348	37,808	40,807	43,821	32,985	38,261	26,489	23,657	26,916	38,998	57,859	35,525	58,141
Number participated in—																		
Boating-motor/power	27,816	15,401	12,415	2,360	3,318	3,349	5,060	4,001	4,797	2,688	2,243	913	1,486	1,570	3,663	6,432	4,355	9,397
Canoeing	10,344	5,843	4,501	1,066	1,257	1,635	1,885	1,768	1,524	731	479	268	361	887	1,447	2,608	1,707	3,065
Cheerleading	2,910	238	2,673	1,209	926	383	90	87	69	86	59	221	257	351	448	545	383	704
Hockey (Ice)	1,911	1,396	515	207	391	337	322	315	214	39	87	97	136	43	247	253	442	694
Hunting with bow and arrow	6,173	5,542	631	341	446	740	1,033	1,631	1,127	479	376	278	395	766	1,152	1,195	969	1,418
Hunting with firearms	18,755	15,874	2,880	711	1,999	2,802	2,924	3,606	3,517	1,934	1,263	791	1,488	2,116	3,762	3,786	2,757	4,055
In-line roller skating	9,306	3,983	5,323	2,871	2,147	1,206	1,338	900	532	117	196	534	637	411	1,366	2,392	1,520	2,445
Mountain biking-off road	10,174	6,727	3,447	1,114	1,458	1,065	2,635	1,869	1,378	411	244	343	473	776	1,617	2,931	1,121	2,912
Muzzle loading	3,403	3,163	240	—	225	538	448	809	699	439	245	153	351	520	667	616	473	623
Paintball games	6,706	5,384	1,322	469	1,883	2,012	1,192	669	297	86	97	318	468	289	1,485	1,632	950	1,565
Scooter riding	10,130	5,707	4,423	4,470	2,523	819	659	611	501	302	244	769	319	546	1,186	2,850	1,414	3,045
Skateboarding	9,771	6,989	2,782	3,577	3,630	1,186	662	391	179	26	120	831	564	593	1,671	2,382	1,127	2,603
Skiing—alpine	6,514	4,059	2,455	850	1,177	1,019	1,006	1,069	1,048	161	184	200	13	300	547	1,149	1,060	3,245
Skiing—cross country	1,578	757	821	85	90	125	210	348	278	231	211	36	102	109	252	391	174	514
Snowboarding	5,854	4,210	1,645	1,166	1,559	1,321	985	463	162	54	144	323	243	42	807	2,010	310	2,120

TABLE 2.1

Participation in selected sports activities, by sex, age group, and income level, 2008 [CONTINUED]

[In thousands (267,586 represents 2 67,586,000), except rank]

Activity	All persons Number	Sex Male	Female	Age 7-11 years	12-17 years	18-24 years	25-34 years	35-44 years	45-54 years	55-64 years	65 and over	Household income (dollars) Under 15,000	15,000-24,999	25,000-34,999	35,000-49,999	50,000-74,999	75,000-99,999	100,000 and over
Target shooting	20,268	15,456	4,811	365	2,050	3,354	4,847	2,976	3,662	1,833	1,180	907	1,534	1,942	3,392	4,851	2,460	5,180
Target shooting-airgun	4,955	3,919	1,036	715	1,091	515	844	640	628	215	308	367	269	665	1,165	1,035	308	1,146
Water skiing	5,592	3,099	2,494	454	969	933	1,260	844	718	244	169	149	184	189	436	1,290	1,153	2,192
Work-out at club	39,349	17,767	21,581	433	2,477	6,824	9,107	6,914	6,278	3,624	3,693	1,118	1,679	2,454	4,218	10,301	6,291	13,288

aParticipant engaged in activity at least six times in the year.
bIncludes wilderness camping.
cVacation/overnight.

source: "Table 1248. Participation in Selected Sports Activities: 2008," in *Statistical Abstract of the United States: 2011*, 130th ed., U.S. Census Bureau, 2010, http://www.census.gov/compendia/statab/2011/tables/11s 1248.xls (accessed June 2, 2011). Data from National Sporting Goods Association, Mt. Prospect, IL, Sports Participation in 2008: Series 1 and Series II.

TABLE 2.2

Team sports participation, selected years 2000–10

Team sports (total participation)	Definition	2000	2007	2008	2009	2010	1 year change	10 year change
Baseball	1+ times	15,848	16,058	15,020	13,837	14,558	5.2%	−8.1%
Basketball	1+ times	26,215	25,961	26,254	24,007	26,304	9.6%	0.3%
Cheerleading	1+ times	2,634	3,279	3,104	3,036	3,232	6.5%	22.7%
Field hockey	1+ times		1,127	1,118	1,066	1,298	21.8%	
Football (flag)	1+ times			7,310	6,553	6,767	3.3%	
Football (touch)	1+ times			10,493	8,959	8,367	−6.6%	
Football (tackle)	1+ times	8,229	7,939	7,692	6,794	6,905	1.6%	−16.1%
Gymnastics	1+ times	4,876	4,066	3,883	4,021	4,815	19.7%	−1.2%
Ice hockey	1+ times	2,432	1,840	1,902	2,134	2,145	0.5%	−11.8%
Lacrosse	1+ times	518	1,058	1,127	1,197	1,648	37.7%	218.1%
Paintball	1+ times	3,615	5,476	4,857	4,552	3,655	−19.7%	1.1%
Roller hockey	1+ times	3,888	1,681	1,456	1,397	1,350	−3.4%	−65.3%
Rugby	1+ times		617	690	750	1,130	50.7%	
Soccer (indoor)	1+ times		4,237	4,737	4,913	4,927	0.3%	
Soccer (outdoor)	1+ times		13,708	14,223	13,691	14,075	2.8%	
Softball (fast pitch)	1+ times	2,693	2,345	2,316	2,636	2,389	−9.4%	−11.3%
Softball (slow pitch)	1+ times	13,577	9,485	9,835	8,525	8,429	−1.1%	−37.9%
Track and field	1+ times		4,691	4,516	4,443	4,322	−2.7%	
Ultimate Frisbee	1+ times		4,038	4,879	4,392	4,749	8.1%	
Volleyball (beach)	1+ times	5,248	3,878	4,171	4,476	5,028	12.3%	−4.2%
Volleyball (court)	1+ times		6,986	8,190	7,283	7,346	0.9%	
Volleyball (grass)	1+ times		4,940	5,086	4,853	4,574	−5.7%	
Wrestling	1+ times	3,743	3,313	3,358	2,982	2,089	−29.9%	−44.2%

Note: All participation figures are in 000s for the U.S. population ages 6 and over.

SOURCE: Adapted from "Team Sports," in *Sports, Fitness & Recreational Activities: Topline Participation Report, 2011*, Sporting Goods Manufacturers Association, 2011, http://www.sgma.com/reports/276_2011-SPORTS,-FITNESS-AND-RECREATIONAL-ACTIVITIES-TOPLINE-PARTICIPATION-REPORT----NEW-RELEASE (accessed July 7, 2011).

Although still among the most popular sports when measured by participation, baseball (−8.1%) and tackle football (−16.1%) have experienced declining participation since 2000. (See Table 2.2.) Other sports that have experienced decreasing participation include gymnastics (−1.2%), beach volleyball (−4.2%), and wrestling (−44.2%). More than 2.1 million people played ice hockey in 2010, yet that figure is 11.8% lower than the 2.4 million who played in 2000.

Sports that grew significantly during this 10-year period include lacrosse (218.1%) and cheerleading (22.7%). (See Table 2.2.) Lacrosse is still played by relatively few people compared to the sports mentioned earlier, but it has been increasing in popularity. Its 1.6 million participants in 2010 were more than triple the 518,000 who played in 2000.

INDIVIDUAL AND RACQUET SPORTS. Table 2.3 and Table 2.4 show data on participation in individual sports. Bowling, pool (cue sports), golf, and tennis remain quite popular pastimes among the American public. According to the SGMA, 55.9 million Americans bowled in 2010—a 7.6% increase since 2000—making it the most popular of all competitive sports in the United States. Bowling has been undergoing a transformation in the form that participation takes. In the past a large percentage of bowlers played on a team that was affiliated with a bowling league. The SGMA estimates that during the 1980s approximately two-thirds of all bowling was done by league bowlers; since the turn of the 21st century about one-third of all bowling takes place under the auspices of a league. The decline in the number of league bowlers has been compensated for by the addition of a large number of young, individual bowlers. However, these bowlers are less serious about the sport than league players. Only 22% of bowlers in 2010 were "core" bowlers, meaning they bowled at least 13 times during the year. As a result of this shift, sales of bowling equipment have stagnated in spite of strong numbers of people who can be counted as participants.

The U.S. Bowling Congress notes that another challenge facing bowling is that the number of places to bowl has been decreasing for several years. This trend is partly the result of consolidation, as older, smaller bowling centers are replaced by larger, state-of-the-art facilities, many of which feature upscale decor and good food service, in contrast to the stereotypical grimy, beer-splashed dens of the mid-20th century. Newer bowling centers usually offer modern, automated scoring, as well as better in-house balls and shoes. Some are mega-centers that offer other activities as well, including golf driving ranges, skating, or even basketball. Efforts to lure a younger crowd to bowling alleys also include special events such as "Rock 'n' Bowl" or "Cosmic Bowling," which features glow-in-the-dark pins and discotheque or ultraviolet lighting.

Proprietors of billiards halls are also attempting to shed the game's rough image in an effort to attract to the sport new players who may have previously been put off

TABLE 2.3

Individual sports participation, selected years 2000–10

Individual sports (total participation)	Definition	2000	2007	2008	2009	2010	1 year change	10 year change
Adventure racing	1+ times		698	920	1,089	1,339	23.0%	
Archery	1+ times	6,285	5,950	6,409	6,326	6,319	−0.1%	0.5%
Billiards/pool	1+ times	46,336	51,089	49,018	43,005	39,385	−8.4%	−15.0%
Bowling	1+ times	51,938	60,184	58,650	57,293	55,877	−2.5%	7.6%
Boxing for fitness*	1+ times					4,788		
Boxing for competition*	1+ times					855		
Darts	1+ times		24,709	23,451	20,022	18,118	−9.5%	
Golf (9/18 hole course)	1+ times	28,844	29,528	28,571	27,103	26,122	−3.6%	−9.4%
Horseback riding	1+ times		12,098	10,816	9,755	9,809	0.6%	
Ice skating	1+ times	11,835	11,430	10,999	10,929	12,024	10.0%	1.6%
Martial arts*	1+ times	6,161	6,865	6,770	6,516	5,488	−15.8%	−10.9%
Mixed martial arts for competition	1+ times					910		
Mixed martial arts for fitness	1+ times					1,745		
Roller skating (2×2 wheels)	1+ times	7,746	8,921	7,855	8,147	8,126	−0.3%	4.9%
Roller skating (inline wheels)	1+ times	21,912	10,814	9,608	8,276	7,980	−3.6%	−63.6%
Scooter riding (non-motorized)	1+ times	9,968	6,782	6,394	5,064	4,861	−4.0%	−51.2%
Skateboarding	1+ times	9,859	8,429	7,807	7,352	6,808	−7.4%	−30.9%
Trail running	1+ times	4,167	4,216	4,857	4,833	5,136	6.3%	23.3%
Triathlon (non-traditional/off road)	1+ times		483	602	666	929	39.5%	
Triathlon (traditional/road)	1+ times		798	1,087	1,208	1,978	63.7%	

Note: All participation figures are in 000s for the U.S. population ages 6 and over.

*Martial arts category was split into 3 to now cover martial arts, martial arts for fitness, and martial arts for competition so this will have impacted the total numbers for the pure martial arts category.

SOURCE: Adapted from "Individual Sports," in *Sports, Fitness & Recreational Activities: Topline Participation Report, 2011*, Sporting Goods Manufacturers Association, 2011, http://www.sgma.com/reports/276_2011-SPORTS,-FITNESS-AND-RECREATIONAL-ACTIVITIES-TOPLINE-PARTICIPATION-REPORT----NEW-RELEASE (accessed July 7, 2011)

TABLE 2.4

Racquet sports participation, selected years 2000–10

Racquet sports (total participation)	Definition	2000	2007	2008	2009	2010	1 year change	10 year change
Badminton	1+ times	8,769	7,057	7,239	7,699	7,590	−1.4%	−13.4%
Cardio tennis	1+ times			830	1,177	1,503	27.7%	
Racquetball	1+ times	4,475	4,229	4,993	4,575	4,630	1.2%	3.5%
Squash	1+ times		612	706	885	1,177	33.0%	
Table tennis	1+ times	12,712	15,955	17,201	19,301	19,446	0.8%	53.0%
Tennis	1+ times	12,974	16,940	18,558	18,534	18,903	2.0%	45.7%

Note: All participation figures are in 000s for the U.S. population ages 6 and over.

SOURCE: Adapted from "Racquet Sports," in *Sports, Fitness & Recreational Activities: Topline Participation Report, 2011*, Sporting Goods Manufacturers Association, 2011, http://www.sgma.com/reports/276_2011-SPORTS,-FITNESS-AND-RECREATIONAL-ACTIVITIES-TOPLINE-PARTICIPATION-REPORT----NEW-RELEASE (accessed July 7, 2011)

by pool's unsavory reputation. According to the SGMA, 39.4 million people shot pool or billiards, collectively called cue sports, in 2010, down 8.4% from the previous year, and down 15% from 2000. (See Table 2.3.) Pool halls were once frequented primarily by older men, but in the 21st century pool is becoming a sport played increasingly by women and young people. Since the 1980s many facilities have upgraded their traditional low-budget style, and most no longer resemble the no-nonsense rooms immortalized in movies such as *The Hustler* (1961). New and refurbished billiards rooms, similar to contemporary bowling centers, are well lit, clean, and frequently part of multiactivity facilities that offer many recreation options.

Table 2.3 shows that golf enjoys widespread popularity, with 26.1 million Americans reporting that they had shot nine or 18 holes of golf at least once in 2010. Tennis has been enjoying an upswing in popularity in recent years, according to SGMA data. In 2000 nearly 13 million tennis enthusiasts hoisted a racket. By 2010 the total had grown by 45.7% to 18.9 million. (See Table 2.4.) One factor in the resurgence of tennis is a conscious effort to democratize the sport. Once played primarily by the wealthy at country clubs, tennis is now available to people at all socioeconomic levels. The U.S. Tennis Association (USTA; 2011, http://www.usta.com/) has helped this trend along by investing heavily in programs that are aimed at growing the sport, including a $50-million initiative launched in 1997 called the USA Tennis Plan for Growth, which offered free lessons around the country. The USTA also has a Diversity Plan aimed at encouraging multicultural participation in a sport that has long been dominated by white players, coaches, and officials. Gains in minority participation have received a boost from the success and popularity of African-American stars such as Serena Williams (1981–), Venus Williams (1980–), and James Blake (1979–). As shown in Table 2.4, in 2010 other widely played racquet sports included table tennis (19.4 million participants), badminton (7.6 million), and racquetball (4.6 million).

Outdoor and Water Sports

Millions of Americans who refrain from competitive sports—individual or team—enjoy engaging in outdoor sports and water sports. Over 39.3 million people bicycled on roads or other paved surfaces in 2010 and 7.2 million went mountain biking. (See Table 2.5.) Fishing is another immensely popular outdoor sport. A combined total of 56.1 million people went fishing in 2010, when the totals for fly, freshwater, and saltwater fishing are combined.

Many water sports have declined significantly in popularity since 2000, according to the SGMA in its 2011 *Topline Participation Report*. Table 2.6 shows that waterskiing, scuba diving, windsurfing, and jet skiing all experienced significant decreases in participation between 2000 and 2010. In contrast, participation in surfing grew by 26.3% during this period. Snorkeling and canoeing

were the top water sports in 2010, with 9.3 million and 10.6 million participants, respectively.

The SGMA reveals in *Topline Participation Report* that a number of strength and conditioning exercise programs became increasingly popular between 2000 and 2010. One activity that saw enormous growth during this span was Pilates training. In 2000 approximately 1.6 million Americans participated in Pilates; by 2010 this number had exploded to 8.2 million, an increase of 424.2%. (See Table 2.7.) Between 2000 and 2010 more and more Americans also participated in a variety of strength training activities, using hand weights, dumbbells, free weights, and weight/resistance machines. (See Table 2.8.)

National Sporting Goods Association Survey

The National Sporting Goods Association (NSGA) also conducts a broad nationwide survey on sports participation. The following are a few highlights from the 2010 NSGA survey.

Table 1.1 in Chapter 1 ranks sports and other physical activities by total participation and provides a useful snapshot of what Americans choose to do when they want to move their bodies, as reported by the NSGA in 2010. Table 2.9 provides a sport-by-sport glance at trends in participation for select years between 2000 and 2010. According to the NSGA, basketball and soccer participation remained relatively stable during this period, while aerobic exercising and hiking enjoyed sizable growth.

TABLE 2.5

Outdoor sports participation, selected years 2000–10

Outdoor sports (total participation)	Definition	2000	2007	2008	2009	2010	1 year change	10 year change
Backpacking overnight—more than 1/4 mile from vehicle/home	1+ times		6,637	7,867	7,647	8,349	9.2%	
Bicycling—BMX*	1+ times	3,213	1,887	1,904	1,811	2,369	30.8%	−26.3%
Bicycling (mountain/non-paved surface)	1+ times		6,892	7,592	7,142	7,161	0.3%	
Bicycling (road/paved surface)	1+ times		38,940	38,114	40,140	39,320	−2.0%	
Birdwatching more than 1/4 mile from home/vehicle	1+ times		13,476	14,399	13,294	13,339	0.3%	
Camping (recreational vehicle)	1+ times	17,893	16,168	16,517	17,436	15,865	−9.0%	−11.3%
Camping within 1/4 mile of vehicle/home	1+ times		31,375	33,686	34,338	30,996	−9.7%	
Climbing (sport/indoor/boulder)	1+ times		4,514	4,769	4,313	4,770	10.6%	
Climbing (traditional/ice/mountaineering)	1+ times		2,062	2,288	1,835	2,198	19.8%	
Fishing (fly)	1+ times	6,717	5,756	5,941	5,568	5,478	−1.6%	−18.4%
Fishing (freshwater—other)	1+ times	43,696	43,859	40,331	40,961	38,860	−5.1%	−11.1%
Fishing (saltwater)	1+ times	14,739	14,437	13,804	12,303	11,809	−4.0%	−19.9%
Hiking (day)	1+ times	30,051	29,965	32,511	32,572	32,496	−0.2%	8.1%
Hunting (bow)	1+ times	4,633	3,818	3,722	4,226	3,908	−7.5%	−15.6%
Hunting (handgun)	1+ times		2,595	2,873	2,276	2,709	19.0%	
Hunting (rifle)	1+ times		10,635	10,344	11,114	10,150	−8.7%	
Hunting (shotgun)	1+ times		8,545	8,731	8,490	8,062	−5.0%	
Shooting (sport clays)	1+ times	4,437	4,115	4,282	4,182	4,399	5.2%	−0.9%
Shooting (trap/skeet)	1+ times	3,416	3,376	3,669	3,368	3,610	7.2%	5.7%
Target shooting (handgun)	1+ times		11,736	13,365	12,473	12,497	0.2%	
Target shooting (rifle)	1+ times	10,022	12,436	13,102	12,730	12,544	−1.5%	25.2%
Wildlife viewing more than 1/4 mile from home/vehicle	1+ times		22,974	24,113	21,291	21,025	−1.2%	

*BMX-Bicycle motorcross
Note: All participation figures are in 000s for the US population ages 6 and over.

SOURCE: Adapted from "Outdoor Sports," in *Sports, Fitness & Recreational Activities: Topline Participation Report, 2011*, Sporting Goods Manufacturers Association, 2011, http://www.sgma.com/reports/276_2011-SPORTS,-FITNESS-AND-RECREATIONAL-ACTIVITIES-TOPLINE-PARTICIPATION-REPORT----NEW-RELEASE (accessed July 7, 2011)

TABLE 2.6

Water sports participation, selected years 2000–10

Water sports (total participation)	Definition	2000	2007	2008	2009	2010	1 year change	10 year change
Boardsailing/windsurfing	1+ times	1,739	1,118	1,307	1,128	1,617	43.4%	−7.0%
Canoeing	1+ times	10,880	9,797	9,935	10,058	10,553	4.9%	−3.0%
Jet skiing	1+ times	9,475	8,055	7,815	7,724	7,753	0.4%	−18.2%
Kayaking (recreational)	1+ times		5,070	6,240	6,212	6,465	4.1%	
Kayaking (sea/touring)	1+ times		1,485	1,780	1,771	2,144	21.1%	
Kayaking (white water)	1+ times		1,207	1,242	1,369	1,842	34.6%	
Rafting	1+ times	5,259	4,340	4,651	4,318	4,460	3.3%	−15.2%
Sailing	1+ times	4,405	3,786	4,226	4,342	3,869	−10.9%	−12.2%
Scuba diving	1+ times	4,305	2,965	3,216	2,723	3,153	15.8%	−26.8%
Snorkeling	1+ times	10,302	9,294	10,296	9,358	9,305	−0.6%	−9.7%
Stand-up paddling	1+ times					1,050		
Surfing	1+ times	2,191	2,206	2,607	2,403	2,767	15.1%	26.3%
Wakeboarding	1+ times	4,558	3,521	3,544	3,577	3,645	1.9%	−20.0%
Water skiing	1+ times	8,765	5,918	5,593	4,862	4,836	−0.5%	−44.8%

Note: All participation figures are in 000s for the U.S. population ages 6 and over.

SOURCE: Adapted from "Water Sports," in *Sports, Fitness & Recreational Activities: Topline Participation Report, 2011*, Sporting Goods Manufacturers Association, 2011, http://www.sgma.com/reports/276_2011-SPORTS,-FITNESS-AND-RECREATIONAL-ACTIVITIES-TOPLINE-PARTICIPATION-REPORT----NEW-RELEASE (accessed July 7, 2011)

TABLE 2.7

Conditioning activities participation, selected years 2000–10

Conditioning activities (total participation)	Definition	2000	2007	2008	2009	2010	1 year change	10 year change
Abdominal machine/device	1+ times	21,354	20,426	19,917	19,465	18,491	−5.0%	−13.4%
Calisthenics	1+ times	7,758	8,629	9,147	9,106	9,088	−0.2%	17.1%
Pilates training	1+ times	1,556	9,192	8,886	8,653	8,154	−5.8%	424.2%
Rowing machine	1+ times	9,407	8,782	9,021	9,174	9,763	6.4%	3.8%
Stretching	1+ times	24,613	36,181	36,288	36,310	35,129	−3.3%	42.7%
Tai Chi	1+ times			3,424	3,205	3,180	−0.8%	
Yoga	1+ times			17,758	20,109	21,886	8.8%	

Note: All participation figures are in 000s for the U.S. population ages 6 and over.

SOURCE: Adapted from "Conditioning Activities," in *Sports, Fitness & Recreational Activities: Topline Participation Report, 2011*, Sporting Goods Manufacturers Association, 2011, http://www.sgma.com/reports/276_2011-SPORTS,-FITNESS-AND-RECREATIONAL-ACTIVITIES-TOPLINE-PARTICIPATION-REPORT----NEW-RELEASE (accessed July 7, 2011)

TABLE 2.8

Strength activities participation, selected years 2000–10

Strength activities (total participation)	Definition	2000	2007	2008	2009	2010	1 year change	10 year change
Free weights (barbells)	1+ times	24,800	25,499	26,142	27,048	27,339	1.1%	10.2%
Free weights (dumbells)	1+ times	27,470	32,371	34,391	35,744	37,388	4.6%	36.1%
Free weights (hand weights)	1+ times	33,784	43,821	42,997	45,934	45,922	0.0%	35.9%
Home gym exercise	1+ times	20,626	25,823	24,514	24,762	24,581	0.7%	19.2%
Weight/resistance machines	1+ times	32,144	39,290	38,397	39,752	38,618	2.9%	20.1%

Note: All participation figures are in 000s for the U.S. population ages 6 and over.

SOURCE: Adapted from "Strength Activities," in *Sports, Fitness & Recreational Activities: Topline Participation Report, 2011*, Sporting Goods Manufacturers Association, 2011, http://www.sgma.com/reports/276_2011-SPORTS,-FITNESS-AND-RECREATIONAL-ACTIVITIES-TOPLINE-PARTICIPATION-REPORT----NEW-RELEASE (accessed July 7, 2011)

YOUTH SPORTS. According to the NSGA, youth participation in many team sports is on the decline. (See Table 2.10.) Youth baseball participation shrank by 15.7% between 2001 and 2010. Softball participation shrank by 18% during this period. Even soccer, which is generally perceived as an emerging sport, saw participation among

TABLE 2.9

Ten-year history of selected sports participation, selected years 2000–10

[Participated more than once (in millions). Seven (7) years of age and older.]

	2010	2008	2006	2004	2002	2000
Aerobic exercising	38.5	36.2	33.7	29.5	29.0	28.6
Backpack/wilderness camp	11.1	13.0	13.3	15.3	14.8	15.4
Baseball	12.5	15.2	14.6	15.9	15.6	15.6
Basketball	26.9	29.7	26.7	27.8	28.9	27.1
Bicycle riding	39.8	44.7	35.6	40.3	39.7	43.1
Billiards/pool	24.0	31.7	31.8	34.2	33.1	32.5
Boating, motor/power	20.0	27.8	29.3	22.8	26.6	24.2
Bowling	39.0	49.5	44.8	43.8	42.4	43.1
Camping (vacation/overnight)	44.7	49.4	48.6	55.3	55.4	49.9
Canoeing	na	10.3	7.1	7.5	7.6	6.2
Cheerleading	na	2.9	3.8	3.8	na	na
Exercise walking	95.8	96.6	87.5	84.7	82.2	86.3
Exercising with equipment	55.3	63.0	52.4	52.2	46.8	44.8
Fishing	33.8	42.2	40.6	41.2	44.2	49.3
Football (tackle)	9.3	10.5	11.9	8.6	7.8	7.5
Golf	21.9	25.6	24.4	24.5	27.1	26.4
Hiking	37.7	38.0	31.0	28.3	27.2	24.3
Hockey (ice)	3.3	1.9	2.6	2.4	2.1	1.9
Hunting w/bow & arrow	5.2	6.2	5.9	5.8	4.6	4.7
Hunting with firearms	16.3	18.8	17.8	17.7	19.5	19.1
In-line roller skating	7.4	9.3	10.5	11.7	18.8	21.8
Mountain biking (off road)	7.2	10.2	8.5	8.0	7.8	7.1
Muzzleloading	3.1	3.4	3.7	3.8	3.6	2.9
Paintball games	6.1	6.7	8.0	9.4	6.9	5.3
Racquetball	na	na	4.0	na	na	3.2
Running/jogging	35.5	35.9	28.8	26.7	24.7	22.8
Scooter riding	7.4	10.1	9.5	12.9	13.4	11.6
Skateboarding	7.7	9.8	9.7	10.3	9.7	9.1
Skiing (alpine)	7.4	6.5	6.4	6.3	7.4	7.4
Skiing (cross country)	2.0	1.6	2.6	2.4	2.2	2.3
Snowboarding	6.1	5.9	5.2	6.6	5.6	4.3
Soccer	13.5	15.5	14.0	13.3	13.7	12.9
Softball	10.8	12.8	12.4	12.5	13.6	14.0
Swimming	51.9	63.5	56.5	53.4	53.1	60.7
Target shooting	19.8	20.3	17.1	19.2	18.9	14.8
Target shooting—airgun	5.3	5.0	5.6	5.1	4.1	3.0
Tennis	12.3	12.6	10.4	9.6	11.0	10.0
Volleyball	10.6	12.2	11.1	11.8	11.5	12.3
Water skiing	5.2	5.6	6.3	5.3	6.9	5.9
Weight lifting	31.5	37.5	32.9	26.2	25.1	24.8
Workout at club	36.3	39.3	37.0	31.8	28.9	24.1
Wrestling	2.9	na	3.8	na	na	na

na = not available.

SOURCE: "Ten-Year History of Sports Participation," in *Research: Sports Participation*, National Sporting Goods Association, 2011, http://www.nsga.org/files/public/Ten-Year_History_of_Sports_Participation_4web_080313.pdf (accessed June 13, 2011)

youth decrease by 2.5%. In contrast, ice hockey enjoyed significant growth during this period, as participation levels grew from 2.2 million in 2001 to 3.3 million in 2010, an increase of 50.4%.

SPORTS PARTICIPATION AND GENDER. According to NSGA survey data, the sports that drew the greatest number of female participants in 2010 (excluding exercise and recreational activities such as walking, aerobics, and camping) were swimming (27.3 million), bowling (18.3 million), and bicycling (17.7 million). (See Table 2.11.) Basketball, at 7.1 million participants, topped the list among team sports, with volleyball (5.9 million participants) not far behind. Tennis, golf, and soccer were also high on the list. Women represent a greater share of participants in some sports than in others. For example, 55.1% of the nation's volleyball players and 52.6% of

swimmers in 2010 were women, whereas women represented only 20.9% of ice hockey players. Table 2.12 shows changes in participation among women between 2005 and 2010. Few sports experienced dramatic shifts in participation among women during this five-year span. One sport that increased in percentage of female participants was hunting with a bow and arrow. In 2005 approximately 11.9% of bow hunters were female, compared to 18% in 2010.

Extreme Sports

As participation in traditional team sports such as baseball and basketball stagnates, especially among youth and young adults, a generation of sports participants is turning instead to a class of activities collectively known as "extreme" or "action" sports. Even though there is no

TABLE 2.10

Youth sports participation, 2010 vs. 2001

	Year	Total	Change vs 2001	Total 7–11	Change vs 2001	Total 12–17	Change vs 2001
Total U.S.	2001	251,239		20,262		23,782	
Total U.S.	2010	280,215	11.5%	20,554	1.4%	24,645	3.6%
Baseball	2001	14,868		4,654		4,095	
Baseball	2010	12,533	−15.7%	3,383	−27.3%	2,882	−29.6%
Basketball	2001	28,104		6,356		7,818	
Basketball	2010	26,875	−4.4%	5,533	−12.9%	6,424	−17.8%
Bicycle riding	2001	39,004		9,753		7,255	
Bicycle riding	2010	39,789	2.0%	8,041	−17.6%	6,546	−9.8%
Bowling	2001	40,302		5,330		5,893	
Bowling	2010	38,980	−3.3%	5,282	−0.9%	4,911	−16.7%
Fishing (fresh water)	2001	39,077		5,124		4,480	
Fishing (fresh water)	2010	29,927	−23.4%	3,354	−34.5%	3,506	−21.7%
Football (tackle)	2001	8,631		1,460		3,593	
Football (tackle)	2010	9,318	8.0%	1,888	29.3%	2,904	−19.2%
Golf	2001	26,637		1,011		2,264	
Golf	2010	21,872	−17.9%	1,297	28.3%	1,388	−38.7%
Hockey (ice)	2001	2,193		384		441	
Hockey (ice)	2010	3,299	50.4%	513	33.6%	607	37.6%
Mountain biking (off road)	2001	6,301		530		1,195	
Mountain biking (off road)	2010	7,242	14.9%	706	33.2%	994	−16.8%
Roller skating (in-line)	2001	19,225		7,108		5,059	
Roller skating (in-line)	2010	7,448	−61.3%	1,868	−73.7%	1,590	−68.6%
Scooter riding	2001	12,675		7,427		3,425	
Scooter riding	2010	7,354	−42.0%	3,570	−51.9%	1,406	−58.9%
Skateboarding	2001	9,623		4,512		3,961	
Skateboarding	2010	7,706	−19.9%	2,302	−49.0%	2,687	−32.2%
Skiing (alpine)	2001	7,660		614		1,453	
Skiing (alpine)	2010	7,383	−3.6%	1,227	99.8%	1,085	−25.3%
Snowboarding	2001	N/A		N/A		N/A	
Snowboarding	2010	6,112		775		1,210	
Soccer	2001	13,886		5,867		3,831	
Soccer	2010	13,534	−2.5%	4,439	−24.3%	3,362	−12.2%
Softball	2001	13,213		2,486		2,286	
Softball	2010	10,841	−18.0%	1,577	−36.6%	2,060	−9.9%
Tennis	2001	10,911		728		1,963	
Tennis	2010	12,250	12.3%	1,474	102.5%	1,859	−5.3%

SOURCE: "2010 Youth Participation in Selected Sports with Comparisons to 2001," in *Research: Sports Participation*, National Sporting Goods Association, 2011, http://www.nsga.org/files/public/2010YouthParticipationInSelectedSportsWithComparisons.pdf (accessed June 13, 2011)

consensus on exactly which sports qualify as extreme, their binding characteristic can be loosely identified as pointing to sports that result in a so-called adrenaline rush, or a degree of risk-taking that is not associated with old-school sports. Most lists include skateboarding, bungee jumping, ice climbing, free running, sand kiting, extreme skiing, mountain biking, BMX bicycling, BASE jumping, wingsuit skydiving, windsurfing, and hang gliding, among others. The boldest of extreme sportspeople will engage in daredevilry such as riding a motorcycle off of a ski jump. Many of these sports saw rapid growth in participation during the first decade of the 21st century.

SKATEBOARDING. Skateboarding is among the oldest and most popular of all the extreme sports. Board-Trac, a leading marketing and research firm for the extreme sports industry, publishes an annual report on the state of skateboarding in the United States. In "2009 Skateboarding Market Facts" (2010, http://www.board-trac.com/images/2009_Skateboard_Fact_Sheet.pdf), Board-Trac estimates that there were roughly 9.3 million skateboarders in 2009. Even though this figure represents a sizable decline

from the sport's peak year of 2002, when there were nearly 13 million skateboarders, it still shows considerable growth compared to the late 1990s, when there were fewer than 8 million skateboarders in the United States. Skateboarders tend to be a youthful group, but the sheer number of people participating indicates that skateboarding and other extreme sports are not just the domain of the young. The numbers suggest that as this youthful core group ages, these sports may continue to outgrow their "alternative" status and become more mainstream.

Skateboarding developed during the mid-20th century in California, where surfers attached small wooden platforms to roller skate wheels and began riding on sidewalks as a pastime when the surf was low. By the mid-1960s skateboards were being commercially manufactured, and by the 1970s improvements had been made in the design and materials so that riders gained increased speed and control over their maneuvers. During a severe drought in California in 1976, some skaters began practicing skateboard tricks in empty swimming pools, thus originating the vertical skating style that would eventually catapult the

TABLE 2.11

Sports participation among women, by total participation, 2010

[Participated more than once (in millions). Seven (7) years of age and older.]

Sport	Total female	Percent female
Exercise walking	58.7	61.3%
Exercising with equipment	29.4	53.2%
Swimming	27.3	52.6%
Aerobic exercising	26.9	69.7%
Camping (vacation/overnight)	21.6	48.3%
Workout at club	18.8	51.8%
Hiking	18.5	49.0%
Bowling	18.3	47.1%
Bicycle riding	17.7	44.4%
Running/jogging	16.9	47.5%
Yoga	16.1	79.6%
Weightlifting	10.9	34.5%
Fishing	10.6	31.3%
Billiards/pool	9.1	37.8%
Boating, motor/power	8.4	41.9%
Basketball	7.1	26.5%
Volleyball	5.9	55.1%
Tennis	5.9	47.9%
Golf	5.4	24.7%
Soccer	4.9	36.2%
Target shooting	4.9	24.7%
Softball	4.8	43.9%
Backpack/wilderness camp	3.9	35.4%
In-line roller skating	3.7	49.4%
Scooter riding	3.1	42.2%
Mountain biking (off road)	2.8	38.9%
Skiing (alpine)	2.8	38.1%
Baseball	2.5	20.1%
Hunting with firearms	2.3	14.3%
Water skiing	2.0	38.6%
Snowboarding	2.0	32.8%
Skateboarding	1.8	23.9%
Paintball games	1.4	23.0%
Football (tackle)	1.1	12.2%
Skiing (cross country)	1.0	47.7%
Hunting w/bow & arrow	0.9	18.0%
Hockey (ice)	0.7	20.9%
Muzzleloading	0.5	17.4%

SOURCE: "2010 Women's Participation Ranked by Total Female Participation," in *Research: Sports Participation*, National Sporting Goods Association, 2011, http://www.nsga.org/files/public/2010Women%27sParticipation-RankedbyTotalFemaleParticipation_4Web.pdf (accessed June 13, 2011)

sport into international significance. Skate teams representing board companies performed and competed to promote their sponsors' products, and stars such as Tony Hawk (1968–) rose to fame during the late 1980s and early 1990s. Hawk leveraged his fame on wheels into a fortune from merchandise and video games bearing his name and image.

SNOWBOARDING. Like skateboarding, snowboarding developed in the United States during the mid-20th century and grew rapidly as technology improved and young enthusiasts adopted the sport. The first snowboards were crudely fashioned wood items made by high school shop students and home hobbyists, all inspired by the idea of surfing or skateboarding on snow. One such creation, the Snurfer, by Sherman Poppen (1930–) of Muskegon, Michigan, gained national distribution through a manufacturing

deal with Brunswick during the mid-1960s. Snurf competitions were held, and other innovators, such as Jake Burton Carpenter (1954–), improved on the design and incorporated boot bindings and laminate materials. In 1982 Suicide Six in Woodstock, Vermont, was the first ski area to open itself to snowboarders when it held the first national competition.

Other ski resorts barred snowboarders due to concerns about safety and insurance coverage. With many younger participants preferring snowboarding to the more expensive downhill skiing, slopes eventually welcomed snowboarders, and the sport increased in popularity. By 2011 nearly all ski areas in the United States allowed snowboarding; exceptions included Alta and Deer Valley in Utah and Mad River Glen in Vermont. Snowboarding became an Olympic sport in 1998, with giant slalom and half-pipe events during the winter games in Nagano, Japan. One of the biggest names in extreme sports involving boards has been the Olympic gold-medalist Shaun White (1986–). Instantly recognizable to fans by his wild shock of flame-red hair, White is unique for having developed into a world-class performer in both skateboarding and snowboarding. Popular female snowboarders include Hannah Teter (1987–) and Kelly Clark (1983–), who won silver and bronze medals, respectively, for the United States at the 2010 Olympic Games in Vancouver, Canada.

CONSUMER PURCHASES OF SPORTING GOODS

Besides asking individuals about their sports participation, the NSGA also tracks nationwide retail sales of sporting goods. As Table 2.13 shows, the economic downturn, which lasted from late 2007 to mid-2009, exerted a significant impact on sporting good purchases in the United States. Americans spent $77.5 billion on sports-related items in 2010, compared to $91.4 billion in 2007. Of the 2010 total, $23.8 billion was spent on what the NSGA calls "recreational transport," a category that includes bicycles, pleasure boats, recreational vehicles, and snowmobiles. This category marked a notable decline from 2007, when Americans spent over $38 billion. The remaining $53.7 billion spent in 2010 went toward sporting goods such as specialized equipment, footwear, and clothing. Footwear accounted for $17.5 billion of this spending and clothing for $10.2 billion.

Excluding apparel, footwear, and exercise equipment, hunting and firearms and golf equipment accounted for the largest shares of sports equipment purchased by Americans in 2010. (See Table 1.2 in Chapter 1.) Consumer purchases of golf gear tallied more than $2.9 billion. Hunting and firearms, one of the fastest-growing categories of consumer purchases, generated even bigger revenues, registering nearly $5.2 billion in equipment sales in 2010.

TABLE 2.12

Female sports participation, 2010 vs. 2005

Sport	2010 total female	2010 percent female	2005 total female	2005 percent female	percent difference
Aerobic exercising	26.9	69.7%	23.7	70.4%	−0.7%
Archery (target)	N/A	N/A	1.4	20.8%	—
Backpack/wilderness camp	3.9	35.4%	4.8	36.0%	−0.6%
Baseball	2.5	20.1%	3.3	22.3%	−2.2%
Basketball	7.1	26.5%	9.4	31.5%	−5.0%
Bicycle riding	17.7	44.4%	18.9	43.9%	0.5%
Billiards/pool	9.1	37.8%	13.7	36.8%	1.0%
Boating, motor/power	8.4	41.9%	11.5	41.9%	0.0%
Bowling	18.3	47.1%	21.5	47.3%	−0.2%
Camping (vacation/overnight)	21.6	48.3%	20.7	44.9%	3.4%
Exercise walking	58.7	61.3%	51.9	60.3%	1.0%
Exercising with equipment	29.4	53.2%	28.7	52.9%	0.3%
Fishing	10.6	31.3%	11.5	30.8%	0.5%
Football (tackle)	1.1	12.2%	1.2	12.4%	−0.2%
Golf	5.4	24.7%	5.2	21.0%	3.7%
Hiking	18.5	49.0%	13.4	44.9%	4.1%
Hockey (ice)	0.7	20.9%	0.4	17.5%	3.4%
Hunting w/bow & arrow	0.9	18.0%	0.8	11.9%	6.1%
Hunting with firearms	2.3	14.3%	3.0	15.5%	−1.2%
In-line roller skating	3.7	49.4%	6.2	47.0%	2.4%
Mountain biking (off road)	2.8	38.9%	3.5	38.0%	0.9%
Muzzleloading	0.5	17.4%	0.3	7.9%	9.5%
Paintball games	1.4	23.0%	1.0	12.3%	10.7%
Running/jogging	16.9	47.5%	12.9	44.0%	3.5%
Scooter riding	3.1	42.2%	4.0	38.5%	3.7%
Skateboarding	1.8	23.9%	3.0	25.3%	−1.4%
Skiing (alpine)	2.8	38.1%	3.4	49.4%	−11.3%
Skiing (cross country)	1.0	47.7%	0.9	49.3%	−1.6%
Snowboarding	2.0	32.8%	1.5	25.8%	7.0%
Soccer	4.9	36.2%	5.8	40.7%	−4.5%
Softball	4.8	43.9%	7.1	50.6%	−6.7%
Swimming	27.3	52.6%	29.4	50.7%	1.9%
Target shooting	4.9	24.7%	5.0	23.0%	1.7%
Tennis	5.9	47.9%	5.3	48.1%	−0.2%
Volleyball	5.9	55.1%	6.9	52.0%	3.1%
Water skiing	2.0	38.6%	2.8	42.1%	−3.5%
Weight lifting	10.9	34.5%	12.8	35.9%	−1.4%
Workout at club	18.8	51.8%	20.1	57.9%	−6.1%

SOURCE: "Female Sports Participation—2010 vs. 2005," in *Research: Sports Participation*, National Sporting Goods Association, 2011, http://www.nsga.org/files/public/2010vs2005Women%27sParticipation_100722.pdf (accessed June 13, 2011)

TABLE 2.13

Sales of sporting goods, by category, 2004–11

[In millions of dollars]

	2004	2005	2006	2007	2008	2009	2010	2011[a]	Change 10 vs '09
Equipment	23,328	23,735	24,497	25,061	24,862	24,421	26,009	26,431	5%
Footwear	14,752	15,719	16,910	17,524	17,190	17,069	17,476	17,639	2%
Clothing	11,201	10,898	10,580	10,834	10,113	9,246	10,172	10,665	0%
Subtotal	49,281	50,352	51,987	53,419	52,165	50,735	53,657	54,735	5%
Recreational transport[b]	36,531	38,082	38,485	38,003	28,266	20,120	23,836	24,975	14%
Total	**85,812**	**88,434**	**90,472**	**91,423**	**80,431**	**70,856**	**77,493**	**79,710**	**8%**

[a]Projected.
[b]Bicycles, pleasure boats, recreational vehicles and snowmobiles; projections provided by other associations.

SOURCE: "Consumer Purchases of Sporting Goods by Category," in *Research: Consumer Purchases/Sporting Goods Market*, National Sporting Goods Association, 2011, http://www.nsga.org/files/public/ConsumerPurchasesofSptGdsbyCategory.pdf (accessed June 13, 2011)

SPORTS FANS

The United States' enthusiasm for professional sports has witnessed a dramatic shift since the 1980s. Table 2.14 offers a breakdown of the United States' favorite sports in select years between 1985 and 2010. Professional football grew steadily in popularity during this 25-year span, with 31% of poll respondents naming it as their favorite sport in 2010. During this same period professional baseball saw its popularity decline. In 1985 football narrowly edged baseball as the United States' favorite sport, with 24% of respondents choosing football and 23% choosing baseball. By 2005 the gap between the two sports had grown to 19 percentage points, with 33% of respondents naming football as their favorite sport, and only 14% naming baseball as their favorite sport. By 2010, however, baseball had begun to enjoy a slight resurgence, with 17% choosing it as their favorite sport that year.

As Table 2.15 shows, professional football enjoys its highest level of popularity among African-American sports fans, with 45% naming it as their favorite sport in 2010. By comparison, only 26% of Hispanics chose professional football as their number-one sport, the lowest among all ethnic categories. In contrast, Hispanics were the most ardent baseball fans in 2010, with 20% naming it as their favorite, the most of any ethnic category. Geographical location also seemed to be a factor in determining a fan's favorite sport.

Table 2.15 further reveals that professional football was substantially more popular in the East (34%) than in the Midwest (26%). Among fans with postgraduate degrees, 18% named college football as their favorite category, whereas only 2% chose auto racing as their sport of choice.

Race

Gallup Organization polls have shown over the years a general shift among American sports fans away from baseball and toward basketball and football, but the pace of this shift has been even more pronounced among African-Americans. In *The Disappearing Black Baseball Fan* (July 15, 2003, http://www.gallup.com/poll/8854/Disappearing-Black-Baseball-Fan.aspx), Jeffrey M. Jones of the Gallup Organization states that 43% of African-Americans named baseball as their favorite sport in 1960, compared to 33% of the overall American public. This strong preference among African-Americans may have been the result of the integration of professional baseball over the previous decade, beginning with Jackie Robinson (1919–1972) crossing baseball's "color line" in 1947, followed by the emergence of African-American stars such as Hank Aaron (1934–), Ernie Banks (1931–), Willie Mays (1931–), and Frank Robinson (1935–).

Jones notes that a Gallup analysis found that by 1985 the percentage of African-Americans calling baseball their favorite sport had fallen to just 17%, a drop that

TABLE 2.14

America's favorite sport, selected years 1985–2010

[Base: All adults who follow one or more sport]

"IF YOU HAD TO CHOOSE, WHICH ONE OF THESE SPORTS WOULD YOU SAY IS YOUR FAVORITE?"

	1985 %	1989 %	1992 %	1993 %	1994 %	1997 %	1998 %	2002 %	2003 %	2004 %	2005 %	2006 %	2007 %	2008 %	2009 %	2010 %	Change 1985–2010 %
Pro football	24	26	28	24	24	28	26	27	29	30	33	29	30	31	35	31	7
Baseball	23	19	21	18	17	17	18	14	13	15	14	14	15	16	16	17	−6
College football	10	6	7	8	7	10	9	9	9	11	13	13	12	12	12	12	2
Auto racing	5	4	5	6	5	5	7	10	9	7	11	9	10	8	9	7	2
Men's pro basketball	6	7	8	12	11	13	13	11	10	7	4	7	4	6	5	6	0
Hockey	2	3	3	3	5	4	3	3	3	4	5	4	5	5	4	5	3
Men's soccer	3	2	2	1	3	3	4	3	3	3	2	2	2	3	2	4	1
Men's college basketball	6	10	8	8	8	6	4	4	6	6	5	5	4	5	3	4	−2
Men's golf	3	4	4	6	5	6	4	4	5	4	4	4	4	4	4	2	−1
Track & field	2	2	1	1	2	2	3	1	3	1	*	2	1	1	1	2	0
Bowling	3	5	2	2	1	1	2	2	1	1	1	1	2	1	1	1	−1
Men's tennis	5	4	4	4	3	3	4	1	2	1	1	2	1	1	1	2	−3
Boxing	NA	NA	NA	NA	NA	NA	NA	NA	NA	2	2	1	1	2	2	1	NA
Horse racing	4	3	3	2	2	2	2	1	2	1	2	1	2	1	2	1	−3
Women's tennis	NA	NA	NA	NA	NA	NA	NA	3	2	2	1	1	*	1	1	1	NA
Swimming	NA	NA	NA	NA	NA	NA	NA	NA	NA	NA	NA	NA	NA	2	1	1	NA
Women's pro basketball	NA	NA	NA	NA	NA	NA	*	1	1	*	*	*	*	*	*	—	NA
Women's soccer	NA	NA	NA	NA	NA	NA	NA	NA	NA	1	*	*	*	*	*	*	NA
Women's college basketball	NA	NA	NA	NA	NA	NA	1	1	*	1	*	1	1	*	*	—	NA
Women's golf	NA	NA	NA	NA	NA	NA	NA	NA	1	*	*	1	*	*	*	*	NA
Not sure	*	1	4	1	2	2	1	3	1	2	2	3	2	1	2	3	NA
Pro football's lead over baseball	**1**	**7**	**7**	**6**	**7**	**11**	**8**	**13**	**16**	**15**	**19**	**15**	**15**	**15**	**19**	**14**	**13**

Notes: NA = Not asked in that year. Men and women's sports were not always distinguished. Percentages may not add up to 100% due to rounding.
*Indicates less than 0.5%.

SOURCE: Regina A. Corso, "Table 1. Favorite Sport,"in "While Gap Narrows, Professional Football Retains Lead over Baseball as Favorite Sport," *The Harris Poll*, no. 7, January 20, 2011, http://www.harrisinteractive.com/vault/HI-Harris-Poll-Favorite-Sport-Football-2011-01-20.pdf (accessed June 1, 2011)

TABLE 2.15

Demographic variations in favorite sports, 2010

[Base: All adults who follow more than one sport]

"IF YOU HAD TO CHOOSE, WHICH ONE OF THESE SPORTS WOULD YOU SAY IS YOUR FAVORITE?"

Sport	All adults %	Highest	%	Lowest	%
Pro football	31	African Americans	45	Hispanics	26
		Those aged 46–64	37	Those aged 18–33	23
		Easterners	34	Mid-westerners	26
Baseball	17	Hispanics	20	African Americans	6
		Those aged 65+	21	Those aged 18–33	13
		High school or less	20	Some college	12
College football	12	Post grads	18	Easterners	4
		Republicans	17	Hispanics	3
		Southerners	17	High school or less	10
Auto racing	7	Income $35K–$49.9K	13	African Americans	—
		High school or less	9	Post grad	2
		Republicans	9	Those aged 18–33	3

SOURCE: Regina A. Corso, "Table 2. Demographic Variations in Favorite Sports," in "While Gap Narrows, Professional Football Retains Lead over Baseball as Favorite Sport," *The Harris Poll*, no. 7, January 20, 2011, http://www.harrisinteractive.com/vault/HI-Harris-Poll-Favorite-Sport-Football-2011-01-20.pdf (accessed June 1, 2011)

far outpaced the decline among white fans, from 32% to 19%. Combined polls from 2000 to 2002 demonstrate a continuation of the decline of baseball's popularity among African-Americans. By this time, only 5% said baseball was their favorite sport. Meanwhile, both basketball and football had gained substantial popularity among African-American sports fans: football was the favorite of 31% and basketball was the favorite of 37%.

The contrast between the sports preferences of white and African-American fans is striking. Jones combines the Gallup data from 2002 and 2003 and shows that when asked simply whether they are baseball fans and whether they are basketball fans, white respondents gave baseball an edge over basketball, 39% to 28%. Nearly twice as many African-American respondents said they were basketball fans (60%) as said they were baseball fans (33%). Jones's analysis of these results suggests two possible reasons for the differences:

- The dominance of professional basketball by African-American players

- The relative lack of baseball facilities and programs in urban areas with predominantly African-American populations

More recent data from Harris Interactive confirm the presence of significant racial differences. By 2010 only 6% of African-Americans named baseball as their favorite sport, the lowest percentage among all ethnic groups. (See Table 2.15.)

Fantasy Sports Leagues

The rise of the Internet during the 1990s and the first decade of the 21st century saw an explosion of interest in fantasy sports leagues, notably baseball and football, but also basketball, hockey, golf, and other sports. In fantasy sports, an individual plays the owner of a fantasy team, which consists of a roster of real professional athletes. A fantasy team's point total is based according to the actual statistical performances of its individual players. For example, if a fantasy football team owner has a star National Football League (NFL) running back on his roster, and that running back rushes for 200 yards (183 m) and three touchdowns in a real NFL game, then the fantasy owner receives credit for those statistics, typically in a head-to-head matchup against another fantasy team owner. Throughout the season, fantasy owners can conduct various transactions, including trades with other owners. According to the Fantasy Sports Trade Association (FSTA; June 10, 2011, http://www.fsta.org/blog/fsta-press-release), by 2011 the number of people participating in fantasy sports leagues had grown to 32 million in the United States and Canada, a 60% increase over the 2007 total of 19.4 million. The popularity of fantasy sports has also seen the proliferation of websites and sports writing dedicated specifically to fantasy sports news and analysis.

SPORTS ATTENDANCE

Attendance trends vary considerably from one sport to another, and in general one sport's loss, whether because of scandal or declining interest, translates into another sport's gain. Professional sports teams rely on revenue from ticket sales to cover much of the cost of the huge salaries they pay their players. At the college level, ticket sales are a big part of what keeps university athletic programs solvent (able to pay all legal debts).

Major Sports

BASEBALL. Even though baseball seems to have lost some of its luster in terms of participation and self-identified fan base over the decades, the public is still attending games. Over 73.3 million fans attended Major League Baseball (MLB) games during the 2009 regular season. (See Table 2.16.) This total represented a decline of 5.2 million compared to 2008 attendance, but it still marked a significant increase over attendance figures in 1995, when just 50.5 million fans attended regular-season games. Interestingly, the National League has seen its attendance totals climb far more dramatically than the American League during this span. In 1995 attendance at American League regular-season games was 25.4 million, slightly higher than the National League total of 25.1 million. Five years later National League teams attracted far more fans to the ballpark. In 2000, 39.9 million people attended National League regular-season games, whereas only 32.9 million attended American League games. By 2009 this gap widened even more, as National League regular-season attendance totals reached 41.1 million, compared to 32.2 million for the American League.

According to ESPN, in "MLB Attendance Report—2010" (2011, http://espn.go.com/mlb/attendance/_/year/2010), in 2010 average attendance at MLB games for the year was 30,082. Nine different teams had attendance figures that exceeded 3 million for home games. The New York Yankees led all MLB organizations with an attendance total of 3.8 million; the Yankees also led the big leagues in attendance average with 46,491 per home game. Other league leaders in attendance included the Philadelphia Phillies (3.6 million), the Los Angeles Dodgers (3.5 million), and the St. Louis Cardinals (3.3 million). The Cleveland Indians posted the worst home attendance figures, attracting only 1.4 million fans in 2010, for an average of 17,435 per game, or only 40.2% of the ballpark's capacity.

BASKETBALL. Professional basketball has been enjoying strong ticket sales since the turn of the 21st century. Michael McCarthy notes in "Trouble Ahead? Looming

TABLE 2.16

Attendance at selected spectator sports, selected years 1990–2009

[55,512 represents 55,512,000]

Sport	Unit	1990	1995	2000	2004	2005	2006	2007	2008	2009
Baseball, major leagues										
Attendance	1,000	55,512	51,288	74,339	74,822	76,286	77,524	80,803	79,975	74,823
Regular season	1,000	54,824	50,469	72,748	73,023	74,926	76,043	79,503	78,588	73,368
National League	1,000	24,492	25,110	39,851	40,221	41,644	44,085	44,114	41,579	41,128
American League	1,000	30,332	25,359	32,898	32,802	33,282	34,503	35,390	34,464	32,239
Playoffs[a]	1,000	479	533	1,314	1,625	1,191	1,218	1,083	1,167	1,166
World Series	1,000	209	286	277	174	168	225	173	219	289
Players' salaries:										
Average	$1,000	598	1,111	1,896	2,313	2,476	2,699	2,825	(NA)	(NA)
Basketball[b]										
NCAA—Men's college:										
Teams	Number	767	868	932	981	983	984	982	1,017	1,017
Attendance	1,000	28,741	28,548	29,025	30,761	30,569	30,940	32,836	33,396	33,111
NCAA—Women's college										
Teams	Number	782	864	956	1,008	1,036	1,018	1,003	1,013	1,032
Attendance[c]	1,000	2,777	4,962	8,698	10,016	9,940	9,903	10,878	11,121	11,160
National hockey league										
Regular season attendance	1,000	12,580	9,234	18,800	20,356	(e)	20,854	20,862	21,236	21,475
Playoffs attendance[d]	1,000	1,356	1,329	1,525	1,709	(e)	1,530	1,497	1,587	1,640
Professional rodeo										
Rodeos	Number	754	739	688	671	662	649	592	609	560
Performances	Number	2,159	2,217	2,081	1,982	1,940	1,884	1,733	1,861	1,656
Members	Number	5,693	6,894	6,255	6,247	6,127	5,892	5,528	5,825	5,653
Permit-holders (rookies)	Number	3,290	3,835	3,249	2,990	2,701	2,468	2,186	2,233	2,042
Total prize money	Mil. dol	**18.2**	**24.5**	**32.3**	**35.5**	**36.6**	**36.2**	**40.5**	**39.1**	**38.0**

NCAA = National Collegiate Athletic Assocation.
[a]Beginning 1997, two rounds of playoffs were played. Prior years had one round.
[b]Season ending in year shown.
[c]For women's attendance total, excludes double-headers with men's teams.
[d]For season ending in year shown.
[e]In September 2004, franchise owners locked out their players upon the expiration of the collective bargaining agreement. The entire season was cancelled in February 2005.

SOURCE: "Table 1244. Selected Spectator Sports: 1990 to 2009," in *Statistical Abstract of the United States: 2011*, 130th ed., U.S. Census Bureau, 2010, http://www.census.gov/compendia/statab/2011/tables/11s1243.pdf (accessed June 1, 2011)

Labor Battle Could Blunt NBA's Boom" (*USA Today*, May 31, 2011) that attendance at National Basketball Association (NBA) games reached 21.3 million during the 2010–11 season, for an average of 17,306 per game. In "NBA Attendance Report—2011" (2011, http://espn.go.com/nba/attendance), ESPN indicates that the Chicago Bulls led the league in home attendance during the 2010–11 season, with an average of 21,791 per game. Other teams that drew an average of more than 20,000 fans to their home games included the Portland Trail Blazers (20,510), the Cleveland Cavaliers (20,112), and the Dallas Mavericks (20,101). In contrast, the Indiana Pacers drew an average of only 13,538 fans to each home game.

On a team-by-team basis, attendance in the NBA has a lot to do with the success of the team and the size of the city. It is not difficult to predict that a winning team in a large city is likely to sell more tickets than a lousy team in a small market. Perhaps more than any other sport, however, professional basketball attendance is influenced by personalities. The acquisition of a truly high-profile player (such as Shaquille O'Neal [1972–] or LeBron James [1984–]) can lead to a spike in ticket sales for the star's new team. Indeed, James's decision to sign with the Miami Heat following the 2009–10 season had a notable impact on Miami's ticket sales. According to ESPN, during the 2009–10 season Miami's average attendance was 17,730, or 15th in the NBA. During the 2010–11 season, James's first season with the Heat, the team attracted an average of 19,778 fans to each game, which was fifth best in the league.

Periodically, a player or set of players emerges with such charisma that the entire league's attendance numbers benefit. This was the case during the 1980s, when the ongoing rivalry between the team of Magic Johnson (1959–; Los Angeles Lakers) and that of Larry Bird (1956–; Boston Celtics) spurred a surge of interest throughout the league. Michael Jordan (1963–) had a similar impact during the 1990s. In 2011 it looked as if a number of emerging rivalries had the potential to boost the league's popularity. Ryan Braun asserts in "Kobe Bryant vs. Dwyane Wade and the Top Player Rivalries in the NBA" (March 5, 2011, http://bleacherreport.com/) that some of the top rivalries during the 2010–11 season included that between Dwyane Wade (1982–) of the Miami Heat and Kobe Bryant (1978–) of the Lakers, Bryant and James, and Derrick Rose (1988–) of the Bulls and Rajon Rondo (1986–) of the Celtics.

FOOTBALL. Professional football saw a slight rise in attendance for the 2010 regular season. According to ESPN, in "NFL Attendance—2010" (2011, http://espn.go.com/nfl/attendance/_/year/2010), the official league tally of total paid attendance for the NFL regular season was 17 million—down from a record 17.4 million in 2007, but up from the 2009 regular-season total of 16.7 million—with an average paid attendance of 66,445 per game. Team-by-team attendance figures show that the Dallas Cowboys led the league in attendance. The Cowboys attracted 696,377 fans to its new state-of-the-art stadium in 2010, for an average of 87,047 fans per game. New York City is a big enough market not only to have two NFL teams—the Jets and the Giants—but also to have these two teams place third (Giants) and fourth (Jets) in attendance. (Both the Jets and the Giants play their home games at Giants Stadium in East Rutherford, New Jersey, just across the Hudson River from New York City. The two teams were scheduled to begin playing in a new venue, New Meadowlands Stadium, during the 2011 season.)

In general, attendance at both college and professional football games has shown significant growth over the long term. Table 2.17 shows attendance figures, along with other relevant data, for college and professional football for select years between 1990 and 2009. Attendance for NFL postseason games peaked in 1990, when a total of 848,000 fans turned out for the playoffs and the Pro Bowl. Attendance at NFL postseason games gradually declined over the next several years, dropping to a low of 776,000 in 2006, before once again climbing to 824,000 in 2009.

HOCKEY. According to ESPN, in "NHL Attendance Report—2010–11" (2011, http://espn.go.com/nhl/attendance), National Hockey League (NHL) attendance for the 2010–11 regular season was nearly 21 million. The NHL continues to regain the fans it lost during the 2004–05 season, which was canceled in its entirety because of labor turmoil. The top draw during the 2010–11 season was the Chicago Blackhawks, with 878,356 spectators over the course of the season, for an average of 21,423 per home game. Only one other team, the Montreal Canadiens, drew more than 20,000 fans per game. The New York Islanders had the poorest turnout for the season, with a total attendance of 453,456.

SOCCER. As soccer emerges as a major sport in the United States, its popularity among fans is steadily growing. Maria Burns Ortiz reports in "Major League Soccer Is Poised to Overtake the NHL as the 4th Most Popular Professional Sports League in the U.S." (Fox News, March 24, 2011) that average attendance at Major League Soccer games was 16,675 in 2010, an increase of 4% over the previous year. The Seattle Sounders attracted an average of 36,173 fans to its home games in 2010. In "Major League Soccer Stats: Team Attendance—2009" (2011, http://soccernet.espn.go.com/stats/attendance/_/league/usa.1/year/2009/major-league-soccer?cc=5901), ESPN indicates the team's average attendance was 31,203 the year before. According to Ortiz, in 2010 nine of the league's 15 returning teams saw increases in attendance.

TABLE 2.17

College and professional football attendance, selected years 1990–2009

[35,330 represents 35,330,000]

Sport	Unit	1990	1995	2000	2005	2006	2007	2008	2009
NCAA college									
Teams	Number	533	565	606	615	615	619	628	630
Attendance	1,000	35,330	35,638	39,059	43,487	47,909	48,752	48,839	48,285
National Football League									
Teams	Number	28	30	31	32	32	32	32	32
Attendance, total[a]	1,000	17,666	19,203	20,954	21,792	22,200	22,256	21,859	21,285
Regular season	1,000	13,960	15,044	16,387	17,012	17,341	17,345	17,057	16,651
Average per game	Number	62,321	62,682	66,078	66,455	67,738	67,755	66,629	65,043
Postseason games[b]	1,000	848	(NA)	809	802	776	792	807	824
Players' salaries									
Average	$1,000	354	584	787	1,400	1,700	1,750	1,824	1,896
Median base salary	$1,000	275	301	441	569	722	772	788	790

NA = Not available. NCAA = National Collegiate Athletic Association.
[a]Preseason attendance data are not shown.
[b]Includes Pro Bowl (a nonchampionship game) and Super Bowl.

SOURCE: "Table 1243. College and Professional Football Summary: 1990 to 2009," in *Statistical Abstract of the United States: 2011*, 130th ed., U.S. Census Bureau, 2010, http://www.census.gov/compendia/statab/2011/tables/11s1243.pdf (accessed June 1, 2011)

AUTO RACING. Auto racing enjoyed a surge in popularity during the first years of the 21st century. The most prominent auto racing event in the United States is the Indianapolis 500 (Indy 500), a 200-lap, 500-mile (805-km) race that is held on Memorial Day weekend each year at Indianapolis Motor Speedway. The 2011 race was the 95th Indy 500. Even though the Indy 500 does not release official attendance figures, the seating capacity at the Indianapolis Motor Speedway is listed at 250,000, making it the largest sports venue in the world, according to World Stadiums, in "100 000+ Stadiums" (2011, http://www.worldstadiums.com/stadium_menu/stadium_list/100000.shtml). CBS Sports reports in "2009 Indianapolis 500 Facts and Figures" (2011, http://www.cbssports.com/nascar/story/11776519) that the speedway also provides space for an additional 100,000 spectators in the infield. According to CBS Sports, the total annual attendance at the Indy 500 is estimated to be roughly 400,000.

However, the Indy Racing League (IndyCar) is only one faction of the broader auto racing scene. There is also the National Association for Stock Car Auto Racing (NASCAR), which has become such a phenomenon that its followers (also known as "NASCAR dads") are now viewed by political analysts as a powerful voting bloc alongside so-called soccer moms. The Super Bowl of the NASCAR circuit is the Daytona 500, which is held in February at the Daytona International Speedway in Florida. Hilary Lehman notes in "Daytona 500 Attendance Up" (*Daytona Beach News-Journal*, April 6, 2011) that an estimated 182,000 fans turned out for the 2011 race, compared to 175,000 the year before. In 2009, roughly 2.1 million racing fans attended at least one NASCAR event per month. (See Table 2.18.)

Besides the IndyCar and NASCAR circuits, there are the Formula One Grand Prix series, the National Hot Rod Association, and various smaller racing circuits. Of these races, NASCAR has by far the greatest overall attendance numbers. Nate Ryan reports in "Action on Track Isn't Helping NASCAR Attendance, Ratings" (*USA Today*, July 21, 2010) that attendance at Sprint Cup events (a series that includes the Daytona 500) peaked in 2005, when an estimated 4.7 million fans turned out for races. However, attendance at NASCAR races began to dip toward the end of the decade. After dropping to 3.9 million in 2009, Sprint Cup attendance was estimated to have fallen even further in 2010, to 3.6 million.

OTHER SPORTS. It can be assumed that what draws these hundreds of thousands of spectators to auto races such as the Indy 500 each year is the speed—the experience of watching people hurtle around a track at well over 200 miles per hour (322 km/h). However, people also jam Boston's streets each year to watch a race in which the fastest entrant averages a mere 12 miles per hour (19 km/h). That race is the Boston Marathon, the most famous marathon in the world. According to the New England Sports Network (April 18, 2011, http://www.nesn.com/2011/04/boston-marathon-draws-approximately-500000-spectators-to-greater-boston-area.html), approximately 500,000 spectators turned out to witness the historic race in 2011. Few other sporting events in the world are witnessed live by as many people as is the Boston Marathon.

TABLE 2.18

Adult attendance at sporting events, by frequency, 2009

[In thousands (2,097 represents 2,097,000), except percent. For fall 2009. Percent is based on total projected population of 225,887,000. Based on survey and subject to sampling error.]

Event	Attend one or more times in a month		Attend less than once a month	
	Number	Percent	Number	Percent
Auto racing—NASCAR	2,097	0.9	16,693	7.4
Auto racing—other	2,332	1.0	14,134	6.3
Baseball	9,442	4.2	27,778	12.3
Basketball				
College games	4,623	2.1	15,615	6.9
Professional games	3,990	1.8	17,893	7.9
Bowling	1,878	0.8	11,478	5.1
Boxing	1,199	0.5	11,124	4.9
Equestrian events	471	0.2	11,111	4.9
Figure skating	554	0.3	11,021	4.9
Fishing tournaments	1,059	0.5	11,094	4.9
Football				
College games	7,522	3.3	18,805	8.3
Monday night professional games	2,998	1.3	13,629	6.0
Weekend professional games	4,715	2.1	18,721	8.3
Golf	1,747	0.8	12,491	5.5
High school sports	11,724	5.2	15,426	6.8
Horse racing				
Flats, runners	1,142	0.5	11,622	5.2
Trotters/harness	802	0.4	10,912	4.8
Ice hockey	2,465	1.1	15,781	7.0
Motorcycle racing	980	0.4	11,434	5.1
Pro beach volleyball	611	0.3	10,695	4.7
Pro bull riding*	716	0.3	11,488	5.1
Rodeo*	1,312	0.6	12,107	5.4
Soccer	3,819	1.7	12,585	5.6
Tennis	1,101	0.5	11,396	5.0
Truck and tractor pull mud racing	1,213	0.5	11,955	5.3
Wrestling—professional	1,651	0.7	11,333	5.0

NASCAR = National Association for Stock Car Auto Racing.
*Both pro bull riding and rodeo were measured as the combined "Rodeo/bull riding".

SOURCE: "Table 1245. Adult Attendance at Sports Events by Frequency: 2009," in *Statistical Abstract of the United States: 2011*, 130th ed., U.S. Census Bureau, 2010, http://www.census.gov/compendia/statab/2011/tables/11s1243.pdf (accessed June 1, 2011)

CHAPTER 3
SPORTS AND THE MEDIA

Sports and the media are so thoroughly intertwined in the United States that it is difficult to think of them as two distinct industries. The financial relationship is complex and reciprocal. Media enterprises, mostly broadcast and cable television stations but also web based, pay the sports leagues millions of dollars for the rights to broadcast their games. Leagues distribute this money to their member teams—the distribution formula varies from sport to sport—which then transfer most of this money to their players in the form of salaries. The media outlets try to recoup their huge expenditures by selling advertising time during sports broadcasts to companies that believe their products will appeal to the kinds of people who like to watch sports on television. These consumer product companies also pay large sums to individual athletes to endorse their products, or in some cases to teams to display their company logo on their uniforms or, in the case of auto racing, on their cars. Consumers then purchase these products, providing the money the companies use to buy advertising and pay for celebrity endorsements. The more people who watch a sport, the more the station can charge for advertising. The more the station can charge for advertising, the more it can offer the league for broadcast rights. The more the league gets for broadcast rights, the more the teams can pay their players.

THE HISTORY OF SPORTS ON TELEVISION

In "Sports and Television" (2011, http://www.museum .tv/archives/etv/S/htmlS/sportsandte/sportsandte.htm), the Museum of Broadcast Communications quotes Harry Coyle, a pioneering television sports director, who explains that "television got off the ground because of sports. Today, maybe, sports need television to survive, but it was just the opposite when it first started. When we (NBC) put on the World Series in 1947, heavyweight fights, the Army-Navy football game, the sales of television sets just spurted."

Even though it may be an exaggeration to credit the explosive growth of television in its early days solely to sports, sports certainly played a significant role. The first-ever televised sporting event was a baseball game between Columbia and Princeton Universities in 1939. It was covered by one camera that was positioned along the third base line. The first network-wide sports broadcast came five years later with the premier of the National Broadcasting Corporation's (NBC) *Gillette Cavalcade of Sports*, the first installment of which featured a featherweight championship boxing match between Willie Pep (1922–2006) and Chalky Wright (1912–1957). Sports quickly became a staple of prime-time network fare, accounting for up to one-third of prime-time programming, but other genres began to catch up during the 1950s, perhaps spurred on by an increase in female viewers. The *Gillette Cavalcade of Sports* remained on the air for 20 years, before giving way to a new model in which sports programs were sponsored by multiple buyers of advertising spots rather than by a single corporation, as the cost of sponsorship became prohibitively expensive during the mid-1960s. The number of hours of sports programming on the networks continued to increase dramatically well into the 1980s, when advertising dollars generated by sports began to decline, making them less profitable for the networks to carry.

The amount of money involved in televising sports was growing fast by the 1970s. According to the Museum of Broadcast Communications, Stanley J. Baran notes that in 1970 the networks paid $50 million for the rights to broadcast National Football League (NFL) games, $18 million for Major League Baseball (MLB) games, and $2 million for National Basketball Association (NBA) games. By 1985 these numbers reached $450 million for football, $160 million for baseball, and $45 million for basketball. This explosive growth was fueled by a combination of increasing public interest, better—and therefore more expensive—coverage of events by the networks, and an effort on the part of the networks to lock in their position of dominance in sports programming in the face of challenges from emerging cable television networks. These skyrocketing fees did not cause much of a problem during the 1970s, as the networks were able to pass the high cost of producing sports programs along to their advertisers. However, things began to change during the early 1980s. According to Baran, between 1980 and 1984 professional football lost 7% of its viewing audience and baseball lost 26% of its viewers. Meanwhile, advertisers became hesitant to pay increasing prices for commercials that would be seen by fewer people. The networks responded by airing more hours of sports. By 1985 the three major networks (NBC, American Broadcasting Company [ABC], and Columbia Broadcasting System [CBS]) broadcast a total of 1,500 hours of sports, about twice as many hours as in 1960. However, by the mid-1980s the market for sports programming appeared saturated, and the presence of more shows made it harder for the networks to sell ads at top prices.

The first half of the 1980s marked the rise of sports coverage on cable. According to Baran, the all-sports station Entertainment and Sports Programming Network (ESPN), first launched in 1979, was reaching 4 million households by the mid-1980s. National stations such as WTBS and WGN, as well as the premium channel Home Box Office (HBO), were also airing a substantial number of sporting events. By 1986, 37 million households were subscribing to ESPN.

Between the early 1990s and the first few years of the first decade of the 21st century broadcast television ratings for the four major professional sports generally trended downward. There is no real consensus as to why this happened. Jere Longman, in "Pro Leagues' Ratings Drop; Nobody Is Quite Sure Why" (Scott R. Rosner and Kenneth L. Shropshire, eds., *The Business of Sports*, 2004), points to "a growing dislocation between fans and traditional sports, as players, coaches and teams move frequently, as athletes misbehave publicly, as salaries skyrocket, and as ticket prices become prohibitively expensive" as possible contributing factors in the decline of ratings during that period.

Even as sports television ratings declined, however, other media forms were attracting the interest of sports fans. The early 21st century saw an explosion of new platforms that enabled people to follow sports over the Internet, from league and team websites to social networking sites such as Facebook and Twitter. In "Survey Spots Social Media Trends among Fans" (*SportsBusiness Journal*, June 27, 2011), David Broughton reports on the results of a survey conducted by Catalyst Public Relations between May and June 2011. Facebook was the most popular social media platform among sports enthusiasts in 2011, with more than 75% of "avid sports fans" choosing the popular networking site as their primary means of following their favorite teams. According

to Broughton, the popularity of social media sites varies from sport to sport. For example, 86% of NFL fans used Facebook to follow their favorite teams. In contrast, NBA fans were the most likely to follow their teams on Twitter (27%) and YouTube (35%). Overall, 40% of survey respondents stated they had become more enthusiastic about their favorite sport since using social media to follow their teams.

The key challenge for all the major sports leagues—beyond the obvious challenge of attracting as many viewers and listeners as possible—is to balance exposure and distribution of their product against consumer demand. In other words, in an era witnessing the emergence of new media such as the Internet, satellite radio, and live feeds to mobile devices, at what point does the coverage of a sport available for consumption outstrip the public's interest in that sport, thereby becoming a losing financial proposition?

BASEBALL AND TELEVISION: THE CONVERGENCE OF OUR TWO NATIONAL PASTIMES

By 1939 baseball was already known as "America's national pastime." Television was still a novelty at the time. The only option for those who could not attend a baseball game in person was to listen to a live broadcast on the radio. The first televised professional baseball game, between the Brooklyn Dodgers and the Cincinnati Reds, took place on August 26 of that year. The broadcast used two cameras: one positioned high above home plate and a second one along the third base line. Such a broadcast would appear primitive by 21st-century standards. To cover the World Series in 2010, the MLB used more than 20 high-definition cameras, capturing each play from multiple angles. In addition, early broadcasts offered none of the additional features that contemporary viewers take for granted, including color, instant replays, and statistics superimposed on the screen.

NBC was the network that first brought televised baseball to the American public. Because NBC used home-team announcers to call the World Series, and because the New York Yankees were in the World Series nearly every year, the Yankees announcer Mel Allen (1913–1996) became the first coast-to-coast voice of baseball. The Hall of Fame pitcher Dizzy Dean (1911–1974) became the first nationwide television baseball announcer when NBC premiered the *Game of the Week* in 1953, thus initiating the long line of former ball players who have transformed themselves into commentators when their playing careers have ended.

By the 1960s baseball had lost a large share of its audience to other sports, particularly football. Baseball nevertheless remains a solid ratings draw, especially when teams with well-known stars located in large markets square off during the postseason. However, the overall ratings for World Series broadcasts have been declining for years. The article "World Series Ratings Tie All-Time Low" (Associated Press, November 2, 2010) notes that ratings for the 2010 World Series, in which the San Francisco Giants triumphed over the Texas Rangers in five games, tied a record low. The series averaged an 8.4 rating (meaning 8.4% of all households were tuned in) and a 14 share (meaning 14% of those watching something were watching the World Series), figures that were identical to those for the 2008 World Series between the Philadelphia Phillies and the Tampa Bay Rays.

Professional baseball has increased its media income substantially in recent years. As of August 2011, the MLB was operating under a round of television deals signed in 2005 and 2006. Danielle Sessa reports in "Baseball Expands TV Coverage with Fox, Turner Deals (Update1)" (Bloomberg.com, July 11, 2006) that in 2005 ESPN agreed to pay $2.4 billion to start a series of Monday night baseball broadcasts as part of an eight-year contract, which runs through 2013. Under the terms of the deal, ESPN may televise up to 80 regular-season games per season. The agreement also affords ESPN substantial flexibility to move some of the games to Sunday nights. In 2006 the MLB also signed deals with Fox for the broadcast rights to the All-Star Game and the World Series through 2013. The MLB's other major television partner is TBS, which is slated to air all regular-season tiebreaker games, Division Series games, and a Sunday afternoon regular-season package through 2013.

Baseball has expanded its radio presence in recent years as well. The 2005 season marked the first year of a six-year contract with ESPN Radio worth an average of $11 million per year, a six-year Internet deal with ESPN for an annual average of $30 million, and a $60 million-per-year deal with XM Satellite Radio to transmit baseball games for 11 years. ESPN and the MLB have also expanded their reach into local radio markets. For example, the article "MLB Rangers Reach Four-Year Rights Deal with ESPN Radio Dallas" (*Sports Business Daily*, December 8, 2010) notes that in December 2010 ESPN Radio Dallas forged a four-year contract with the Texas Rangers to broadcast the team's games. ESPN Dallas took over the rights from the local CBS-affiliate KRLD-AM, which had been broadcasting Rangers games since 1995.

Since the turn of the 21st century the MLB has been working to expand its presence on the Internet. In 2000 the league formed MLB Advanced Media (MLBAM) as a way of consolidating the online businesses of individual teams into a single centralized location, MLB.com. Maury Brown reports in "MLB Advanced Media Rejects $1B in Offers from Private Equity" (Bizofbaseball.com, January 20, 2011) that within its first year of operation the new website had already become profitable. By 2005

Wall Street analysts were forecasting that an initial public offering for MLB.com would generate a revenue of between $2 billion and $2.5 billion. In spite of pleas from a number of major investment banking firms, including Goldman Sachs and Bank of America, the MLB refused to go public. In 2011 the league, intent on retaining complete control of its lucrative and rapidly growing online enterprise, again refused to accept $1 billion in investment capital from private equity firms.

FOOTBALL: BIGGEST ATHLETES, BIGGEST AUDIENCE
Professional Football

It is not an exaggeration to say that television put football where it is today. Before the era of televised sports, baseball was much more popular than football. Stirring television moments such as the 1958 NFL Championship, a thrilling overtime victory by the Baltimore Colts over the New York Giants, helped establish professional football as a big-time spectator sport. A few years later, when *Time* put the Green Bay Packers coach Vince Lombardi (1913–1970) on its cover in 1962—accompanied by the pronouncement that football was "The Sport of the '60s"—it was clear that the sport had come of age as a media phenomenon.

In April 2005 the NFL signed a deal for $1.1 billion per year to move *Monday Night Football* from its long-standing home with ABC—which was paying about half that sum under its expiring contract—to ESPN from 2006 to the 2013 season. (See Table 1.4 in Chapter 1.) Under the terms of the deal, ESPN would continue to make its NFL games available on regular broadcast television in the markets of the participating teams each week. However, unlike basketball, which experienced a loss of casual viewers when games were moved to cable in 2002, regular network television would continue to play a large role in bringing football to the viewing public.

The same day it shook hands with ESPN, the league reached an agreement with NBC, which had not broadcast NFL games since 1997. The NBC contract provides $603 million per year for the rights to carry 17 Sunday night games each season through 2011. (See Table 1.4 in Chapter 1.) The NBC deal was later extended through 2013, and the league granted the network the rights to broadcast Super Bowl games in 2009 and 2012. Meanwhile, the NFL had agreed in November 2004 to extend its existing relationships with CBS and Fox to carry regular-season American Football Conference and National Football Conference games, respectively. The new CBS agreement included two Super Bowls and guaranteed $620 million per year through 2011; the new Fox contract called for five years at $720 million per year, with two Super Bowls included in the deal. As with NBC, the NFL later extended its deals with both CBS and Fox through 2013.

During this period the league received another $700 million from DirecTV Satellite in a five-year agreement covering satellite transmission rights. This deal was later extended through 2014, with the price tag rising to $1 billion per year.

What do the networks get for all this money? They get plenty because advertisers know how firmly football is entrenched in U.S. households and sports bars. Football is by far the most popular sport to watch on television in the United States. Indeed, the NFL's showcase event, the Super Bowl, owns the record for the most-watched broadcast in television history. (See Table 3.1.) In a poll conducted in January 2011, Harris Interactive found that 69% of Americans planned on watching Super Bowl XLV between the Pittsburgh Steelers and the Green Bay Packers. (See Table 3.2.) As Table 3.3 shows, the magnitude of these television audiences generates enormous sums in advertising revenues for the NFL.

The United States' fascination with the Super Bowl extends far beyond the actual contest on the field. Every year, companies produce highly original, memorable television advertisements to air during the big game, pouring millions of dollars into 30- and 60-second spots. As Table 3.4, Table 3.5, and Table 3.6 show, these advertisements generate substantial buzz among consumers. According to Harris Interactive, 59% of Super Bowl viewers look forward to seeing the advertisements; another 30% who do not express enthusiasm about the advertisements in advance claim to enjoy watching them during the game. (See Table 3.7.) By comparison, the Super Bowl halftime show is not nearly as popular with viewers. Only 33% of fans look forward to the halftime show, with a higher proportion of women (37%) than men (29%) expressing enthusiasm about watching it. (See Table 3.8.)

In spite of professional football's widespread appeal among television viewers, the NFL labor dispute of 2011 threatened to erode the sport's popularity considerably. In March of that year the league imposed a lockout that prohibited players from using team facilities or signing new contracts. One month later, as negotiations between players and owners became more contentious, Harris Interactive conducted a survey of NFL fans. As Table 3.9 shows, distaste for the labor dispute was relatively widespread among football viewers, with 19% of fans claiming they would be less likely to follow the NFL on television if the lockout resulted in the cancellation of even a portion of the 2011 season. The lockout was resolved in July 2011, so the full season was scheduled to be played.

TABLE 3.1

Most-watched telecasts, all-time, as of February 2011

Program	Date	Network	Avg. # of viewers (000)
Super Bowl XLV	February 6, 2011	FOX	111,010
Super Bowl XLIV	February 7, 2010	CBS	106,476
M*A*S*H Special	February 28, 1983	CBS	105,970
Super Bowl XLIII	February 1, 2009	NBC	98,732
Super Bowl XLII	February 3, 2008	FOX	97,448
Super Bowl XXX	January 28, 1996	NBC	94,076

SOURCE: Adapted from "Most-Watched Telecasts of All-Time (U.S.)," in *Super Bowl XLV Most Viewed Telecast in U.S. Broadcast History*, The Nielsen Company, February 7, 2011, http://blog.nielsen.com/nielsenwire/media_entertainment/super-bowl-xlv-most-viewed-telecast-in-broadcast-history/ (accessed June 1, 2011)

TABLE 3.2

Where respondents plan to watch Super Bowl XLV, by gender and team preference, January 2011

[Base: All adults]

"WHICH OF THE FOLLOWING BEST DESCRIBES WHERE YOU WILL BE WHILE WATCHING THE SUPER BOWL?"

	Total	Gender		Team preference		
		Male	Female	Rooting for steelers	Rooting for packers	Just enjoy Super Bowl
	%	%	%	%	%	%
Watching the Super Bowl (NET)	69	75	63	100	100	100
I will be hosting friends and/or family at my house	14	16	13	22	26	14
I will be joining friends and/or family at someone else's house	14	15	12	27	26	18
I have other plans for watching the Super Bowl (e.g., at a bar, restaurant)	4	4	3	6	6	3
I am not sure what my plans are yet, but I do plan to watch the Super Bowl	38	40	35	45	51	65
I will not be watching the Super Bowl	31	25	37	—	—	—

Note: Percentages may not add up exactly to 100% due to rounding. NET represents the combined value of the following statements.

SOURCE: Regina A. Corso, "Table 1. Watching the Super Bowl," in "Over Two-Thirds of Americans Planning to Watch the Super Bowl," *The Harris Poll*, no. 14, February 3, 2011, http://www.harrisinteractive.com/vault/HI-Harris-Poll-SuperBowl-Ads-Football-2011–02–03.pdf (accessed June 9, 2011)

College Football

Televised college sports have nearly as much appeal as professional sports for American audiences, and since the 1980s they have become the subject of large media contracts as well. In the early days of televised sports, the National Collegiate Athletic Association (NCAA) determined which college teams could play on television. Officially, the NCAA's goal in making these decisions was to protect the schools from the loss of ticket-buying fans who were lured by the glowing screen in a warm home. The NCAA's dominance over the right to broadcast football games went virtually unquestioned for years. According to Welch Suggs, in "Football, Television, and the Supreme Court" (*Chronicle of Higher Education*, July 9, 2004), the only case of a college losing its membership in the NCAA came in 1951, when the University of Pennsylvania was dismissed for attempting to schedule its own broadcasts in defiance of the NCAA. The school quickly repented, and its membership was restored.

The networks, however, aware of the potential audience for games between large universities with esteemed football programs, kept courting college athletic departments. By the 1970s several universities with top football programs had become frustrated with the limits the NCAA was placing on their television exposure. In

TABLE 3.3

Top Super Bowl advertising categories, 2010

Rank	Product category	Ad expenditure (000's)
1	Automotives	$32,715.10
2	Beer	$32,715.10
3	Motion picture	$16,357.55
4	Regular soft drinks	$14,870.50
5	Tortilla chips	$11,896.40

SOURCE: Adapted from "Top 5 Product Categories (2010 Super Bowl Advertising)," in *Chips, Beer, and Lip Gloss? Which Super Bowl Advertisers Will Drive Consumer Spending?* The Nielsen Company, February 3, 2011, http://blog.nielsen.com/nielsenwire/consumer/chips-beer-and-lip-gloss-which-super-bowl-advertisers-will-drive-consumer-spending/ (accessed June 1, 2011)

TABLE 3.4

Top 10 most-recalled commercials, Super Bowl XLV

Recall rank	Brand	Ad description	Game quarter	Recall index
1	Doritos	Pug knocks down door (:30)	Q1	179
2	Budweiser	Cowboy in Western saloon (:60)	Q2	166
3	Doritos	Man licks cheese crumbs off of coworker's fingers (:30)	Q1	159
4	Pepsi	Pepsi Max—Couple on first date (:30)	Q4	153
5	Pepsi	Pepsi Max—Soda cans shoot out of cooler (:30)	Q1	150
6	Snickers	Richard Lewis and Roseanne Barr complain while working (:30)	Q2	149
7	Doritos	Housesitter brings grandpa back to life (:30)	Q1	148
8	NFL	TV clips montage (:60)	Q3	147
9	GoDaddy.com	GoDaddy.co—New spokesperson Joan Rivers (:30)	Q1	146
10	Budweiser	Bud Light—Kitchen redesigned with a bucket of beer (:30)	Q1	145

Note: The recall score is the percentage of viewers who can recall the brand of an ad they were exposed to during the normal course of viewing the Super Bowl. These scores are then indexed against the average score for all Super Bowl ads (recall index). 100 equals average. For example, with a recall index of 179, the Doritos "Pug" ad was 79% better-recalled than the average Super Bowl spot.

SOURCE: Adapted from "Nielsen's Top 10 Most-Recalled Commercials in Super Bowl XLV," in *'Wild Ride' Most-Watched Ad of All Time While 'Little Darth Vader' Is Super Bowl Favorite*, The Nielsen Company, February 9, 2011, http://blog.nielsen.com/nielsenwire/media_entertainment/chevys-wild-ride-most-watched-ad-of-all-time-while-little-darth-vader-is-super-bowl-favorite/ (accessed June 1, 2011)

TABLE 3.5

Top 10 most-liked commercials, Super Bowl XLV

Likeability rank	Brand	Ad description	Game quarter	Likeability index
1	Volkswagen	Passat—Little Darth Vader starts car (:30)	Q2	186
2	Bridgestone	Woodchuck saves driver (:30)	Q4	171
3	E*Trade	Baby talks next to sneezing cat (:30)	Q4	168
4	Doritos	Man licks cheese crumbs off of coworker's fingers (:30)	Q1	159
5	Doritos	Housesitter brings grandpa back to life (:30)	Q1	151
6	Volkswagen	Beetle—Beetle navigates the wild (:30)	Q4	146
7	NFL	TV clips montage (:60)	Q3	141
8	Chrysler	200—Eminem represents Detroit (:120)	Q3	138
9	Budweiser	Bud Light—Dogs work at party (:30)	Q4	133
10	Audi	A8—Men break out of old luxury (:60)	Q1	127

SOURCE: Adapted from "Nielsen's Top 10 Most-Liked Commercials in Super Bowl XLV," in *'Wild Ride' Most-Watched Ad of All Time While 'Little Darth Vader' Is Super Bowl Favorite*, The Nielsen Company, February 9, 2011, http://blog.nielsen.com/nielsenwire/media_entertainment/chevys-wild-ride-most-watched-ad-of-all-time-while-little-darth-vader-is-super-bowl-favorite/ (accessed June 1, 2011)

TABLE 3.6

Most-watched commercials, Super Bowl XLV

Time of air (ET)	Game quarter	Brand description	# of viewers (000)
9:56:21 PM	Q4	Chevrolet Camaro (autos)	119,628
9:59:31 PM	Q4	Chevrolet Cruze (autos)	119,333
9:21:19 PM	Q3	National Football League Sporting Association	118,155
9:31:38 PM	Q4	*Rango* (motion picture)	117,565
9:44:00 PM	Q4	Bridgestone (tires)	117,565
9:44:30 PM	Q4	Godaddy.Com (Website-Internet services)	117,565
10:00:01 PM	Q4	*Limitless* (motion picture)	117,565
10:00:31 PM	Q4	Skechers Shape-Ups (women's sporting footwear)	117,565
9:57:21 PM	Q4	Verizon Wireless (wireless telephone services-Web access)	116,976
9:45:00 PM	Q4	Volkswagen Beetle (autos)	116,092
9:45:30 PM	Q4	Fox *Raising Hope* (television program, prime entertainment)	116,092
9:46:30 PM	Q4	Mercedes-Benz (autos and trucks)	116,092
9:47:30 PM	Q4	Fox *Chicago Code* (television program, prime entertainment)	116,092
9:47:40 PM	Q4	Fox *House* (television program, prime entertainment)	116,092

SOURCE: Adapted from "Nielsen's Most Watched Commercials in Super Bowl XLV," in *'Wild Ride' Most-Watched Ad of All Time While 'Little Darth Vader' Is Super Bowl Favorite*, The Nielsen Company, February 9, 2011, http://blog.nielsen.com/nielsenwire/media_entertainment/chevys-wild-ride-most-watched-ad-of-all-time-while-little-darth-vader-is-super-bowl-favorite/ (accessed June 1, 2011)

TABLE 3.7

Attitudes of respondents toward Super Bowl ads, January 2011

[Base: Plan to watch the Super Bowl]

"NOW I WOULD LIKE TO ASK YOU ABOUT ADVERTISING ON THE SUPER BOWL. OF THE FOLLOWING STATEMENTS, WHICH BEST DESCRIBES YOUR OPINION OF SUPER BOWL ADS?"

	Total %
I look forward to watching Super Bowl ads	59
I don't necessarily look forward to Super Bowl ads, but I enjoy watching them when they come on	30
I don't pay any special attention to Super Bowl ads	8
I wish they didn't have advertising on the Super Bowl	3

Note: Percentages may not add up exactly to 100% due to rounding.

SOURCE: Adapted from Regina A. Corso, "Table 2. Super Bowl Ads," in "Over Two-Thirds of Americans Planning to Watch the Super Bowl," *The Harris Poll*, no. 14, February 3, 2011, http://www.harrisinteractive.com/vault/HI-Harris-Poll-SuperBowl-Ads-Football-2011–02–03.pdf (accessed June 9, 2011)

TABLE 3.8

Attitudes of respondents toward Super Bowl halftime show, by gender, January 2011

[Base: Plan to watch the Super Bowl]

"OF THE FOLLOWING STATEMENTS, WHICH BEST DESCRIBES YOUR FEELINGS ABOUT THE SUPER BOWL HALFTIME SHOW?"

	Total %	Gender Men %	Gender Women %
I look forward to watching the halftime show	33	29	37
I don't necessarily look forward to the halftime show, but I enjoy watching it once it comes on	27	23	32
I don't pay any special attention to the halftime show	29	35	23
I think the halftime show is a distraction from the main event and could do without it	10	13	7

Note: Percentages may not add up exactly to 100% due to rounding.

SOURCE: Adapted from Regina A. Corso, "Table 3. Super Bowl Halftime Show," in "Over Two-Thirds of Americans Planning to Watch the Super Bowl," *The Harris Poll*, no. 14, February 3, 2011, http://www.harrisinteractive.com/vault/HI-Harris-Poll-SuperBowl-Ads-Football-2011–02–03.pdf (accessed June 9, 2011)

1977 five major conferences, along with a handful of high-profile independents, formed their own group, the College Football Association (CFA), to fight for their interests within the NCAA. A few years later the CFA signed its own television agreement with NBC, the second-largest sports television contract ever signed up to that time. Naturally, the NCAA was unhappy about this development and moved to ban the teams involved from all championship events. The University of Georgia and Oklahoma University sued the NCAA, and the case was eventually decided by the U.S. Supreme Court in *NCAA v. Board of Regents of the University of Oklahoma* (468 U.S. 85 [1984]). In the end, the NCAA was found to be in violation of antitrust laws. Thus, the NCAA's stranglehold on television broadcast of college football was broken.

In the wake of the Supreme Court decision, the CFA took on the role of coordinating the television coverage of most of the nation's leading football conferences. Still, some teams found the arrangement too restrictive. Following the defection of a handful of teams and conferences, the CFA folded in 1994, and the conferences were on their own to negotiate television contracts with the networks. The dollars began to flow in an ever-greater volume during this period. Suggs notes that the Southeastern Conference (SEC) signed a contract in 1990 that brought in $16 million to be divided among its members. In "SEC, ESPN Agree to Milestone Contract" (August 25, 2008, http://blogs.tampabay.com/gators/2008/08/sec-espn-agree.html), Antonya English notes that in 2008 the SEC signed broadcast contracts with CBS and ESPN that extended

TABLE 3.9

Likelihood of respondents watching NFL following 2011 lockout, by age, gender, and income level, April 2011

[Base: All U.S. adults]

"THERE IS SOME TALK THAT THE UPCOMING NFL SEASON MAY BE DELAYED BECAUSE THE CURRENT LABOR LOCKOUT WILL CONTINUE. IF THIS HAPPENS, HOW MUCH MORE OR LESS LIKELY, IF AT ALL, WILL YOU BE TO WATCH FOOTBALL WHEN THE SEASON BEGINS?"

	Total	Age				Gender		Income			
		18–34	35–44	45–54	55+	Male	Female	Less than $35K	$35K–$49.9K	$50K–$74.9K	$75K+
	%	%	%	%	%	%	%	%	%	%	%
More likely (NET[a])	4	5	5	3	4	4	4	5	5	7	2
Much more likely	2	2	3	2	3	3	2	3	3	6	1
Somewhat more likely	2	3	2	1	1	1	2	2	3	2	1
No change in likelihood	67	70	64	67	65	65	68	65	71	64	72
Less likely (NET[b])	19	12	19	18	25	22	16	16	21	18	20
Somewhat less likely	8	7	10	6	8	11	5	5	6	10	9
Much less likely	11	6	9	12	17	11	11	12	15	8	11
Not at all sure	10	12	11	12	6	8	11	14	2	10	5

Note: Percentages may not add up to 100% due to rounding. NFL = National Football League.
[a]NET is the combined values for "Much more likely" and "Somewhat more likely."
[b]NET is the combined values for "Somewhat less likely" and "Much less likely."

SOURCE: Samantha Braverman, "Table 1. Likelihood of Watching NFL When It Returns," in "The Future of Football: One in Five Americans Less Likely to Watch When the NFL Begins," *The Harris Poll*, no. 56, May 10, 2011, http://www.harrisinteractive.com/vault/HI-Harris-Poll-Adweek-Football-2011–05–10.pdf (accessed June 9, 2011).

for 15 years and guaranteed participating schools such as the University of Alabama, the University of Florida, and Louisiana State University an estimated $20 million each per year. With so much money at stake, the nation's leading college conferences also began to explore possibilities for expansion. Dennis Dodd reports in "Whenever Big Ten Expands, College Football Will Feel Trickle-down Effect" (CBS Sports, April 21, 2010) that in 2010 the Big 10 Conference and the SEC were by far the two largest conferences in the United States, together accounting for roughly 50% of the nation's college football television audience. As the two conferences jockeyed for dominance, they began exploring ways to attract more teams. According to the Big 10 Conference, in the press release "University of Nebraska Becomes Official Member of Big Ten Conference" (June 30, 2011, http://www.bigten.org/genrel/070111aaa.html), in July 2011 the University of Nebraska officially joined the Big 10 Conference, after years being a member of the rival Big 12 Conference.

With about a thousand universities participating in over 150,000 sporting events each year, competition for the right to put these events on television is fierce. In 2003 a network devoted strictly to collegiate athletics was launched under the name College Sports Television (CSTV). According to CSTV (http://www.cstv.com/online/), in 2011 the network was available in more than 21 million homes via cable and satellite. CSTV also operates a network of 215 official athletic websites for top colleges and streams audio and/or video for thousands of events per year on high-speed Internet to online subscribers. CSTV was purchased by CBS in January 2006. As often happens in the media world, success breeds competition. According to the article "BCS, ESPN Reach Deal to Air Games from 2011–14" (Associated Press, November 18, 2008), in 2008 ESPN entered into an agreement with the NCAA to cover Bowl Championship Series (BCS) football games from 2011 to 2014, in a deal worth $125 million per year. Two years later the NCAA signed a 14-year, $10.8 billion deal with Turner Broadcasting and CBS to provide expanded television coverage of its annual Division I basketball tournament, known as "March Madness." Brad Wolverton notes in "NCAA Agrees to $10.8-Billion Deal to Broadcast Its Men's Basketball Tournament" (*Chronicle of Higher Education*, April 22, 2010) that the agreement would generate a minimum of $740 million for member colleges and universities each year.

The highlight of the college football season comes each December, when the annual bowl game season gets underway. Traditionally, the most prestigious bowl games included the Rose Bowl, the Orange Bowl, and the Sugar Bowl. In recent years, however, the college bowl game schedule has expanded significantly. According to the article "Do We Really Need 35 NCAA Bowl Games?" (ThePigskinReport.com, June 18, 2011), there were a record 35 bowl games slated for the 2011–12 season, beginning on December 17. Each year the college bowl game season concludes with the BCS, culminating with the BCS National Championship Game to determine the top college football team in the country. Even though the more prestigious bowl games garner a great deal of media attention, the vast majority of bowl contests attract relatively small television viewing audiences. In "TV Ratings" (February 28, 2011, http://www.bcsfootball.org/news/story?id=4819384), the BCS indicates that during the 2010–11 season only two bowl contests, the BCS National Championship Game (15.3) and the Rose Bowl (11.3), earned television ratings higher than 10. In comparison, the New Orleans Bowl between Troy University and Ohio University earned the lowest ratings of any bowl game (1.5), followed closely by the Armed Forces Bowl between the U.S. Army and Southern Methodist University (1.6).

BASKETBALL

NBA regular-season games have never drawn the kind of television audiences that NFL games routinely attract, simply because there are so many of them—the NBA season has 82 games, whereas the NFL season has just 16 games. In basketball, viewership increases significantly during the playoffs and is greatly influenced by the specific teams or personalities involved in a game. The NBA's television ratings have generally been sliding since Michael Jordan (1963–) retired in 1999, although there were signs that ratings were beginning to rebound during the latter part of the first decade of the 21st century. Ratings for NBA regular-season broadcasts in 2010–11 saw a sharp increase over the previous season. In "What's behind Jump in NBA's TV Ratings?" (*USA Today*, February 23, 2011), Michael Hiestand reports that by the midpoint of the season ratings had improved on all three of the NBA's main television networks. ABC's ratings increased by 32% compared to 2009–10, TNT's ratings climbed by 26%, and ESPN's ratings grew by 15%. Much of this growth was attributed to the number of young players beginning to emerge as NBA stars. For example, Hiestand points out that TNT's ratings in Oklahoma City, Oklahoma, home to the basketball star Kevin Durant (1988–), grew by 150% over the previous season, the highest increase in the league.

Table 3.10 shows the history of the NBA's television contracts since 1953. The rate at which the money involved has increased is striking. The set of deals the league signed in 1990 with TNT and NBC were worth well under $1 billion for four years. The most recent contracts, signed in 2007 with ABC/ESPN and TNT, cover eight years (from the 2008–09 season to the 2015–16 season) and have a total value of $7.4 billion. Under these contracts ABC airs 15 regular-season games and the entire NBA finals, along with several early-round playoff games. ESPN broadcasts up to 75 regular-season games and one of the conference finals, as well as some early-round playoff games. TNT airs 52 regular-season games, the All-Star Game, and playoff games, including one of the conference finals.

In 2003 Time Warner Cable, Cox Communications, and Cablevision Systems teamed up on a multiyear agreement with the NBA for distribution of NBA TV, the league's own 24-hour network, which as of 2011 was

TABLE 3.10

NBA television contracts, by cable channel or broadcast network, 1953–2016

NBA cable television contracts

Seasons	Station	Contracts amount
1979–80 to 1981–82	USA	$1.5 million/3 years
1982–83 to 1983–84	USA/ESPN	$11 million/2 years
1984–85 to 1985–86	TBS	$20 million/2 years
1986–87 to 1987–88	TBS	$25 million/2 years
1988–89 to 1989–90	TBS/TNT	$50 million/2 years
1990–91 to 1993–94	TNT	$275 million/4 years
1994–95 to 1997–98	TNT/TBS	$397 million/4 years
1998–99 to 2001–02	TNT/TBS	$840 million/4 years
2002–03 to 2007–08	TNT	$2.2 billion/6 years
NBA network television contracts		
1953–54	DUMONT	$39,000/13 games
1954–55 to 1961–62	NBC	N/A
1962–63 to 1972–73	ABC	N/A
1973–74 to 1975–76	CBS	$27 million/3 years
1976–77 to 1977–78	CBS	$21 million/2 years
1978–79 to 1981–82	CBS	$74 million/4 years
1982–83 to 1985–86	CBS	$91.9 million/4 years
1986–87 to 1989–90	CBS	$173 million/4 years
1990–91 to 1993–94	NBC	$601 million/4 years
1994–95 to 1997–98	NBC	$892 million/4 years
1998–99 to 2001–02	NBC	$1.616 billion/4 years
2002–03 to 2007–08	ABC/ESPN	$2.4 billion/6 years
Current contracts, combined cable and network		
2008–16	ABC/ESPN and TNT	$7.44 billion/8 years

SOURCE: Adapted from National Basketball Association, http://www.nba.com/ (accessed July 7, 2011)

available via cable systems across the United States and in 79 other countries. In January 2008 Turner Sports, part of Time Warner, took over management of all of the NBA's digital assets, including both NBA TV and NBA .com, under a deal to run through 2016.

HOCKEY

Even though the National Hockey League (NHL) has experienced a general downturn in television ratings since the 1990s, there are signs that viewers are coming back. The article "NBC and NHL Agree to 10-Year TV Rights Deal" (Reuters, April 19, 2011) reveals that between 2005 and 2009 the NHL's television ratings grew by 84%. Among the most popular television events for the NHL is the Winter Classic, an annual outdoor game that is played on New Year's Day. According to the article "Game 7 Preliminary TV Rating Ties Best on Record" (Associated Press, June 16, 2011), game seven of the 2010–11 Stanley Cup Finals between the Boston Bruins and the Vancouver Canucks earned a 5.7 rating and a 10 share, equaling a league television record set in 2003. The NHL reports in the press release "Best-Ever Business Year Highlighted by Record Revenue" (April 13, 2011, http://www.nhl.com/ice/news.htm?id=559630) that the 2011 Winter Classic between the Pittsburgh Penguins and the Washington Capitals was the most-watched regular-season hockey game in 36 years.

The article "NBC and NHL Agree to 10-Year TV Rights Deal" reports that in April 2011 the NHL signed a new 10-year, $2 billion deal with NBC that granted the network the right to broadcast 100 regular-season games per year. As part of the deal, NBC will begin airing a nationally televised NHL game annually on the day after Thanksgiving. In "NBC, Versus Win NHL TV Rights in War vs. ESPN; Sources Say 10 Years" (April 19, 2011, http://sports.yahoo.com/), Greg Wyshynski notes that NBC outbid ESPN, which had expressed strong interest in forging its own television deal with the league. As part of the agreement, the cable channel Versus, which had broadcast professional hockey games since 2005 and had since been acquired by NBC, will continue to televise the NHL throughout the regular season and the playoffs.

AUTO RACING

In "NASCAR TV Deals Done" (December 7, 2005, http://www.multichannel.com/article/CA6289818.html), Mike Reynolds reports that in 2005 the National Association for Stock Car Auto Racing (NASCAR) signed a set of eight-year television rights contracts with ESPN/ABC Sports ($270 million per year) and Turner Broadcasting's TNT network ($80 million per year). Soon after these lucrative deals were signed, NASCAR's television ratings began to sag. According to Nate Ryan, in "NASCAR's Growth Slows after 15 Years in the Fast Lane" (*USA Today*, November 15, 2006), in 30 of the first 34 races of 2006, ratings were lower than they were the previous year. NASCAR's television ratings continued to fall through 2010. Ryan reports in "Action on Track Isn't Helping NASCAR Attendance, Ratings" (*USA Today*, July 21, 2010) that much of NASCAR's slump could be attributed to a decline in interest among males between the ages of 18 and 34 years. According to Ryan, Fox's ratings in that key demographic fell 29% in 2010. Meanwhile, TNT's overall ratings for NASCAR events fell 9.1% between 2009 and 2010.

EXTREME SPORTS

Even though television ratings for extreme sports still have a long way to go before they are in the same league as professional football and basketball, the audience is growing. More important, at least from the perspective of advertisers, the audience watching extreme sports is youthful and predominantly male, with a lot of buying power. Not many sports can take credit for completely altering the public image of a soft drink, but extreme sports have done just that for Mountain Dew. Once perceived as a "hillbilly" drink, Mountain Dew is now almost universally associated with the youth culture as personified by practitioners of extreme sports. In "Going to Extremes" (*Advertising Age*, June 1, 2002), Joan Raymond explains that the transformation started in 1992 with the appearance of the "Do the Dew" advertising

campaign. The campaign, which featured attractive young people engaging in a variety of extreme activities, helped make Mountain Dew the fastest-growing soft drink during the 1990s.

Raymond notes that by the turn of the millennium, while *Monday Night Football*'s ratings were declining—viewership dropped from an average of 12.7% of the nation's households in 2000 to 11.5% in 2001—ratings for the two premier extreme sports events, the Gravity Games and the X Games, were increasing quickly. The average household rating was 1.7 for the 2001 Gravity Games, up from 1.6 the previous year. However, Chris Isidore states in "X-treme Marks the Spot" (CNN Money, August 6, 2004) that even though the best ratings for the 2003 Summer X Games on ABC showed 2.2% of the nation's households watching, that number was still barely half the rating ABC achieved for the final game of the NHL's Stanley Cup Finals, which were themselves considered a ratings disappointment.

Still, the audience for extreme sports remained steady, and by the end of the decade ESPN was offering Summer X Games coverage in a variety of television and online platforms. ESPN notes in "X16 Sees High Attendance and Sets Record" (August 11, 2010, http://sports.espn.go.com/action/xgames/summer/2010/news/story?id=5455079) that for the Summer X Games 16 of 2010 the network expanded its broadcast coverage from 20 hours to 31 hours on its two principal television channels, in addition to airing eight hours of the games on ESPN3D. The network also saw increased traffic on its online network, ESPN3.com, as viewership more than doubled over the previous year. Overall, ESPN estimated that 35.4 million Americans managed to view some portion of the games. Regardless, audiences remained quite small relative to other sporting events, as the games finished with a ratings share of only 0.7.

Broadcasters and advertisers are nevertheless optimistic about the future of extreme sports programming. According to Isidore, the sports' median (half are higher and half are lower) viewership age is 27, compared to a median age of 42 for ESPN's NFL football broadcasts. The ages for some other sports are even higher: baseball's median age is 48 and golf's is 55. Media companies are scrambling to ride this youthful wave. On July 1, 2003, Fox launched the digital cable channel FuelTV (2011, http://www.fuel.tv/), which is devoted to skateboarding, snowboarding, surfing, BMX, freestyle motocross, wakeboarding, and other action sports programming that targets the under-40 demographic. Moreover, this young audience tends to be more comfortable with new media than their parents are. The emergence of mixed martial arts as a popular television sport also holds promise for attracting more viewers in this younger demographic group.

ADVERTISING

Plunkett Research, Ltd., estimates in "Sports Industry Overview" (2011, http://www.plunkettresearch.com/sports%20recreation%20leisure%20market%20research/industry%20statistics) that sports in the United States was a $422 billion industry in 2011. Furthermore, approximately $27.8 billion was spent by U.S. companies on sports advertising, a large portion of which was dedicated to television advertising. David Broughton reports in "Sports Ad Spending Roars Back" (*SportsBusiness Journal*, May 2, 2011) that the top-50 sports advertisers spent a combined $6.6 billion on television advertising in 2010, an increase of 27% over the previous year. The top advertiser during sporting events was the automobile industry, which accounted for 23.8% of all sports advertising spending in 2010. This figure was more than double the share of the next largest sports advertiser, the telecom industry, at 11.9%.

Many companies devote the vast bulk of their advertising budgets to promoting their products and services during sporting events. Broughton provides a list of the fifty top sports advertisers in 2010. Of these, the company that devoted the largest proportion of advertising money to sporting events was Nike. In 2010 Nike, a manufacturer of athletic shoes and apparel, spent $67.8 million (91.5%) out of a total advertising budget of $74.1 million on sports. Beer companies such as Anheuser-Busch (80.8%) and MillerCoors (75.3%) also spent large percentages of their advertising money on sports in 2010. By comparison, Procter and Gamble spent $118.5 million (6.5%) out of $1.8 billion on sports advertising.

A significant portion of sports advertising spending is on commercials that are aired during noteworthy games. The most expensive television advertisements of any kind are those placed during the NFL's Super Bowl games. Kevin Baumer explains in "Here's a Look at the Cost of Super Bowl Ads through the Years" (February 3, 2011, http://www.businessinsider.com/cost-super-bowl-ads-through-the-years-2011-2) that a 30-second television spot during Super Bowl XLV cost $3 million, compared to only $40,000 (or about $261,100 in 2011 dollars) in 1967.

Sports Advertising and Alcohol

Sports advertising is dominated by products that appeal to young adult males. One product in particular, beer, is the undisputed king of the sports advertising jungle. In "Sports Ad Spending Roars Back," Broughton points out that Anheuser-Busch was the top sports advertiser in the United States 15 times between 1994 and 2010; in 2006 and 2010 the company placed second behind Chevrolet and AT&T Mobility, respectively. Proportionally, however, the beer giant has typically spent more of its total budget on sports advertising than other companies. In 2010 Anheuser-Busch dedicated $356.2 million out of $440.7 million to marketing its products during sporting events.

The Center on Alcohol Marketing and Youth (CAMY) has studied the relationship between sports programming and alcohol advertising. In *Alcohol Advertising on Sports Television, 2001 to 2003* (October 2004, http://www.camy.org/bin/s/a/Alcohol_Advertising_on_Sports_Television.pdf), the most recent report on this topic as of August 2011, the CAMY indicates that even though sports programming accounted for only 16% to 18% of overall television advertising spending and only 4% of all ads between 2001 and 2003, 60.3% of the alcohol industry's advertising spending and 30.5% of its ads were on sports programs. Overall, the alcohol industry spent $540.8 million to place 90,817 ads on television sports programming in 2003. The CAMY notes that the percentage of commercials on sports programs that are for alcohol products is triple the percentage of commercials on all programming that are for alcohol products. Even though beer advertisements have long been omnipresent on sports television, in recent years ads for hard liquor have been appearing with greater frequency. Sports television advertising for distilled spirits increased 350% between 2001 and 2003. The CAMY also finds that alcohol advertising increased for the Super Bowl, *Monday Night Football*, and other top-rated games.

The CAMY states that soccer outranked all other sports in terms of the percentage of its advertising that was for alcohol products in 2003; 8.3% of the commercials on televised soccer games were for alcohol. Hockey was second at 7.2%, followed by professional basketball at 6.8%. Overall, 3.2% of all commercials shown during televised sporting events in 2003 were for alcohol products. Among professional sports, hockey games had the highest number of alcohol commercials per broadcast. A typical televised hockey game featured 5.3 alcohol commercials in 2003. Boxing matches averaged 4.5 alcohol commercials, followed closely by professional basketball with 4.4 alcohol commercials.

According to the CAMY, advertising on college sports presentations is at least as alcohol-oriented as on professional sports programming. In 2003 alcohol companies spent $52.2 million to place 4,747 ads on college sports programs. College basketball, at $28.3 million, accounted for more than half of this spending.

SPORTS VIEWING AND GENDER

In "Olympics Bridge Gender Divide in Sports Interest" (February 1, 2010, http://pewresearch.org/pubs/1481/interest-men-women-winter-olympics-super-bowl-world-cup), the Pew Research Center examines men's and women's levels of interest for various sporting events. In a survey that was conducted in January 2010, Pew finds that a larger percentage of women (63%) than men (59%) were looking forward to following the 2010 Winter Olympics in Vancouver, Canada. A similar survey conducted in December 2007 found that 54% of women were excited to watch the 2008 Summer Olympics in Beijing, China, compared to 51% of men. By comparison, the 2010 survey showed that 67% of men were looking forward to watching Super Bowl XLIV, whereas only 50% of women expressed the same view. Likewise, a higher proportion of men (28%) than women (18%) stated they were eager to follow the 2010 World Cup soccer tournament on television.

Even though female athletes generally fail to generate the same television ratings as male athletes, during the first decade of the 21st century there were signs that the audience for women's sports was growing. The article "Women's Basketball Sees Higher Attendance, TV Ratings" (Reuters, September 16, 2008) reports that in 2007 the Women's National Basketball Association (WNBA) signed an eight-year, $30 million deal to extend its television contract with ABC and ESPN2, as the league continued to expand its fan base. The WNBA's television ratings rose 19% between 2007 and 2008, and its attendance increased by 2.2%. WNBA games also posted a record 46 sellouts in 2008, twice its previous high of 23 in 2004. According to the article "Attendance, TV Ratings up for WNBA" (Associated Press, August 13, 2010), attendance at WNBA games rose each year between 2007 and 2010. At the same time, viewership for WNBA games broadcast on ESPN2 rose 23% between 2009 and 2010.

Nowhere was the increasing popularity of women's sports more apparent than during the U.S. soccer team's run to the women's World Cup final in 2011. Sports Media Watch notes in "World Cup: USA/Brazil Third Most-Viewed WWC Match Ever" (July 12, 2011, http://www.sportsmediawatch.com/2011/07/world-cup-usabrazil-third-most-viewed-wwc-match-ever/) that the women's quarterfinal match against Brazil in July 2011 attracted nearly 3.9 million viewers, the third-largest television audience for a women's World Cup game in U.S. history and the highest rating in over a decade. Martin Rogers reports in "U.S. Women Lauded with Celebrity Tweets" (July 11, 2011, http://sports.yahoo.com/soccer/news?slug=ro-rogers_usa_women_soccer_celebrity_tweets_071111) that the U.S. team's dramatic victory over Brazil also elicited a wave of national pride among a wide range of celebrities and athletes, many of them male. Among the luminaries to post congratulatory messages were the actor Tom Hanks (1956–), who declared "I love these women" on his Twitter page; the hip-hop musician Lil Wayne (1982–); and the NBA star LeBron James (1984–). In the aftermath of this outpouring, the U.S. goalie Hope Solo (1981–), who blocked a critical penalty kick during the final shootout, spoke of the team's gratitude. "Go ahead, jump on the bandwagon and let's do this together," she told the press. "Thank you for standing behind us." Even though the United States ultimately lost the final to Japan, the article "Tweets-per-Second Mark Set during Final" (Associated Press, July 18, 2011) reports that the game inspired a frenzy on Twitter, as users sent a record 7,196 tweets per second during the game's thrilling conclusion.

GAMING

Not long ago there were only two options for sports enthusiasts: playing a sport yourself or watching others play it live or onscreen. In recent years, a third way has emerged in the form of sports gaming.

Sports-oriented video games have been around for years, but until the mid-1980s the graphics were mediocre and the action unexciting for a true sports buff. A big change took place during the late 1980s, when Electronic Arts (EA), at the time a relatively new company making interactive entertainment software, introduced the first-ever football video game to offer realistic 11-on-11 action. To make the game as realistic as possible, the company consulted extensively with the former NFL coach and current football commentator John Madden (1936–). EA eventually named the game after Madden, and in 1989 the first version of *John Madden Football* was released for Apple II computers. The game was an instant sensation. A version for the Sega Genesis home entertainment system was introduced the following year. Over the next few years the gaming industry grew exponentially, split about evenly between computer games and television-based systems. By the release of the 1995 version of the game *Madden NFL '95*, EA had hashed out licensing deals with the NFL and the NFL Players Association, allowing it to use the likenesses of real players and the official league and team logos and uniforms. *Madden NFL* was eventually made available for every major gaming system. John Gaudiosi reports in "'Madden NFL 12' Sales Will Suffer with Players' Lockout" (*Hollywood Reporter*, March 14, 2011) that total sales of *Madden NFL* had topped 90 million units by 2010. With the NFL owners and players caught in a bitter labor dispute, however, Gaudiosi also indicates that many analysts believed sales of the next version of the game, *Madden NFL 12*, could fall by as much as 50% if the 2011 NFL season was canceled. In the end, the lockout was resolved, and the 2011 season was scheduled to be played in its entirety.

CURRENT ISSUES IN SPORTS AND MEDIA
Violence and Athlete Role Models

Violence in sports is often a focus of media scrutiny and academic research because the behavior of high-profile athletes can have an impact on fan behavior, according to social scientists. In "Violence in Sports Reflects Society, Says IU Professor" (July 3, 2002, http://newsinfo.iu.edu/news/page/normal/449.html),

Lynn Jamieson of Indiana University explains that "sport tends to reflect society, and we live in a violent era. We have a violent society where people use violence to solve problems instead of using other means.... The violence issue is not limited to professional sports. It filters down to the high schools and even to recreational activities.... This is because if it occurs at the professional level, it is likely to be imitated at the lower levels like Little League and city recreational programs."

Some sports include a measure of violence that is held in check by the rules of fair play and by officials who can enforce penalties or regulate the players' behavior to some extent. However, the violence below the surface can often erupt, and violent events involving professional athletes—either on or off the playing field—become major stories that are covered by news and entertainment organizations in addition to the sports media. The 2004–05 NBA season was marred by a huge brawl during a game between the Detroit Pistons and the Indiana Pacers; the fracas spilled into the stands, resulting in the involvement of both spectators and players. Several players received long suspensions, and the entire season took place under the cloud of the melee.

Basketball is not alone in contending with image problems stemming from extended media coverage of the actions of its players. In October 2005 several members of the NFL's Minnesota Vikings were allegedly involved in a party aboard a chartered boat that erupted into a drunken sex orgy. In August 2007 Michael Vick (1980–) of the Atlanta Falcons was suspended by the NFL after he pleaded guilty to felony charges stemming from his involvement in an illegal dog-fighting ring. According to Michael MacCambridge, in *America's Game: The Epic Story of How Pro Football Captured a Nation* (2004), such incidents result from the unique position athletes are afforded within U.S. society. In "Goodell Is Keeping the N.F.L. Inbounds" (*New York Times*, September 16, 2007), Judy Battista quotes Mac-Cambridge, who stated, "There is a tremendous amount of money, free time and scrutiny in the lives of most pro football players, and the combination is more pronounced and more combustible than it was a generation ago." Vick's suspension indicated a no-nonsense response from Roger Goodell (1959–), who in his first year as commissioner of the NFL instituted a strict code of conduct for players and coaches. Goodell reinstated Vick following completion of his sentence in 2009, and Vick joined the Philadelphia Eagles, returning to play in September 2009.

Incidents in college sports also abound. In a Conference USA basketball game in January 2009, the University of Houston's Aubrey Coleman (1987–) stepped on the face of University of Arizona's Chase Budinger (1988–). The video of the incident spread quickly around the Internet. Ultimately, Coleman was suspended for one

game. During the first weekend of the 2009 college football season, LeGarrette Blount (1986–) of the University of Oregon punched Boise State defensive end Byron Hout (1990–) and was suspended for the rest of the season. However, Blount was eventually reinstated after 10 games.

Even more concerning to college officials is the rise in criminal behavior among student athletes. In "Out of Bounds: College Athletes and Crime" (CBS News, March 2, 2011), Armen Keteyian examines the results of an investigation into the criminal backgrounds of top college athletes. Of 2,837 total players on the rosters of the nation's top-25 football teams, 200, or 7%, had been arrested or cited for a crime. More than 25% (56) of these incidents involved violent crimes, including assault and battery, rape, and robbery. The University of Pittsburgh held the dubious distinction of having 22 student athletes with criminal records, the most for any American college or university. Keteyian points out that only two of the 25 universities surveyed performed any kind of criminal background check on its athletic recruits, and none conducted research into the juvenile records of their players.

ATHLETES AND GUNS. A related issue is the prevalence of professional athletes who carry guns. A large number of professional athletes feel they need to carry a weapon for self-protection given their high profile. The public knows the players are likely to be carrying a lot of money and wearing expensive jewelry, and they are often robbery targets for that reason. The problem is that the athletes sometimes use their guns. In August 2009 Plaxico Burress (1977–) of the New York Giants was indicted for offenses related to an incident that took place in November 2008, in which he accidentally shot himself in the thigh at a Manhattan nightclub. Burress pleaded guilty to the weapons charge and was sentenced to two years in prison. On Christmas Eve 2009 Gilbert Arenas (1982–) and Javaris Crittenton (1987–) of the Washington Wizards drew guns on each other in the team locker room following a dispute over a gambling debt. Both players received probation and were suspended for the remainder of the season.

ATHLETES AND DOMESTIC VIOLENCE. Domestic violence is also a cause of concern in professional sports. Numerous examples of violence are reported in the media, and incidents are not limited to athletes who participate in contact sports or whose physical strength sets them apart from mainstream society. In 1992 the professional golfer John Daly (1966–) was arrested and charged with third-degree assault on his wife following an argument. The NBA guard Ron Artest (1979–), who had previously been suspended for 73 games after taking part in the infamous brawl with Detroit Pistons fans in Auburn Hills, Michigan, in 2004, was suspended for the first seven games of the 2007–08 season after he pleaded no contest to domestic violence charges. In *Breaking into Baseball: Women and the National Pastime* (2005), Jean Hastings Ardell quotes the law professor Phyllis Goldfarb of George Washington University, who noted that domestic violence is the leading cause of arrest among professional athletes. According to Goldfarb, "A celebrity athlete may simply be taught by the culture that he is superior to his wife, that she can ask nothing of him that he doesn't want to give, that if she persists in doing so, she deserves mistreatment, and moreover, is expendable, as there are countless women out there for him."

CHAPTER 4
PROFESSIONAL TEAM SPORTS

For decades baseball, football, basketball, and hockey have been considered the four major professional team sports in the United States. Even though other sports such as auto racing and soccer are gaining ground in terms of popularity, and hockey is struggling to maintain its status, it most likely will be some time before major league sports in the United States means anything other than the four core sports.

Besides being popular spectator events, professional league sports are also major industries that generate huge amounts of money—for team owners and managers, companies that sponsor teams, equipment and athletic gear manufacturers, and the athletes themselves.

MAJOR LEAGUE BASEBALL

Major League Baseball (MLB) is no longer as popular as professional football and is losing ground to other sports, yet it remains firmly ingrained in the American imagination, retaining the title of "national pastime." In 2004, 2005, and 2007, two teams with long histories of futility, the Boston Red Sox and the Chicago White Sox, saw World Series victories. Their success evoked an emotional response in fans across the United States and seemed to spark renewed interest in a sport that has had more than its share of bad publicity since the 1990s, partly because of steroid scandals. Baseball's steroid problem was magnified in 2007, as Barry Bonds (1964–), the player most closely associated with the scandal, approached the all-time home-run record held by Hank Aaron (1934–) since 1974. Bonds broke Aaron's record on August 7, 2007, eliciting an ambivalent response from fans and the national media. It remains to be seen if the renewed interest in baseball will translate into long-term gains in attendance and television viewership in the face of stiff competition from other sports, old and new. The steroid problem flared up again in

2009, when information emerged that in 2003 a number of elite players had tested positive for steroids during a round of testing the players union had agreed to under a set of conditions that included anonymity. Among the top players revealed to have tested positive were Alex Rodriguez (1975–) of the New York Yankees, Manny Ramirez (1972–) of the Los Angeles Dodgers, and David Ortiz (1975–) of the Boston Red Sox. Ramirez served a 50-game suspension in 2009 as a result of his steroid violations. In 2011 Ramirez once again tested positive for steroid use; he decided to retire from the game rather than face another suspension.

MLB Structure and Administration

Technically speaking, "Major League Baseball" refers to the entity that operates the National League and the American League, the two top professional baseball leagues in North America. The MLB operates these two leagues under a joint organizational structure that was established in 1920 with the creation of the Major League Constitution. This constitution has been overhauled many times since then. MLB team owners appoint a commissioner, under whose direction the MLB hires and maintains umpiring crews, negotiates marketing and television deals, and establishes labor agreements with the MLB Players Association.

As of 2011 the MLB consisted of 30 teams. (See Table 4.1.) These teams are divided into two leagues: 14 in the American League and 16 in the National League. Each of these leagues is further split into three divisions— East, Central, and West—that are loosely based on geography. The MLB season normally runs from early April through late September and consists of 162 games. Following the regular season, the champions of each division (three teams in each league) plus a wild-card team—the team with the best record among those not winning their division—from each league compete in the playoffs. The playoffs consist of three rounds: two best-of-five Division Series in each league; a best-of-seven Championship Series in each league; and finally the World Series, a best-of-seven game series between the champions of each league, to determine the major league champion team.

The MLB maintains a level of control over baseball that is somewhat unique among the major sports. This comes as a result of a 1922 U.S. Supreme Court decision in which baseball was deemed not to be "interstate commerce" and therefore not subject to federal antitrust law. Consequently, the MLB is allowed to operate in monopolistic ways that would not be legal in most other industries. This privileged status allowed baseball to stave off player free agency (a professional athlete who is free to sign a contract with any team), and the high salaries that accompanied it, until the mid-1970s.

TABLE 4.1

Major League Baseball teams and divisions

American League	National League
East Division	**East Division**
Baltimore Orioles	Atlanta Braves
Boston Red Sox	Florida Marlins
New York Yankees	New York Mets
Tampa Bay Rays	Philadelphia Phillies
Toronto Blue Jays	Washington Nationals
Central Division	**Central Division**
Chicago White Sox	Chicago Cubs
Cleveland Indians	Cincinnati Reds
Detroit Tigers	Houston Astros
Kansas City Royals	Milwaukee Brewers
Minnesota Twins	Pittsburgh Pirates
West Division	St. Louis Cardinals
Los Angeles Angels of Anaheim	**West Division**
Oakland Athletics	Arizona Diamondbacks
Seattle Mariners	Colorado Rockies
Texas Rangers	Los Angeles Dodgers
	San Diego Padres
	San Francisco Giants

SOURCE: Created by Stephen Meyer for Gale, 2011

According to Kurt Badenhausen, in "Yankees Soar, Mets Plunge on List of Baseball's Most Valuable Teams" (*Forbes*, March 23, 2011), the MLB took in $6.1 billion in revenue in 2010. Table 4.2 shows the values and revenues of select MLB teams in 2010. The New York Yankees were worth $1.7 billion that year. This sum was nearly double that of the second-most valuable team, the Boston Red Sox; in 2010 the Red Sox were worth a relatively modest $912 million. The Yankees also dwarfed the rest of the league in revenues, at $427 million. Again, the Red Sox placed second behind the Yankees in this category, generating $272 million in revenues in 2010. According to CBS Sports, in "MLB Salaries" (2011, http://www.cbssports.com/mlb/salaries/avgsalaries), average MLB player salaries topped $3.3 million in 2011, compared to an average of just $512,804 in 1989.

MLB History

The first professional baseball team was the Cincinnati Red Stockings, founded in 1869. That year the team—which still exists as the Cincinnati Reds—embarked on a 57-game national tour and went undefeated against local amateur teams. The team's success led in 1871 to the creation of the first professional baseball league, the nine-team, eight-city National Association of Professional Baseball Players. Various other competing leagues were formed over the next decade, including a precursor to the modern National League. The American League was founded in 1901. The champions of the American League and the National League faced off in what became the first World Series in 1903. The popularity of professional baseball continued to grow over the next several years. A crisis unfolded in 1919, when several members of the Chicago White Sox were paid by gamblers to throw the World Series in the so-called Black Sox scandal. In the wake of the scandal, club owners hired baseball's first commissioner, Kenesaw Landis (1866–1944), to clean up the game. As of August 2011,

TABLE 4.2

Selected baseball team values and revenue, 2010

Rank	Team	Current value ($mil)	1-year value change (%)	Debt/value (%)	Revenue ($mil)	Operating income ($mil)
1	New York Yankees	1,700	6	4	427	25.7
2	Boston Red Sox	912	5	26	272	−1.1
3	Los Angeles Dodgers	800	10	54	246	32.8
4	Chicago Cubs	773	6	75	258	23.4
5	New York Mets	747	−13	60	233	−6.2
6	Philadelphia Phillies	609	13	29	239	8.9
7	San Francisco Giants	563	16	21	230	29.9
8	Texas Rangers	561	25	66	206	22.6
9	Los Angeles Angels of Anaheim	554	6	10	222	11.8
10	Chicago White Sox	526	13	8	210	27.6

SOURCE: Adapted from Kurt Badenhausen, Michael K. Ozanian, and Christina Settimi, eds., "MLB Team Values: The Business of Baseball," in *Forbes*, March 22, 2011, http://www.forbes.com/lists/2011/33/baseball-valuations-11_land.html (accessed June 1, 2011). Reprinted by Permission of Forbes Media LLC © 2011.

the commissioner was Bud Selig (1934–), a founder of the Milwaukee Brewers. Selig, the ninth commissioner in MLB history, was appointed to the post by the team owners in 1998.

Baseball's golden era took place between the two world wars, which was marked by the rise of all-time greats such as Babe Ruth (1895–1948), Ty Cobb (1886–1961), and Lou Gehrig (1903–1941). The major leagues survived the Great Depression (1929–1939) by introducing night games, which soon became the norm for games played during the week; weekend games were still played during the day. From its beginnings through World War II (1939–1945), the MLB was racially segregated. That changed in 1947, when the African-American player Jackie Robinson (1919–1972) joined the Brooklyn Dodgers. Legends such as Willie Mays (1931–) and Hank Aaron followed over the next decade, and by the mid-1950s African-American players were fairly common on major league rosters. More recently, the number of African-American players in baseball has plummeted, as young African-American athletes have flocked to other sports. The 2005 World Series roster of the Houston Astros did not include a single African-American player; it was the first team to compete for the MLB championship without an African-American player in half a century.

After 50 years of stability, the 1950s brought changes to the MLB in response to demographic shifts in the United States. The Boston Braves moved to Milwaukee in 1953. Two New York teams moved to the West Coast in 1957: the Brooklyn Dodgers departing to Los Angeles and the New York Giants to San Francisco.

Baseball started losing fans, especially younger ones, in big numbers during the 1960s and 1970s as labor conflicts and other challenges plagued the sport. In 1966 the MLB Players Association was formed. The association's main goal was to end the reserve clause, a contractual provision that essentially gave teams ownership of players, meaning they were bound to a particular team until they were traded or released. The reserve clause was finally overturned in 1975, ushering in the era of free agency in baseball, wherein players were free to negotiate with any team they wanted once their existing contract had expired. Labor squabbles continued over the next 20 years, and parts of several seasons were lost to work stoppages. The worst of these took place in 1994, when the final third of the season, including the World Series, was canceled.

The sport survived in spite of these distractions, however, thanks partly to a handful of individual accomplishments. These included Cal Ripken Jr.'s (1960–) destruction of Gehrig's long-standing record for consecutive games played, and Mark McGwire's (1963–) and Sammy Sosa's (1968–) 1998 competition to break the record for home runs in a season—a record that was finally broken by Bonds just three years later. Since then, enthusiasm over these feats has been muted by ongoing scandals involving performance-enhancing drugs, which call into question the validity of the exploits of Bonds, McGwire, Sosa, and others who just a few years earlier had been credited with reviving public interest in the sport.

The Labor History of the MLB: Players versus Owners

The MLB's first major strike took place in 1981, as owners sought to blunt the impact of free agency. Team owners wanted to receive compensation when one of their players was signed by another team. The players went on strike in protest, and more than 700 games were canceled before the two sides agreed on a limited form of compensation for free-agent signings.

In 1990 owners proposed a sort of salary cap and the elimination of the arbitration system in place for resolving salary disputes. A 32-day lockout ensued, resulting in the cancellation of spring training that year. The owners finally dropped their demands, and the full regular season took place, though its start was postponed by one week.

In "The Baseball Strike of 1994–95" (*Monthly Labor Review*, vol. 120, no. 3, March 1997), Paul D. Staudohar of California State University reports that in June 1994 the owners proposed a salary cap that would have limited the players to 50% of total industry revenues. This represented a pay cut of about 15% for the players; not surprisingly, they declined the offer and went on strike in August. This strike resulted in the cancellation of the 1994 postseason, including the World Series. A ruling by the federal judge Sonia Sotomayor (1954–) ended the strike in March 1995. Sotomayor reinstated the 1990 contract, and the 1995 and 1996 seasons were played under the terms of the expired agreement.

In 2002 the MLB appeared to be on the brink of another strike, the causes of which were mainly rooted in imbalances between teams in large and small markets that resulted in some financial disparities. The team owners lobbied for salary caps, but the players were understandably opposed to this. Instead, the owners came up with the idea of a luxury tax, which would be imposed on any team that spent more than a predetermined amount on player salaries. A strike was thus averted. The impact of the luxury tax, however, has been questionable. For example, the New York Yankees continued to spend vast sums to lure top players; in 2005 the Yankees became the first team in the history of sports to spend more than $200 million on salaries in a season. According to Barry M. Bloom, in "Yanks, Red Sox Hit with Luxury Tax Bills" (December 21, 2005, http://mlb.mlb.com/content/printer _friendly/mlb/y2005/m12/d21/c1286225.jsp), this was about $80 million over the luxury tax threshold, triggering a $34 million tax bill for the team owner George Steinbrenner (1930–2010). Indeed, since 2003 the Yankees have been the biggest spender in the league. Cork Gaines indicates in "The MLB Luxury Tax Should Really Be Called 'The Yankees Tax'" (*Business Insider*, April 6, 2011) that between 2003 and 2011 the Yankees accounted for 91.6% of all MLB luxury tax expenditures, paying a total of $192.2 million during this span.

The other part of the 2002 deal was increased revenue sharing, meaning a greater share of each team's revenue was put into a pot to be divided among all major league teams. The biggest difference between baseball's revenue sharing system and football's is that baseball teams earn significant revenue from local television broadcasts, whereas almost all football coverage is national. The MLB's 2002 contract brought a sharp increase in the amount of local revenue that teams must share. The 2002 collective bargaining agreement ran through the 2006 season; a new agreement, signed during the fall of 2006 and running through the 2011 season, preserved the luxury tax and revenue sharing systems with only minor alterations.

Current Issues in Baseball

By 2011, with the National Football League and the National Basketball Association mired in rancorous labor disputes, baseball had emerged as a model of owner-player harmony. During the summer of 2011, as the two sides met weekly to negotiate a new labor contract, a number of issues dominated the discussions. Phil Rogers reports in "MLB Looks to Remain Beacon of Labor Peace" (*Chicago Tribune*, July 12, 2011) that one of the key points for both the league and the players was realignment. According to Rogers, both sides advocated moving one team from the National League to the American League, so that both leagues had 15 teams. (See Table 4.1.) However, as of September 2011, the American League continued to operate with 14 teams and the National League with 16. As in previous years, competitive balance was also an issue, as the financial gap between high-value teams such as the New York Yankees and small-market teams such as the Kansas City Royals continued to widen.

In 2011 Selig was also preoccupied with the disastrous financial situations confronting two of the league's leading franchises: the New York Mets and the Los Angeles Dodgers. In "Yankees Soar, Mets Plunge on List of Baseball's Most Valuable Teams," Badenhausen notes that the Mets and the Dodgers owed $450 million and $433 million, respectively, before opening day 2011. In the case of the Dodgers, much of the organization's financial trouble stemmed from the messy divorce proceedings between the team's owner, Frank McCourt (1953–), and his wife, Jamie McCourt (1953–). In April 2011 the MLB took the surprise step of assuming control over the organization's business activities. Two months later McCourt filed for bankruptcy protection in a bid to retain ownership of the team. According to Bill Shaikin, in "In Filing for Bankruptcy, Dodgers

Will Ask Judge to Override MLB Rules" (*Los Angeles Times*, June 27, 2011), the league attempted to provide the Dodgers an alternative means of financing to prevent McCourt from regaining control of the organization. As the case continued to drag through the summer, league members began to speculate whether Selig would invoke a unique clause in the MLB constitution, which empowers the commissioner to strip away franchise privileges from any owner who declares bankruptcy.

Diversity in Baseball

Diversity has long been an issue in major league sports in the United States. The MLB was entirely white until Robinson crossed the color line in 1947. Over the next few decades the number of prominent African-American players grew, and baseball took on the appearance of an inclusive sport (at least on the field; managerial jobs for African-Americans remained scarce). However, the trend has reversed itself. Once again, MLB teams have few African-Americans on their rosters, although the number of Hispanic players has increased dramatically. The Baseball Almanac notes in "Major League Baseball Players by Birthplace during the 2010 Season" (2011, http://www.baseball-almanac.com/players/birthplace.php?y=2010) that the country that has produced the greatest number of players born outside the United States is the Dominican Republic, with 139 players in 2010. Venezuela was second with 85. In recent years the MLB has also earned praise for hiring minorities to management and front office positions. In *The 2011 Racial and Gender Report Card: Major League Baseball* (April 21, 2011, http://web.bus.ucf.edu/documents/sport/2011_MLB_RGRC_FINAL.pdf), the University of Central Florida's Institute for Diversity and Ethics in Sport gave professional baseball an A for racial diversity in its hiring practices. However, it also gave the league a B− for gender diversity in its hiring practices.

NATIONAL FOOTBALL LEAGUE

The National Football League (NFL) is the premier U.S. professional sports league, both in terms of popularity and monetary value. Table 4.3 provides an overview of NFL franchise values and revenues. Half of the NFL's 32 teams were worth more than $1 billion during the 2009 season. By comparison, in the MLB only the New York Yankees were valued at over $1 billion in 2010. (See Table 4.2.) The NFL's least valuable team, the Jacksonville Jaguars, was worth $725 million during the 2009 season, a figure that would place it in the top-six among the MLB teams in 2010. Kurt Badenhausen indicates in "The World's 50 Most Valuable Sports Teams" (July 12, 2011, http://blogs.forbes.com/kurtbadenhausen/2011/07/12/the-worlds-50-most-valuable-sports-teams/) that all 32 NFL franchises placed in the top 50 among the most valuable sports teams in the world in 2011. With a

TABLE 4.3

Football team values and revenue, 2009 season

Rank	Team	Current value ($mil)	1-year value change (%)	Debt/value (%)	Revenue ($mil)	Operating income ($mil)
1	Dallas Cowboys	1,805	9	11	420	143.3
2	Washington Redskins	1,550	0	15	353	103.7
3	New England Patriots	1,367	0	20	318	66.5
4	New York Giants	1,182	0	55	241	2.1
5	Houston Texans	1,171	2	17	272	36.5
6	New York Jets	1,144	−2	66	238	7.6
7	Philadelphia Eagles	1,119	0	16	260	34.7
8	Baltimore Ravens	1,073	−1	25	255	44.9
9	Chicago Bears	1,067	−1	9	254	37.3
10	Denver Broncos	1,049	−3	14	250	22.0
11	Indianapolis Colts	1,040	1	4	248	43.2
12	Carolina Panthers	1,037	−1	18	247	15.0
13	Tampa Bay Buccaneers	1,032	−5	14	246	56.1
14	Green Bay Packers	1,018	0	2	242	9.8
15	Cleveland Browns	1,015	−2	15	242	36.1
16	Miami Dolphins	1,011	0	40	247	−7.7
17	Pittsburgh Steelers	996	−2	25	243	17.9
18	Tennessee Titans	994	−1	13	242	23.3
19	Seattle Seahawks	989	0	12	241	34.0
20	Kansas City Chiefs	965	−6	14	235	47.8
21	New Orleans Saints	955	1	13	245	36.7
22	San Francisco 49ers	925	6	14	226	21.0
23	Arizona Cardinals	919	−2	16	236	28.1
24	San Diego Chargers	907	−1	14	233	24.7
25	Cincinnati Bengals	905	−5	11	232	49.4
26	Atlanta Falcons	831	−3	33	231	34.5
27	Detroit Lions	817	−6	43	210	−2.9
28	Buffalo Bills	799	−12	16	228	28.2
29	St Louis Rams	779	−15	8	223	29.0
30	Minnesota Vikings	774	−7	36	221	17.9
31	Oakland Raiders	758	−5	7	217	2.2
32	Jacksonville Jaguars	725	−16	17	220	25.9

SOURCE: Adapted from "Special Report: NFL Team Valuations," in *Forbes*, August 25, 2010, http://www.forbes.com/lists/2010/30/football-valuations-10_NFL-Team-Valuations_Rank.html (accessed June 1, 2011). Reprinted by Permission of Forbes Media LLC © 2011.

total worth of $1.8 billion, the Dallas Cowboys was the second-most valuable team worldwide, slightly behind the British soccer juggernaut Manchester United ($1.9 billion).

With so much money at stake, it is perhaps understandable that owners and players would become embroiled in a highly contentious dispute over revenues, following the expiration of the collective bargaining agreement in early 2011. Further analysis of these negotiations will be discussed later in the chapter.

NFL Structure and Administration

As of 2011 there were 32 teams in the NFL, 16 each in the American Football Conference and the National Football Conference. (See Table 4.4.) Each conference is divided into four divisions—East, North, South, and West—and each division has four teams. The NFL teams play a 16-game regular season, which begins the weekend of Labor Day. Each team also has a weekend off, or bye weekend, during the season; therefore, the full regular season lasts 17 weeks. Sunday afternoons have long been the traditional time for professional football games. The exceptions have been one game per week on Sunday night and another on Monday night, although in recent years the league has also begun scheduling games on Thursday

TABLE 4.4

National Football League teams and divisions

American Football Conference (AFC)	National Football Conference (NFC)
East Division	**East Division**
Buffalo Bills	Dallas Cowboys
Miami Dolphins	New York Giants
New England Patriots	Philadelphia Eagles
New York Jets	Washington Redskins
North Division	**North Division**
Baltimore Ravens	Chicago Bears
Cincinnati Bengals	Detroit Lions
Cleveland Browns	Green Bay Packers
Pittsburgh Steelers	Minnesota Vikings
South Division	**South Division**
Houston Texans	Atlanta Falcons
Indianapolis Colts	Carolina Panthers
Jacksonville Jaguars	New Orleans Saints
Tennessee Titans	Tampa Bay Buccaneers
West Division	**West Division**
Denver Broncos	Arizona Cardinals
Kansas City Chiefs	St. Louis Rams
Oakland Raiders	San Francisco 49ers
San Diego Chargers	Seattle Seahawks

SOURCE: Created by Robert Jacobson for Gale, 2011

nights, and on Saturday nights late in the season. In addition, three games are played annually on Thanksgiving Day. Two teams, the Dallas Cowboys and the Detroit Lions, always host a game on the holiday.

At the end of the regular season, six teams from each conference qualify for the playoffs: the four division champions and two wild-card teams (those with the best record that did not win their division). The champions of the two conferences square off in the Super Bowl. For much of its history, the Super Bowl has taken place in January; however, since 2004 it has been played in early February.

The NFL is administered by the Office of the Commissioner. The first commissioner of the NFL was Elmer Layden (1903–1973), who had been a star player and later a coach at the University of Notre Dame. Layden held the post from 1941 until 1946, guiding the league through the difficult years of World War II, when most able-bodied American men had either joined or were drafted into the armed services. Layden was succeeded by Bert Bell (1895–1959), the cofounder of the Philadelphia Eagles. Under Bell, whose term as commissioner lasted until his death in 1959, NFL attendance grew every year. Bell is famous for his oft-quoted statement, "On any given Sunday, any team can beat any other team."

However, it was Bell's successor, Pete Rozelle (1926–1996), who led the league through its period of dramatic growth during the 1960s and 1970s. Rozelle introduced the concept of long-term network broadcast contracts and applied sophisticated marketing techniques to sell the NFL brand to the American public. Rozelle oversaw the merger between the American Football League (AFL) and the NFL and guided the league to what is generally considered a victory over the players' union during the 1987 labor strike. Rozelle retired in 1989 and was replaced by Paul Tagliabue (1940–). Under Tagliabue the NFL was marked by a great deal of team movement between cities, as owners sought to maximize the revenue they could generate from the sale of stadium naming rights and luxury skybox seating. During Tagliabue's tenure the NFL largely avoided the labor disputes that plagued the other major sports. Tagliabue retired after the 2005 season and was replaced by Roger Goodell (1959–). One of the key issues confronting the new commissioner involved the future of the NFL's revenue-sharing system. The revenue-sharing system is inextricably tied to the team owners' contract with the NFL Players Union. In 2008 the owners unanimously voted to end the players' contract two years early, largely due to their dissatisfaction with the cut of league revenue that was going to the players. This move ultimately set the stage for the 2011 lockout.

NFL History

The NFL came to life in 1920 as the American Professional Football Association (APFA). The league adopted its current name two years later, but professional football actually dates back to 1892, when a Pittsburgh club paid Pudge Heffelfinger (1867–1954) $500 to play in a game.

The APFA—which was based in a Canton, Ohio, automobile dealership—consisted of 11 teams, all but one of them located in the Midwest. In its original form the APFA was not really a league in the modern sense; it was essentially an agreement among member teams not to steal players from each other. Even though professional football remained secondary to the college version during its early years, it gradually gained in popularity when former college stars such as Red Grange (1903–1991) and Benny Friedman (1905–1982) turned professional. An annual championship game was established in 1933. By this time most of the league's teams, with the notable exception of the Green Bay Packers, had left the small towns of their birth for bigger cities.

Professional football began to challenge college football's dominance in the years following World War II, as a faster-paced, higher-scoring style drew new fans. The NFL expanded to the West Coast in 1945, when the Cleveland Rams relocated to Los Angeles. By the 1950s professional football was firmly entrenched as a major sport in the United States, as television effectively captured the heroics of glamorous stars such as Bobby Layne (1926–1986), Paul Hornung (1935–), and Johnny Unitas (1933–2002). The explosive growth of professional football led to the creation of a rival league, the AFL, in 1960, resulting in a costly bidding war for the services of top players. By the mid-1960s professional football had eclipsed baseball as the nation's favorite sport. In 1970 the two football leagues merged. The AFL's 10 teams plus three NFL teams became the American Football Conference; the remaining 13 NFL teams became the National Football Conference. The champions of the two conferences would meet in the newly created Super Bowl to determine the world champion of professional football.

The NFL was the biggest spectator sport in the United States during the 1970s and 1980s. In most years the Super Bowl was the most watched television show of any kind, and *Monday Night Football* set a new standard for sports broadcasting with its innovative mixture of sports and entertainment. Since the 1990s the popularity of football has spread internationally. In 1993 the NFL launched the World League of American Football, whose name was changed to NFL Europe in 1997. NFL Europe, with teams in Germany and the Netherlands, served as a sort of development league in which a player's skills could be honed to reach NFL standards. In June 2007 the NFL abruptly announced that it was shutting down NFL Europe. Its final game, the World Bowl Championship match in which the Hamburg Sea Devils defeated the Frankfurt Galaxy by a score of 37–28, drew a crowd of more than 48,000.

The NFL Salary Cap

Unlike the MLB and the National Basketball Association (NBA), the NFL has a hard salary cap, meaning teams cannot spend more than a specified amount on salaries under any circumstances. For the players and their union, free agency is considered an acceptable trade-off for the introduction of salary caps. With each new contract, the size of the salary cap is a subject of intense negotiation, but to date there have not been any work stoppages over it. Salary caps are considered an important way to ensure competition across the league: They stop the large-market teams from buying their way to the Super Bowl, and they give the smaller-market teams such as Kansas City, Cincinnati, and Green Bay the ability to afford high-performing players.

Studies in sports economics show a strong correlation between total team salary and winning percentage. In "Buying Success: Relationships between Team Performance and Wage Bills in the U.S. and European Sports Leagues" (Rodney Fort and John Fizel, eds., *International Sports Economics Comparisons*, 2004), Robert Simmons and David Forrest analyze salary expenditures and percentages of wins in seven professional sports leagues during the 1980s and 1990s: three European soccer leagues, the MLB, the National Hockey League (NHL), the NBA, and the NFL. The results show that, in general, a higher overall team salary was associated with a greater likelihood of higher point scoring (in the European leagues) and of entering playoffs (in the North American leagues). Salary caps were invented precisely to mitigate this effect, and by and large they have been effective at balancing the wealth within leagues. The NFL's cap is the "hardest" (it has the fewest loopholes) and as such has had the biggest balancing effect. Of course, wealth parity does not always translate into winning percentage parity because there are so many other variables involved, such as whether management makes good decisions about how to distribute its limited payroll.

Labor Disputes in the NFL

The NFL Players Union was formed in 1956, when players on the Green Bay Packers and the Cleveland Browns used a collective approach to demand minimum salaries, team-paid uniforms and equipment, and other benefits from owners. The owners refused to respond to any of these demands. The union threatened to sue, a threat strengthened by *Radovich v. National Football League* (352 U.S. 445 [1957]), in which the U.S. Supreme Court ruled that the NFL did not enjoy the same special status as the MLB did with regard to antitrust laws. The owners eventually gave in to most of the players' demands but did not formally recognize the union for collective bargaining purposes. The NFL Players Association (NFLPA), as it was by then named, did not become the official bargaining agent for players until 1968, following a brief lockout and strike.

After the merger of the NFL and the AFL, the NFLPA focused on antitrust litigation that challenged the so-called Rozelle Rule, which required a team signing a free agent to compensate the team losing the player, thereby severely limiting players' ability to benefit from free agency. The union succeeded in getting the Rozelle Rule eliminated in 1977.

When the NFLPA went on strike for a month in 1987, the owners responded by carrying on with the schedule by using replacement players and a handful of veterans who chose to cross the picket line. With support weakening, the union ended its strike in October 1987. Free agency finally came to the NFL in 1992, and this was balanced by the introduction of salary caps during the mid-1990s. The NFL has experienced relatively smooth labor relations since then. The most recent collective bargaining agreement, which was renewed in March 2006, was supposed to be active through the 2011 season. The owners, however, abruptly opted out of the agreement in 2008, setting the stage for the NFL's first genuine labor strife since the mid-1990s.

In August 2008, with a standoff between players and owners looming on the horizon, the NFLPA executive director Gene Upshaw (1945–2008) died of cancer. The following March the NFLPA unanimously elected DeMaurice Smith (1964–), a District of Columbia lawyer, as Upshaw's successor. As the expiration of the collective bargaining agreement approached, a number of key issues dividing players and owners materialized. At the heart of the dispute was the question of revenue sharing. With the league generating roughly $9 billion in annual revenues by decade's end, the stakes for both sides were high. Owners also wanted to expand the regular-season schedule by two games, from 16 to 18, something the players adamantly opposed. The players, for their part, wanted to increase pensions and expand medical benefits for retired players, while also implementing stricter safety provisions for active players.

Serious negotiations between the NFLPA and NFL owners began in February 2011, shortly after Super Bowl XLV. As talks faltered, it emerged that the league had included a clause in its latest round of television contracts that guaranteed the owners $4 billion in broadcast revenues, regardless of whether a single game was played during the 2011 season. In the eyes of many, this guaranteed money put the owners at a significant advantage in the talks. The NFLPA strenuously objected to this provision in the television contracts, arguing that the league was legally required to provide benefits for both owners and players when entering into any contract. According to CBS Sports, in "Federal Judge: NFL Can't Keep TV Revenue" (March 2, 2011, http://www.cbssports.com/nfl/story/14757584/federal-judge-nfl-cant-keep-tv-revenue), on March 1, 2011, Judge David Singleton Doty (1929–) of the U.S. District Court ruled in favor of the players, deeming that the television contracts were in violation of the former collective bargaining agreement. As discussions intensified, the league and the players agreed to extend the collective bargaining agreement expiration date by more than a week, in the hope of forging a deal. However, the two sides were unable to resolve their differences, so on March 11 the players union voted to decertify.

On March 12 the NFL owners imposed a lockout, which prohibited players from using team facilities or signing new contracts. That same day the players filed an antitrust suit against the league in federal court, seeking an injunction against the lockout. The case was titled *Brady v. NFL*, after Tom Brady (1977–), the star quarterback of the New England Patriots and one of the league's high-profile players. On April 25 Judge Susan Richard Nelson (1952–) of the U.S. Court of Appeals for the Eighth Circuit ruled in favor of the players and ordered the owners to lift the lockout. The NFL owners subsequently filed for a stay of Judge Nelson's order, pending an appeal; the stay was eventually granted by the Court of Appeals for the Eighth Circuit.

Talks continued intermittently into the summer, but with little progress. Finally, on July 14 the two sides came to an agreement on a new wage scale for rookie players, which would lower the cap on contract amounts for top draft picks. The following week, on July 21, the owners ratified a new collective bargaining agreement. Mark Maske reports in "NFL Back in Business after Player Leaders Recommend Ratification of CBA" (*Washington Post*, July 25, 2011) that the players unanimously approved the new collective bargaining agreement on July 25. Key provisions of the 10-year agreement included a new revenue sharing split, which granted the owners 53% of total revenues and the players 47%; a fund of between $900 million and $1 billion for retired players, $620 million of which was earmarked for the Legacy Fund, a newly formed program aimed at assisting players who retired prior to 1993; and a protection benefit for injured players, with a value of up to $1.5 million over two years. The question of extending the regular season to 18 games was shelved until 2013. With the new collective bargaining agreement in place, the four-and-a-half-month lockout ended and the 2011 NFL season was saved.

Issues Surrounding Retired Players

Since the beginning of the 21st century greater attention has been focused on the well-being of former players suffering from physical problems resulting from the pounding their bodies took during their active playing careers. Many players with disabilities severe enough to prevent them from working have faced financial hardships besides physical pain. One story that received a great deal of media attention is the case of Mike Webster

(1952–2002), a Hall of Fame–caliber player for the Pittsburgh Steelers. Webster died homeless and destitute at the age of 50 after years of drug addiction and dementia that he believed was caused by the many concussions he suffered during his 17-year career. The NFL denied that Webster's injuries were football-related and withheld assistance. A court later ordered the league to pay Webster's estate more than $1 million.

In June 2007 congressional hearings revealed that the NFL's disability compensation system provided assistance to a shockingly low number of former players who had suffered debilitating injuries, ranging from multiple concussions to severe arthritis necessitating joint replacement. In 2007, in response to this problem, a number of former players—led by Jerry Kramer (1936–) and Mike Ditka (1939–)—formed the Gridiron Greats Assistance Fund (GGAF), a nonprofit foundation that provides financial assistance to former players who need help with medical or domestic issues. According to the GGAF (http://gridirongreats.org/stories/), as of 2011 it had distributed more than $2.5 million in direct assistance and medical aid to needy former NFL players. In spite of these measures, many former players remained angry about their treatment by the league. In July 2011, as owners and players were finalizing terms on the new collective bargaining agreement, a group of 75 former players filed a lawsuit against the league. ESPN reports in "Ex-Players Sue NFL over Concussions" (July 20, 2011, http://espn.go.com/nfl/story/_/id/6785702/seventy-five-ex-players-sue-nfl-concussions) that the retired players accused the NFL of deliberately withholding information about the harmful effects of concussions for decades. As a result, the players were seeking unspecified compensation from the league.

NATIONAL BASKETBALL ASSOCIATION

Professional basketball has changed drastically since its early days; in fact, its evolution has perhaps been more pronounced than that of any other major sport—in dress, style of play, and, most noticeably, the racial composition of teams. Once a sport that featured white men in close-fitting uniforms hoisting up set shots from chest level, by the late 20th century basketball was largely an African-American phenomenon, featuring loose-fitting uniforms, a hip-hop sensibility, and an emphasis on the shortest-range shot of all: the slam dunk. Even though a sport such as hockey, for example, has always been dominated by white fans and players, basketball's racial shift has led to an identity crisis of sorts, with the issue of race becoming a major feature of discussion about the game.

NBA Structure and Administration

The 30-team NBA is divided into two conferences: the Eastern Conference, which consists of the Atlantic, Central, and Southeast Divisions; and the Western Conference, which consists of the Southwest, Northwest, and Pacific Divisions. (See Table 4.5.) Each division contains five teams.

The NBA regular season begins in early November. A season consists of 82 games for each team, divided evenly between home and away games. Teams play each of the other teams in their own division four times per season; they play teams in the other divisions of their own conference three or four times; and they play teams in the other conference twice each. The NBA is currently the only one of the major sports leagues in which all teams play each other over the course of the regular season.

The NBA Playoffs begin in late April. Eight teams from each conference qualify: the winners of each of the three divisions plus the five teams with the next best records. Each round of the playoffs is a best-of-seven series. The third round of the playoffs is for the Conference Championship, and the winners of these two series compete against each other in the NBA Finals, the winner receiving the Larry O'Brien Trophy.

In "NBA Lockout Begins after Negotiations between Players, Owners Fail" (*Washington Post*, June 30, 2011), Amy Shipley reports that the NBA generated a record $4.3 billion in revenues during the 2010–11 season. According to Brett Marshall, in "Pro Athletes Should Start Counting Their Blessings" (*Garden City [KS] Telegram*, July 14, 2011), the average annual player salary was over $5.5 million; the league's top-30 players earned an average of $16.5 million per season. During the 2010–11 season the NBA's highest-paid player was Kobe Bryant (1978–), who earned more than $24.8 million, or an average of $302,500 per game. Not surprisingly, Bryant's team, the Los Angeles Lakers, was among the league's most valuable franchises. Table 4.6 shows the values and revenues of select NBA teams for the 2010–11 season.

NBA History

Basketball was invented in 1891 by James Naismith (1861–1939), a Canadian physical education instructor and physician. Working at a Young Men's Christian Association (YMCA) in Springfield, Massachusetts, Naismith was directed by the head of the physical education department to create an indoor athletic game that would keep a class of young men occupied during the winter months. In two weeks Naismith had developed the game, including the original 13 rules of basketball. Among them: "A player cannot run with the ball" and "The referee shall be judge of the ball and shall decide when the ball is in play, in bounds, to which side it belongs, and shall keep the time." Even though he never sought recognition for his invention, Naismith was present at the 1936 Olympic Games in Berlin, Germany, basketball's first appearance as an Olympic event.

TABLE 4.5

National Basketball Association teams and divisions

Eastern Conference	Western Conference
Atlantic Division	**Southwest Division**
Boston Celtics	Dallas Mavericks
New Jersey Nets	Houston Rockets
New York Knicks	Memphis Grizzlies
Philadelphia 76ers	New Orleans Hornets
Toronto Raptors	San Antonio Spurs
Central Division	**Northwest Division**
Chicago Bulls	Denver Nuggets
Cleveland Cavaliers	Minnesota Timberwolves
Detroit Pistons	Oklahoma City Thunder
Indiana Pacers	Portland Trail Blazers
Milwaukee Bucks	Utah Jazz
Southeast Division	**Pacific Division**
Atlanta Hawks	Golden State Warriors
Charlotte Bobcats	Los Angeles Clippers
Miami Heat	Los Angeles Lakers
Orlando Magic	Phoenix Suns
Washington Wizards	Sacramento Kings

SOURCE: Created by Stephen Meyer for Gale, 2011

TABLE 4.6

Selected basketball team values and revenue, 2010–11 season

Rank	Team	Current value ($mil)	1-year value change (%)	Debt/value (%)	Revenue ($mil)	Operating income ($mil)
1	New York Knicks	655	12	0	226	64.0
2	Los Angeles Lakers	643	6	19	214	33.4
3	Chicago Bulls	511	0	11	169	51.3
4	Boston Celtics	452	5	40	151	4.2
5	Houston Rockets	443	−6	16	153	35.9
6	Dallas Mavericks	438	−2	46	146	−7.8
7	Miami Heat	425	17	38	124	−5.9
8	Phoenix Suns	411	−4	45	147	20.4
9	San Antonio Spurs	404	1	10	135	−4.7
10	Toronto Raptors	399	3	34	138	25.3

SOURCE: Adapted from Kurt Badenhausen, Michael K. Ozanian, and Christina Settimi, eds., "NBA Team Values: The Business of Basketball," in *Forbes*, January 26, 2011, http://www.forbes.com/lists/2011/32/basketball-valuations-11_land.html (accessed June 1, 2011). Reprinted by Permission of Forbes Media LLC © 2011.

Basketball was first played professionally in 1896, when members of a YMCA team in Trenton, New Jersey, left to form a squad that would play for money. Two years later a group of New Jersey sports journalists founded the National Basketball League (NBL), which consisted of six teams based in Pennsylvania and New Jersey. The NBL petered out after several years, but during the mid-1930s a new league with the same name was founded. A second professional league, the Basketball Association of America (BAA), was formed by a group of New York entrepreneurs. The BAA, which was in direct competition with the NBL, had teams in New York, Boston, Philadelphia, Chicago, and Detroit. Right before the start of the 1948–49 season, four NBL teams—Minneapolis, Rochester, Fort Wayne, and Indianapolis—joined the BAA, and the following year the NBL's six surviving teams followed suit. The BAA was then divided into three divisions and renamed the National Basketball Association. One division was eliminated the following year, leaving the two that became the forerunners of the modern Eastern Conference and Western Conference of the NBA.

The NBA had no serious competition for the next two decades. That changed in 1967 with the formation of the American Basketball Association (ABA). The ABA lured fans, and quite a few players, away from the NBA with a flashier style of play that featured a red, white, and blue ball. The ABA disbanded in 1976, and several of its teams became part of the NBA. However, by the late 1970s professional basketball's popularity was sagging. Revenue and television ratings were down, and the game had become dull. The league received a huge boost with the emergence of two new stars: Magic Johnson (1959–) of the Los Angeles Lakers and Larry Bird (1956–) of the Boston Celtics, who together are credited with ushering in a new era of popularity and prosperity to the NBA. Behind Johnson and Bird, the Lakers and the Celtics completely dominated the NBA throughout the 1980s. During the 1990s the game was dominated by Michael Jordan (1963–) and the Chicago Bulls. With the charismatic Jordan leading the way, the NBA continued to thrive through most of the decade.

After the 1997–98 season, tensions between players and owners began to heighten, as the salary cap and other issues came to a head. The owners instituted a player lockout, and the two sides did not reach an agreement until January 1999, by which time more than a third of the regular season had been canceled.

At the turn of the 21st century there was a dramatic increase in the number of foreign-born players in the NBA. Mariama Diallo notes in "International Players' Impact on NBA Grows in Past Two Decades" (Voice of America, February 17, 2011) that the number of foreign-born NBA players tripled between 1992, when there were only 21 international players on professional rosters, and

2011, when they accounted for 20% of all players in the league. The NBA reports in "Breaking down the 2011 NBA Draft" (2011, http://www.nba.com/home/global/breakdown_draft_2011_06_28.html) that four of the top-seven picks in the 2011 NBA draft were foreign-born players.

The flow of players across national borders has become a two-way street in recent years. In August 2008 the Atlanta Hawks forward Josh Childress (1983–) signed a three-year, $32.5 million deal with the Greek club Olympiakos. Childress's decision to play in Europe came shortly after the July 2008 announcement by the California high school star Brandon Jennings (1989–) that he would play Italian league basketball after he failed to qualify academically to play at the University of Arizona. In July 2011, with NBA owners and players entrenched in a labor dispute, the New Jersey Nets point guard Deron Williams (1984–) shocked the league when he signed a contract to play with the BC Besiktas in Istanbul, Turkey. The article "NBA Players See Overseas Options as Real Threat to Owners" (*SportingNews*, 2011, http://aol.sportingnews.com/nba/feed/2011-07/nba-overseas/story/nba-players-see-overseas-options-as-real-threat-to-owners) indicates that with the 2011–12 NBA season in jeopardy, more and more players were beginning to explore the possibility of playing overseas.

Current Issues in the NBA

SALARY CAPS. Basketball has a soft salary cap, meaning the amount a team can spend on salaries is limited, but there are loopholes and complications. As a result, there are still great disparities in how much the teams spend. According to Hoops Hype, in "Salaries" (2011, http://hoopshype.com/salaries.htm), the Los Angeles Lakers spent $91.3 million on player salaries during the 2010–11 season, the most in the league. By comparison, the Denver Nuggets paid its players a total of only $28.9 million. For the season, 20 NBA teams were below the $58 million salary cap. Figure 4.1 shows the history of the NBA salary cap since 1984.

Beginning in the late 1980s it became increasingly common for top college players to leave school before graduating and enter the NBA draft. By the mid-1990s the best high school players were foregoing college altogether and moving straight into the professional ranks. The NBA has long sought to discourage players from making the jump from high school to the pros. Toward that end, in 1995 the league enacted a salary limit for rookies, in the hopes of making the move less enticing.

In June 2005, as another labor dispute seemed possible, the league and the players union reached a new collective bargaining agreement. In "The NBA's New Labor Deal: What It Means, Who It Impacts" (*SportsBusiness Journal*,

FIGURE 4.1

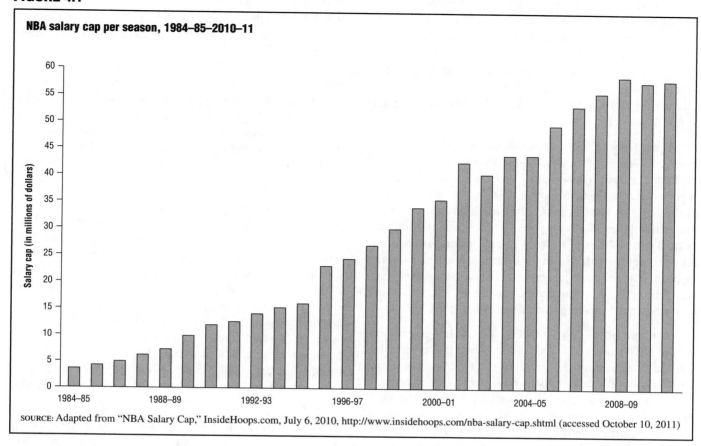

NBA salary cap per season, 1984–85–2010–11

SOURCE: Adapted from "NBA Salary Cap," InsideHoops.com, July 6, 2010, http://www.insidehoops.com/nba-salary-cap.shtml (accessed October 10, 2011)

June 27, 2005), Liz Mullen and John Lombardo explain that the agreement's key provisions included a new rule that prevented players from entering the NBA straight out of high school, increased drug testing, set a 3% increase in the salary cap, and reduced the maximum length of free-agent contracts from seven to six years. This deal remained in effect through the 2010–11 season, after which NBA players and owners once again found themselves in negotiations over a new collective bargaining agreement. Chris Sheridan reports in "Sources: NBA, Union to Meet Monday" (ESPN, July 28, 2011) that NBA players wanted a six-year deal and agreed to reduce their share of league revenues from 57% to 54.6%, a pay cut of roughly $100 million per season. Owners, for their part, insisted on implementing a hard salary cap, like the one that was adopted by the NFL. On July 1, after the two sides failed to forge a deal, the league imposed a lockout. Players and owners later agreed to resume talks on August 1. However, the prospects of a resolution still seemed remote, and the possibility that at least a portion of the 2011–12 season would be canceled became more imminent.

RACE AND THE NBA. Because the NBA is dominated by young African-American males, it struggles with the image the league projects to a predominantly white American public. Some basketball executives, particularly David

Stern (1942–), the commissioner of the NBA, express concern about the message sent by the appearance and behavior of certain players. The arrests of high-profile players on sexual assault, drugs, and weapons charges have not helped matters. According to Jeff Benedict, in *Out of Bounds: Inside the NBA's Culture of Rape, Violence, and Crime* (2004), a startling 40% of NBA players have police records, although, not surprisingly, the NBA disputes this claim.

Nonetheless, over the years the league has taken measures to improve its public image. As one way of addressing this perceived problem, Stern announced in October 2005 a new dress code that would apply to all players when they are participating in NBA-related activities, including arriving at and leaving games, participating in interviews, and making promotional appearances. The new rules banned sleeveless shirts, shorts, T-shirts, chains or medallions worn over the clothes, sunglasses while indoors, and headphones (except on a team bus or plane or in the locker room). The code also required players to wear a sport coat when on the bench but not in uniform. Reactions to the code among players were at best mixed. Some players applauded the league's effort to clean up the game's image. Others were outraged. For example, Janny Hu reports in "Some Players Chafe over Stern

Fashion Statement" (*San Francisco Chronicle*, October 30, 2005) that Tim Duncan (1976–) of the San Antonio Spurs, a player often touted by the league as a model citizen, called the dress code "a load of crap." Hu also quotes Duncan as saying, "I understand what they're trying to do with the hats and do-rags and jerseys and stuff. That's fine. But I don't understand why they would take it to this level."

The article "Pacers' Jackson: Dress Code Is 'Racist': Forward Wears Jewelry to Protest Rules, Which He Says Attacks Culture" (Associated Press, October 20, 2005) reports that Stephen Jackson (1978–), a former member of the Indiana Pacers, openly accused the league of targeting African-American players. Jackson was particularly critical of the ban on wearing chains, noting that chains are associated with hip-hop culture and are a common fashion choice among young African-American men. According to Hu, Stern took issue with the criticism, asserting that "hip-hop doesn't mean sloppy."

THE TIM DONAGHY SCANDAL. A new image problem for the NBA emerged in July 2007, when it was revealed that the veteran referee Tim Donaghy (1967–) was under investigation for allegedly betting on the outcome of NBA games, including games in which he had officiated. The following month he pleaded guilty to two felony charges, admitting that he personally bet on NBA games and that he provided inside information to associates about likely game outcomes. In 2008 Donaghy was sentenced to 15 months in prison. After serving 11 months in a federal prison camp in Florida, Donaghy was released to a halfway house in June 2009 to serve out the rest of his sentence.

THE DECISION. Arguably the most controversial event in recent NBA history came on July 8, 2010, when LeBron James (1984–) announced on live television his decision to leave the Cleveland Cavaliers for the Miami Heat. The ESPN program, known as *The Decision*, attracted nearly 10 million viewers, according to Russell Adams, in "James's Decision Heats up ESPN's Ratings" (*Wall Street Journal*, July 12, 2010). In spite of the ratings, many NBA observers were critical of the broadcast. For example, in "ESPN Sells Its LeSoul" (*Los Angeles Times*, July 10, 2010), James Rainey called the program "loathsomely self-serving" and symptomatic of the "self-absorption and personal branding" that has come to characterize modern professional sports. James himself came under intense criticism for the manner in which he announced his choice to go to Miami—particularly in Cleveland, where he had played the first seven years of his career. Even though James enjoyed great success in Miami by helping lead the Heat to within two wins of an NBA title during his first season in Miami, the negative scrutiny surrounding *The Decision* inflicted significant damage to his public image.

WOMEN'S NATIONAL BASKETBALL ASSOCIATION

The Women's National Basketball Association (WNBA) started play in June 1997 following the celebrated gold medal run of the U.S. women's basketball team in the 1996 Olympics. There had been other professional women's basketball leagues before, but the WNBA was launched with the full support of the NBA, making it much more viable than other upstart leagues. At its inception, the WNBA already had television deals in place with the National Broadcasting Corporation, ESPN, and the Lifetime network.

During its first season the WNBA had eight teams. By 1999 four more teams had joined the league. That same year the players and the league signed the first collective bargaining agreement in the history of women's professional sports. Four more teams were added in 2000. Following the 2002 season, the league's ownership structure was changed. Before that, the NBA owned all the teams in the WNBA. In 2002, however, the NBA sold the women's teams either to their NBA counterparts in the same city or to outside parties. As a result of this restructuring, two teams moved to other cities, and two teams folded. Another team dropped out after the 2003 season.

As of 2011 there were 12 teams in the WNBA: six in the Eastern Conference and six in the Western Conference. (See Table 4.7.) Each team plays a 34-game regular-season schedule, with the top-four teams in each conference competing in the playoffs. The first and second rounds of the playoffs are best-of-three series. The WNBA Finals are best of five. The WNBA season starts in the summer, when the NBA season ends.

Even though the WNBA has gained in popularity, it has been slow to achieve financial success. The league did reach a significant milestone in 2010, when the Connecticut Sun became the first team in WNBA history to turn a profit. Pat Eaton-Robb indicates in "WNBA Hoping to Take Lessons from Sun's Profit" (Associated Press, June 6, 2011) that Laurel J. Richie, the incoming league president, saw the Sun as a valuable model for all WNBA franchises. "I think the league, as well as the teams

TABLE 4.7

WNBA teams and conferences

Eastern Conference	Western Conference
Atlanta Dream	Los Angeles Sparks
Chicago Sky	Minnesota Lynx
Connecticut Sun	Phoenix Mercury
Indiana Fever	San Antonio Silver Stars
New York Liberty	Seattle Storm
Washington Mystics	Tulsa Shock

SOURCE: Created by Stephen Meyer for Gale, 2011

themselves, are always looking for best practices and successes that can be replicated," Richie was quoted as saying. "One of the lessons that I take from Connecticut that it's important having a good venue that attracts a lot of people, that is easy to fill, that is easy to get to."

NATIONAL HOCKEY LEAGUE

Even though professional hockey suffered a major public relations blow following the cancellation of the 2004–05 season, it has recently enjoyed a resurgence in popularity among fans. Rich Thomaselli reports in "NBC and Versus Re-up with Growing NHL" (AdAge.com, April 19, 2011) that by April 2011 the league was expected to generate record revenues for the fifth consecutive season, with earnings projected to approach $2.9 billion. At the same time, sponsorship sales increased 33% between the 2009–10 and 2010–11 seasons, driven largely by a seven-year, $400 million deal with Molson Coors and MillerCoors. Player salaries also grew steadily during this span. Kurt Badenhausen indicates in "The Highest-Paid NHL Players" (*Forbes*, December 1, 2010) that the average NHL player earned $2.4 million during the 2010–11 season, while 10 players earned more than $8 million annually. According to Kurt Badenhausen, Michael K. Ozanian, and Christina Settimi, in "Hockey's Most Valuable Teams" (*Forbes*, December 1, 2010), the average NHL team also increased in value in 2010–11, to $228 million. However, 14 teams saw their values decline in 2010–11, as sponsorship revenues and ticket sales continued to be affected by the depressed economy that followed the economic recession (which lasted from late 2007 to mid-2009). Table 4.8 lists the values and revenues of select hockey teams for the 2009–10 season.

NHL Structure and Administration

The NHL is divided into the Eastern Conference and the Western Conference. (See Table 4.9.) Each conference consists of three divisions, and each division has five teams. The Eastern Conference is split into the Atlantic, Northeast, and Southeast Divisions. The divisions that make up the Western Conference are the Central, Northwest, and Pacific. NHL teams play an 82-game regular season that is split evenly between home and away games. Before the 2004–05 season lockout each team played all the others at least once during the season, but this is no longer the case. Besides playing 32 games against their division rivals, NHL teams now play 10 games against opponents outside of their own conference and 40 games against teams in a different division within their own conference.

At the conclusion of the regular season, the champion of each division plus the five teams in each conference with the next best records compete in the Stanley Cup Playoffs. The structure is similar to that of the NBA: a single-elimination tournament consisting of four rounds of best-of-seven series, culminating in the Stanley Cup Finals, which is usually played in the late spring.

NHL History

Even though hockey in North America started in Canada, the first professional version of the game was launched in the United States. In 1904 the International Pro Hockey League was founded in the iron-mining areas of Michigan's Upper Peninsula. That league lasted only a few years, but in 1910 a new league, the National Hockey Association (NHA), arose. The Pacific Coast League (PCL) was founded soon after the NHA. It was arranged that the champions of the two leagues would play a championship series, the winner gaining possession of the coveted Stanley Cup, a trophy named for Frederick A. Stanley (1841–1908), a former British governor-general of Canada.

World War I (1914–1918) put a temporary halt to the fledgling sport, but when the war ended professional hockey reorganized itself as the National Hockey League. At first the NHL was strictly a Canadian affair. The league initially consisted of five teams: the Montreal

TABLE 4.8

Selected hockey team values and revenue, 2009–10

Rank	Team	Current value ($mil)	1-year value change (%)	Debt/value (%)	Revenue ($mil)	Operating income ($mil)
1	Toronto Maple Leafs	505	8	27	187	82.5
2	New York Rangers	461	11	0	154	41.4
3	Montreal Canadiens	408	20	70	163	53.1
4	Detroit Red Wings	315	−6	0	119	15.3
5	Boston Bruins	302	11	40	110	2.6
6	Philadelphia Flyers	301	10	22	121	13.3
7	Chicago Blackhawks	300	16	0	120	17.6
8	Vancouver Canucks	262	10	42	119	17.6
9	Pittsburgh Penguins	235	6	42	91	−1.6
10	Dallas Stars	227	−8	88	95	6.4

SOURCE: Adapted from Kurt Badenhausen and Michael K. Ozanian, eds., "NHL Team Values 2010: The Business of Hockey," in *Forbes*, December 1, 2010, http://www.forbes.com/lists/2010/31/hockey-valuations-10_land.html (accessed June 1, 2011). Reprinted by Permission of Forbes Media LLC © 2011.

TABLE 4.9

National Hockey League teams and divisions

Eastern Conference	Western Conference
Atlantic Division	**Central Division**
New Jersey Devils	Chicago Blackhawks
New York Islanders	Columbus Blue Jackets
New York Rangers	Detroit Red Wings
Philadelphia Flyers	Nashville Predators
Pittsburgh Penguins	St. Louis Blues
Northeast Division	**Northwest Division**
Boston Bruins	Calgary Flames
Buffalo Sabres	Colorado Avalanche
Montreal Canadiens	Edmonton Oilers
Ottawa Senators	Minnesota Wild
Toronto Maple Leafs	Vancouver Canucks
Southeast Division	**Pacific Division**
Carolina Hurricanes	Anaheim Ducks
Florida Panthers	Dallas Stars
Tampa Bay Lightning	Los Angeles Kings
Washington Capitals	Phoenix Coyotes
Winnipeg Jets	San Jose Sharks

SOURCE: Created by Stephen Meyer for Gale, 2011

Canadiens, Montreal Wanderers, Ottawa Senators, Quebec Bulldogs, and Toronto Arenas (later renamed the Maple Leafs). The first game took place in December 1917. The NHL expanded into the United States during the 1920s, adding the Boston Bruins in 1924; the New York Americans and the Pittsburgh Pirates in 1925; and the New York Rangers, the Chicago Blackhawks, and the Detroit Cougars (which later became the Red Wings) in 1926. By the end of the 1930–31 season there were 10 teams in the NHL. The Great Depression and World War II took their toll on the league, however, and by its 25th birthday the NHL was reduced to six teams. Those six teams—the Canadiens, Maple Leafs, Red Wings, Bruins, Rangers, and Blackhawks—are commonly referred to, though not very accurately, as the "Original Six" of the NHL.

The NHL did not expand again until 1967, when six new teams were added, forming their own division. Two other franchises came on board three years later. In 1972 a new rival league, the World Hockey Association (WHA), was formed. In response, the NHL accelerated its own plans for expansion, adding four new teams over the next three years. This double-barreled expansion of professional hockey in North America diluted the pool of available players, however, and the quality of play suffered as a result. The WHA folded in 1979, and four of its teams joined the NHL. The league continued to expand over the next two decades, as league officials sought to follow demographic trends in the United States. The NHL reached its current total of 30 teams in 2000. Prior to 2011 there was a trend that saw a number of NHL franchises relocate to warmer locations. However, in 2011 there was a slight reversal, when True North Sports

and Entertainment, a Canadian business group, acquired the Atlanta Thrashers and announced plans to move the franchise to Winnipeg, Manitoba. According to ESPN, in "Thrashers Headed to Winnipeg" (June 1, 2011, http://sports.espn.go.com/nhl/news/story?id=6610414), the transaction occurred 15 years after Winnipeg's former NHL team, the Jets, moved to Phoenix, Arizona, to become the Coyotes. Soon after moving the Thrashers to Winnipeg, True North officially renamed the team the Jets.

Labor Issues in the NHL: A Season on Ice

In its long history the NHL has been interrupted only three times by labor strife. The first, a 1992 strike by the NHL Players Association (NHLPA), lasted only 10 days, short enough for all missed games to be made up. A lockout at the start of the 1994–95 season was more disruptive. It lasted three months and resulted in the cancellation of 36 games, nearly half of the regular season.

With the 1995 deal moving toward its 2004 expiration date, negotiations between players and owners turned bitter. Unlike the 1994 lockout, which came at a time when the NHL was enjoying strong fan support and rising popularity, interest in the league had been waning for several years by 2004. As in other major sports, one of the biggest points of contention was proposed limits on the amount teams could spend on player salaries. The league proposed what it called cost certainty, which the NHLPA argued was just a fancy term for a salary cap. The union rejected the idea and instead proposed a luxury tax. Not surprisingly, the owners were opposed. The two sides failed to reach an agreement, and the entire 2004–05 season, from preseason training through the Stanley Cup Finals, was canceled—the first time a major sport had lost a whole season to labor unrest.

In July 2005 the NHLPA and the league finally agreed to the terms of a new collective bargaining agreement, which was published as the *Collective Bargaining Agreement, 2005* (http://www.nhlpa.com/CBA/2005CBA.asp). The deal, which runs through the 2010–11 season, gives players 54% to 57% of league-wide revenues, depending on the total. The agreement includes a salary cap—which according to ESPN was $64.3 million for the 2011–12 season—and enhances revenue sharing to help the smaller market teams remain competitive. It does not include a luxury tax.

Naturally, hockey fans across North America were greatly disappointed by the loss of an entire season. In response, the NHL took measures to try to lure back fans—both those who had wandered away from the sport before the lockout and those who lost interest directly because of it. These measures included a handful of rule changes that were designed to speed up the pace of the game and increase scoring.

MAJOR LEAGUE SOCCER

Major League Soccer (MLS), the premier professional soccer league in the United States, was launched in April 1996. The MLS has a unique ownership and operating structure that is unlike those of other major U.S. sports leagues. Even though the other leagues are confederations of independent franchise owners, the MLS has a single-entity structure, which allows investors to own a share of the league as well as individual teams.

As of the 2011 season, the MLS consisted of 18 teams that were divided into two conferences: Eastern and Western. (See Table 4.10.) Teams compete through a season that runs from April through the MLS Cup championship in November. Each team plays 30 regular-season games, which are evenly divided between home and away matches. Each team plays against every other team in its conference twice, once at home and once away, for a total of 28 games. The remaining two games are against nonconference opponents. Eight teams advance to the MLS Cup Playoffs, which begin in mid-October and culminate in the crowning of a new MLS Cup champion.

Plans to start up the MLS were first announced in December 1993. Twenty-two cities submitted bids to secure teams, of which 10 were selected. A player draft was conducted in February 1996, and the league's first game took place a few months later in April 1996. Two additional teams were added in 1998. The following year the Columbus Crew built the first major league stadium ever constructed specifically for soccer in the United States. The Crew ended up leading the league in attendance for the year.

In 2002 the league was forced to cut two teams for financial reasons, returning the MLS to its original 10-team size. Two new teams were added in 2005, bringing the league to 12 teams once again. The addition of the Toronto FC before the 2007 season made the league 13 strong. The San Jose Earthquakes morphed into the expansion Houston Dynamo in 2005, but a new version of the Earthquakes was formed in San Jose in 2008. The Seattle Sounders FC joined the league in 2009, followed by the Philadelphia Union in 2010 and the Portland Timbers and the Vancouver Whitecaps in 2011.

The MLS is far more ethnically diverse than any of the traditional four major sports in the United States. According to Don Ruiz, in "Sounders FC, MLS Seeking Mass Appeal" (*Olympian* [WA], June 3, 2011), by 2011 there were 390 players born outside the United States on MLS rosters, representing 56 different countries. The MLS has also played a huge role in preparing American players for greater impact on the international soccer scene.

Women's Professional Soccer

Women's professional soccer in the United States has not met with great success, but players and fans are hopeful that its most recent incarnation, Women's Professional Soccer, will catch on. The first women's professional outdoor league to be sanctioned by U.S. Soccer, the Women's United Soccer Association, was launched in 2001. It featured stars from the popular 2000 U.S. Olympic team, including Mia Hamm (1972–), Brandi Chastain (1968–), and Julie Foudy (1971–). Faced with financial struggles, the association suspended operations in September 2003.

In 2004 a new nonprofit organization, the Women's Soccer Initiative, was established with the goal of reviving women's professional soccer in the United States. In September 2007 the Women's Soccer Initiative announced plans to relaunch a professional women's league in 2009. As scheduled, Women's Professional Soccer (2011, http://www.womensprosoccer.com/) opened its inaugural season in March 2009, with seven teams each playing 20 regular-season games. As of August 2011, the league had been reduced to six teams.

THE STADIUM SCRAMBLE

Since the early 1990s there has been an unprecedented boom in the construction of new stadiums for U.S. sports teams. The main reason is that team owners believe they can make more money selling skyboxes to wealthy corporate customers than they can by selling cheaper seats to the masses, and many older stadiums lack luxury accommodations. A skybox can sell for more than $300,000 per season. Table 4.11 shows the typical cost of a luxury skybox at venues that host each of the major sports. An additional incentive is that the revenue from sales of these luxury skyboxes is exempt from the revenue-sharing formulas of both the MLB and the NFL, meaning that teams get to keep all the money that is generated by skybox sales.

Public Funding for Stadiums

The use of public funds in the construction of professional sports venues remains highly controversial. In "The Public Dollars Fueling the NFL Dispute" (*RealClearMarkets*, June 1, 2011), Steven Malanga reveals that the NFL

TABLE 4.10

Major League Soccer teams and conferences

Eastern Conference	Western Conference
Chicago Fire	Chivas USA
Columbus Crew	Colorado Rapids
D.C. United	FC Dallas
Houston Dynamo	Los Angeles Galaxy
New England Revolution	Portland Timbers
New York Red Bulls	Real Salt Lake
Philadelphia Union	San Jose Earthquakes
Sporting Kansas City	Seattle Sounders
Toronto FC	Vancouver Whitecaps FC

SOURCE: Created by Stephen Meyer for Gale, 2011

TABLE 4.11

Average prices for luxury suites within major sports leagues, 2011

Sport/league	Averages		
	Qty	Low	High
Major League Baseball (MLB)	70	$119,010	$233,666
National Football League (NFL)	142	$69,281	$223,250
National Basketball Association (NBA)	90	$144,885	$307,820
National Hockey League (NHL)	95	$129,500	$283,166

SOURCE: Adapted from "Luxury Suites," in *Free Venue Information*, Revenues from Sports Venues, 2011, http://www.sportsvenues.com/info.htm (accessed June 21, 2011)

built or renovated 13 stadiums between 1993 and 1999 at a cost of $3.3 billion. Of this, $2.4 billion (73%) came from public funds. Even after the league created a stadium loan program, known as the G-3 fund, in 1999, public financing continued to play a major role in the construction and renovation of new NFL venues. According to Malanga, the NFL built or renovated 12 more stadiums between 1999 and 2011, at a total cost of nearly $8 billion; of this sum, roughly 40% came from public funding. One of the most impressive NFL venues ever built, Cowboys Stadium in Arlington, Texas, opened in 2009 at a total cost of $1.2 billion, according to Ballparks.com (2011, http://football .ballparks.com/NFL/DallasCowboys/newindex.htm). To help finance construction, the Dallas Cowboys received $325 million from the city of Arlington. As a result, sales tax in the city rose by 0.5%, while the hotel tax rose by 2% and the car rental tax rose by 5%. The Cowboys also obtained an additional $150 million from the league, of which it still owed $71.4 million in 2010. Maury Brown reports in "Leaked NFL Documents Show 13 Teams Owe Hundreds of Millions to League for Stadium Debt" (Bizoffootball.com, July 9, 2011) that the 13 NFL franchises that had borrowed from the G-3 fund still owed the league a total of $771.9 million in 2010.

NFL owners usually argue that a new stadium will generate additional tax revenue because as fans flock to the new facility they will spend vast sums of money at nearby businesses. However, opponents of public funding for stadiums have challenged the view that stadiums provide economic benefits to the surrounding region. In *Do Economists Reach a Conclusion on Subsidies for Sports Franchises, Stadiums, and Mega-Events?* (September 2008,

http://www.aier.org/ejw/archive/doc_view/3626-ejw-200809), Dennis Coates and Brad R. Humphreys report on survey data and economic research measuring the benefits of subsidies for sports facilities and conclude that from an economic standpoint, most research does not support subsidies. They state, "The large and growing peer-reviewed economics literature on the economic impacts of stadiums, arenas, sports franchises, and sport megaevents has consistently found no substantial evidence of increased jobs, incomes, or tax revenues for a community associated with any of these things. . . . If professional sports franchises and facilities do not have any important positive economic impact in the local economy, then subsidies for the construction and operation of these facilities are even more difficult to justify."

Corporate Sponsorship of Stadiums

Another source of revenue from stadiums comes from the sale of naming rights. Where in the past most stadiums had straightforward names such as Tiger Stadium or the Houston Astrodome, in the 21st century an increasing number of facilities bear the name of a corporate sponsor that has paid millions of dollars for the privilege. The following are only three out of several examples that Revenues from Sports Venues cites in *Free Venue Information* (July 22, 2011, http://www.sports venues.com/pdf/names.pdf):

- Comerica Park in Detroit, home of the MLB's Detroit Tigers ($66 million for 30 years)

- American Airlines Center in Dallas, home of both basketball's Mavericks and hockey's Stars ($195 million for 30 years)

- Citi Field in Flushing, New York, home of baseball's New York Mets ($400 million for 20 years)

Sometimes these deals backfire. For example, Darren Rovell reports in "Astros Stuck with Enron Name—For Now" (January 25, 2002, http://espn.go.com/sportsbusiness/ s/2002/0124/1316712.html) that in 1999 Enron, a U.S. energy company, signed a 30-year, $100 million deal with the Houston Astros. In 2001 Enron filed for bankruptcy following an accounting scandal. The collapse of the company forced the Astros to buy their way out of the deal to get Enron's name off their stadium. In 2002 a new sponsor was found, and the stadium was rechristened Minute Maid Park.

CHAPTER 5
OTHER PROFESSIONAL SPORTS

As important as professional team sports are in the United States, Americans' sports obsession extends well beyond them. Not every sports enthusiast is engrossed by the hoopla of *Monday Night Football* or the high-flying acrobatics of the National Basketball Association. Some fans prefer the quiet beauty of a perfect putt or the battle of wills that takes place across the Centre Court net at Wimbledon. Others are attracted to the blunt truth of boxing or the raw speed of the National Association for Stock Car Auto Racing. This chapter considers several sports that fall below the top tier of U.S. sports in terms of audience or revenue but are nevertheless important components of the nation's professional sports culture.

GOLF

Professional golf in the United States is coordinated by the Professional Golfers' Association (PGA) of America, a nonprofit organization that promotes the sport while enhancing golf's professional standards. The PGA of America (http://www.pga.com/pga-america) states that in 2011 there were more than 28,000 PGA professionals in the United States, both men and women, making it the largest working sports organization in the world. However, most of these members were primarily golf instructors; only a small fraction competed in high-profile tournaments.

The PGA of America traces its roots to 1916, when a group of golf professionals and serious amateurs in the New York area got together at a luncheon that was sponsored by the department store magnate Lewis Rodman Wanamaker (1863–1928). The point of the meeting was to discuss forming a national organization to promote golf and elevate the occupation of golf professionals. The meeting led to the organization of the first PGA Championship tournament, which was played later that year. The PGA Championship has grown to become one of professional golf's four major championships, along with the British Open, the Masters, and the U.S.

Open. Together, these four tournaments make up the unofficial Grand Slam of Golf. (See Table 5.1.) Besides the PGA Championship, the PGA of America sponsors three other top golf events: the Senior PGA Championship; the Ryder Cup, which every two years pits a team of top American golfers against their European counterparts; and the PGA Grand Slam of Golf, an annual event in which the winners of the four major championships compete head to head. Besides these championships, the PGA of America also conducts about 40 tournaments for PGA professionals.

However, while professional golfers in the United States are members of the PGA of America, most of the actual golf they play is under the auspices of other organizations. Worldwide, professional golf is organized into several regional tours, each of which usually holds a series of tournaments over the course of a season. There are approximately 20 of these tours around the world, each run by a national or regional PGA or by an independent tour organization. Each tour has members who may compete in as many of its events as they want. Joining a tour usually requires that a golfer achieve some specified level of success, often by performing well in a qualifying tournament. A player can be a member of multiple tours.

The History of the PGA

According to the PGA Tour (2011, http://www.pgatour.com/company/pgatour_history.html), the first U.S. Open took place in 1895 in Newport, Rhode Island. Ten professionals and one amateur competed in the event. The Western Open made its debut in Chicago, Illinois, four years later. Tournaments were initiated throughout the country at about this time, although there was no coordination or continuity among them. English players dominated the competition in U.S. tournaments. As interest in golf continued to grow, American players improved. Enthusiasm for the sport began to increase after Johnny McDermott (1891–1971) became

TABLE 5.1

Golf Grand Slam events

Event	Location	Scheduled time
The Masters	Augusta, Georgia	April
U.S. Open	Location varies	June
British Open	Location varies	July
PGA Championship	Location varies	August

SOURCE: Created by Robert Jacobson for Gale, 2011

the first U.S.-born player to win the U.S. Open in 1911. By the 1920s professional golf had spread to the West Coast and southward to Florida, and the prize money was becoming substantial.

The PGA Tour was formally launched in late 1968, when the Tournament Players Division of the PGA broke away from the parent organization. The tour grew during the 1970s and 1980s, with its total annual revenue increasing from $3.9 million in 1974 to $229 million in 1993. In "PGA Tour's Investments Suffer in '08" (*SportsBusiness Journal*, September 7, 2009), Jon Show reports that even though the PGA Tour lost financial value due to the economic downturn (which lasted from late 2007 to mid-2009), "combined revenue from tournaments and supporting business" was still "creeping closer to the $1 billion mark" by 2008.

To a large extent, PGA revenues during these years were driven by the popularity of Tiger Woods (1975–), the world's premier golfer of the early 21st century. Indeed, Woods's impact on tournament television ratings and attendance was enormous. Michael McCarthy notes in "Financial Impact for Golf Felt All around with Tiger Woods Gone" (*USA Today*, January 28, 2010) that when Woods missed the 2008 PGA Championship due to a knee injury, the tournament's final round attracted roughly 4 million television viewers. When Woods returned to competition a year later, television viewership for the final round of the PGA Championship rose to 10.1 million. In December 2009, amid revelations that he had been cheating on his wife, Elin Nordegren (1980–), Woods announced that he was taking an indefinite hiatus from the game. His absence hurt the tour almost immediately. According to McCarthy, when Woods withdrew from the Chevron World Challenge, tournament organizers refunded $20,000 worth of tickets and reduced the price on 2010 tickets by 20%. In the aftermath of his infidelity scandal, Woods himself lost lucrative sponsorship deals with Accenture, AT&T, and Gillette.

Even after Woods returned to tournament play the following spring, he continued to struggle with injuries, causing the sport's popularity to decline further. When Woods failed to finish in the top 10 of the 2010 PGA Championship, ratings for the tournament's final round

fell by 3.6 million viewers compared to the previous year, according to Richard Sandomir, in "PGA Says Viewership Decline Shouldn't Be Costly in TV Talks" (*New York Times*, August 20, 2010). Woods returned to form in the 2011 Masters, launching an impressive comeback bid in the final round before finishing tied for fourth. However, he also suffered injuries to both his knee and Achilles tendon during the tournament, which subsequently forced him to miss the 2011 U.S. and British Opens. In July 2011, in the midst of these health woes, Woods surprised many in the golf world by firing Steve Williams (1963–), his longtime caddy. Gene Wojciechowski suggests in "Where Is Golf Going?" (ESPN, July 19, 2011) that Woods's continued struggles have left professional golf in a state of deep uncertainty.

The Champions Tour

The Champions Tour, which is run by the PGA Tour, hosts 30 events each year in the United States and Canada for golfers at least 50 years old. Many of the most successful players on the PGA Tour go on to play on the Champions Tour when they reach age 50. The tour grew out of a highly successful 1978 event called the Legends of Golf, which featured two-member teams composed of some of the game's best-known former champions. Following the success of the Legends event, the Senior PGA Tour was established in 1980. The Senior Tour proved remarkably popular, as fans flocked to golf courses and tuned in on television to see legendary competitors such as Arnold Palmer (1929–) and Sam Snead (1912–2002) in action. At the start of the 2003 season, the Senior Tour changed its name to the Champions Tour.

Most tournaments on the Champions Tour are played over three rounds (54 holes) rather than the customary four rounds (72 holes) of PGA tournaments. The five majors of the senior circuit are exceptions; they are played over four rounds. The major tournaments of the Champions Tour are the Senior PGA Championship, the Senior Players Championship, the Senior British Open, the U.S. Senior Open, and the Tradition. Due to corporate sponsorship, the Senior Players Championship has been known as the Constellation Energy Senior Players Championship since 2007. In 2011 the Regions Financial Corporation began sponsoring the Tradition, which subsequently became known as the Regions Tradition.

The Nationwide Tour

The Nationwide Tour is the developmental tour for the PGA Tour. Its players are professionals who have missed the criteria to get into the main tour by failing to score well enough in the PGA Tour's qualifying tournament, known as the Qualifying School, or who have made it into the main tour but failed to win enough money to stay there. The Nationwide Tour gets its name from the company that bought the naming rights in 2003, the Nationwide Mutual Insurance Company of Columbus, Ohio. It was called the Nike Tour and the Buy.com Tour before that. When the tour was first launched in its original form in 1990, it was known as the Ben Hogan Tour. In 2011 the Nationwide Tour (http://www.pgatour.com/h/schedule/) consisted of 26 regular-season events.

Other Men's Tours

In 1996 the International Federation of PGA Tours was formed by golf's five chief governing bodies around the world. As of 2011 the International Federation (http://www.worldgolfchampionships.com/wgc/international federation/index.html) had six members: the Asian Tour (Singapore), the Japan Golf Tour Organization, the PGA European Tour, the PGA Tour (United States), the PGA Tour of Australasia, and the Sunshine Tour (South Africa). Together, these tours sanction the Official World Golf Rankings. The federation also had two associate members: the Canadian Tour and the Tour de las Americas (Venezuela).

The PGA European Tour, headquartered in England, is the premier professional golf tour in Europe and is second only to the PGA Tour in money and international prestige. The European Tour was established by the British PGA, but in 1984 it became a separate entity. In 2011 the European Tour (2011, http://www.european tour.com/europeantour/tournament/index.html) consisted of 54 tournaments. Most of the top players on the European Tour, including Ernie Els (1969–), Sergio Garcia (1980–), and Padraig Harrington (1971–), are also members of the PGA Tour. Like the PGA Tour, the European Tour has a developmental tour, called the Challenge Tour, and a senior tour, called the European Seniors Tour. In 2008 the European Tour introduced the Race to Dubai, a season-long competition over 51 tournaments in 26 destinations featuring players from at least 40 countries, culminating in the extremely lucrative Dubai World Championship.

Women's Tours

Women's professional golf, like men's golf, is organized into several regional tours. The top tour for female professional golfers is the Ladies Professional Golf Association (LPGA), which operates the LPGA Tour. Unlike the PGA Tour, the LPGA Tour and the LPGA are not distinct organizations. Both of these terms generally refer to the LPGA that is based in the United States. Internationally, there are other regional LPGAs and tours, including the LPGA of Japan, the LPGA of Korea, the Australian Ladies Professional Golf Tour, and the Ladies European Tour.

Founded in 1950 by a group of 13 golfers, the LPGA is the oldest continuing women's professional sports organization in the United States. It features the best female golfers from all over the world. The 2011 LPGA Tour (http://www.lpga.com/tournaments_index.aspx) consisted of 27 regular-season tournaments, as well as four majors: the Kraft Nabisco Championship, the Wegmans LPGA Championship, the U.S. Women's Open, and the Ricoh Women's British Open (held jointly with the Ladies European Tour).

Besides the main tour, the LPGA also coordinates a developmental tour called the Duramed Futures Tour. The Futures Tour began in Florida in 1981 as the Tampa Bay Mini Tour but is now a national tour that functions as a feeder system for the LPGA, filling the same role as the Nationwide Tour does for the men. In 2001 the LPGA also created the Women's Senior Golf Tour for players over the age of 45 years. Its name was changed to the Legends Tour before the 2006 season. In 2011 the Legends Tour (http://www.thelegendstour.com/tournaments.htm) showcased six events.

Women in the PGA

Ever since Babe Didrikson Zaharias (1914–1956) played in the 1938 Los Angeles Open, there have been women who seek to achieve crossover success competing against men in PGA events. Since 2000 most of the attention has focused on Annika Sorenstam (1970–) and Michelle Wie (1989–). In 2003 Sorenstam was dominating women's golf almost as thoroughly as Woods was towering over the other male competitors. That year, she accepted a sponsor's invitation to compete in the Bank of America Colonial tournament. She missed the cut (failed to achieve a good enough score to continue in the second portion of the tournament) by four strokes. Wie has played against men in eight PGA events since 2006, but has failed to make the cut each time.

TENNIS

The modern sport of tennis developed out of various games that involved hitting a ball with a racket or the hand dating back to ancient times. Lawn tennis was developed in 1873 in Wales by Walter C. Wingfield (1833–1912). It is based on the older sport of Real tennis (French for "Royal tennis"), which was itself based on earlier forms of racket sports. Tennis gained popularity across Great Britain, and the first world tennis championship was held just four years later at the All England Croquet Club (which eventually became known as the All England Lawn Tennis and Croquet Club) at Wimbledon. This tournament evolved into the famous Wimbledon Championships, which remain the most prestigious tennis titles to this day. A women's championship was added at Wimbledon in 1884. Over the next several years, tennis spread across many parts of the British Empire, becoming especially popular in Australia.

In the United States, the first National Championship for men's tennis was held in 1881 in Newport, Rhode Island. A women's championship was added six years later. The National Championship moved to Forest Hills, New York, in 1915, where it remained under various names for more than 60 years. Now known as the U.S. Open, the event has been held at the National Tennis Center in Flushing, New York, since 1978.

The Development of Professional Tennis

As tennis spread throughout the British Empire early in the 20th century, national federations were formed in countries where the sport caught on. These federations eventually joined forces to form the International Tennis Federation (ITF), which was the worldwide sanctioning authority for tennis. International competitions between national teams soon arose, the most important being the Davis Cup tournament, founded in 1900, and the Wightman Cup, an annual competition between women's teams from England and the United States, founded in 1923.

Most sports turned professional during the first half of the 20th century, but tennis largely remained an amateur endeavor, a pastime for wealthy country club members. By the late 1920s it became economically feasible for a top player to make a decent living on the professional tour, but it meant giving up the sport's most prestigious, amateur-only events, such as those at Wimbledon and Forest Hills. The move toward professionalism accelerated after Will T. Tilden II (1893–1953), the best player of his time and a winner of seven U.S. singles championships and three Wimbledon titles as an amateur, turned professional in 1931. Over the next few decades more and more top players trickled into the professional ranks, although the professional tour was not glamorous and the money was mediocre. The ITF fought hard against the professionalization of tennis. In 1968 the All England Lawn Tennis and Croquet Club decided to open Wimbledon to professional players, thus ushering in the "open era" of tennis in which professional players are allowed to compete in the sport's biggest tournaments.

About this time women players became frustrated at the gender disparity in tennis prize money. Women winning a tournament often received a mere fraction of what the men's champion in the same tournament took home. In 1971 a women-only professional tour was formed to address these inequities. This new Virginia Slims Tour was an instant hit. It made Billie Jean King (1943–) the first woman athlete in any sport to earn more than $100,000 in a single year.

The most important professional tennis tournaments for both men and women are those that consist of the Grand Slam: the Australian Open, the French Open, Wimbledon, and the U.S. Open. (See Table 5.2.) Only two men have ever won the Grand Slam of tennis: Don Budge

TABLE 5.2

Tennis Grand Slam events

Event	Location	Scheduled time
Australian Open	Melbourne	Last fortnight of January
French Open	Paris	May/June
Wimbledon	Wimbledon, England	June/July
U.S. Open	Flushing Meadows, Queens, New York	August/September

SOURCE: Created by Robert Jacobson for Gale, 2011

(1915–2000) in 1938 and Rod Laver (1938–) in both 1962 and 1969. The total prize money for Wimbledon in 2011 was approximately $23.5 million, with the men's and women's singles champions each receiving a prize of about $1.8 million (based on 2011 exchange rates; http://aeltc2011.wimbledon.com/footer/about/prize-money .html). According to the U.S. Open, in the press release "2011 US Open Base Prize Money Reaches Record $23.7 million" (July 13, 2011, http://www.usopen.org/2011_us _open_base_prize_money_reaches_record_237_million/), the 2011 tournament offered a payout of $23.7 million, with the men's and women's singles champions taking home $1.8 million each.

Men's professional tennis is coordinated by the Association of Tennis Professionals (ATP), which organizes the ATP Tour (the principal worldwide tennis tour), and the ITF, which coordinates international play including the Davis Cup and the Grand Slam tournaments. The ATP was originally formed in 1972 as a sort of trade union to protect the interests of male professional tennis players. The organization assumed its role as the chief coordinating body of the professional tour in 1990. The ATP also operates the Challenger Series, a second-tier professional circuit in which many top players have started their professional careers.

Women's professional tennis is coordinated by the Women's Tennis Association (WTA). The WTA was formed in 1973 as a professional organization to protect the interests of the players. The tour itself, which started out as the Virginia Slims Tour, was originally formed out of protest at the disparity between the prize money for men and women. By 1980 more than 250 women were playing professionally all over the world in a tour consisting of 47 global events. The tour remained under the governance of the Women's Tennis Council, an umbrella agency run by representatives from the ITF, the tournament promoters, and the players, into the 1990s. The WTA Tour in its current form was created in 1995 through the merger of the WTA Players Association and the Women's Tennis Council. The WTA runs the premier professional women's tour, which in 2005 became known as the Sony Ericsson WTA Tour.

TABLE 5.3

Top-10 tennis players, men and women, by earnings, 2010

Player	Nationality	Total earnings 2010*	Major corporate sponsors
Roger Federer	Switzerland	$43.0 million	Nike, Credit Suisse, Gillete
Maria Sharapova	Russia	$24.5 million	Nike, Prince, Tiffany
Rafael Nadal	Spain	$21.0 million	Nike, Kia Motors, Babolat
Serena Williams	United States	$20.0 million	Nike, Hewlett-Packard, Kraft
Venus Williams	United States	$15.0 million	Wilson, American Express, Kraft
Andy Roddick	United States	$14.0 million	Lacoste, Lagardere
Novak Djokovic	Serbia	$10.0 million (tie)	Sergio Tacchini, Head, FitLine
Andy Murray	United Kingdom	$10.0 million (tie)	Adidas, Head, Royal Bank of Scotland
Ana Ivanovic	Serbia	$7.0 million	Adidas, Yonex, Rolex
Jelena Jankovic	Serbia	$5.0 million	Anta, Orbit

*Earnings include prize winnings, endorsements, appearances fees, and exhibitions.

SOURCE: Adapted from Kurt Badenhausen, "The World's Highest-Paid Tennis Players," *Forbes*, August 30, 2010, http://www.forbes.com/2010/08/30/best-paid-tennis-players-business-sports-tennis.html (accessed June 13, 2011)

Besides prize money, professional tennis players also earn large sums through endorsement deals and corporate sponsorships. Table 5.3 shows the top-10 men and women tennis players, based on earnings, in 2010.

AUTO RACING

There are several different top-level auto-racing circuits in the United States, in which different kinds of cars race. The two most popular types of race cars are stock cars and open-wheeled racers. From the outside, stock cars essentially look like the regular cars that populate U.S. highways, except that they are covered with corporate logos. Stock car racing is dominated by the National Association for Stock Car Auto Racing (NASCAR). Open-wheeled cars are single-seat vehicles with special aerodynamic features that allow them to travel at speeds well over 200 miles per hour (322 km/h) without flying off the track. Open-wheeled racing was in a state of civil war between two chief circuits, the Indy Racing League (IRL) and the Champ Car Series, for several years until Champ Car was merged into the IRL in 2008. Another open-wheeled circuit, the Formula One Grand Prix, is dominant in Europe.

NASCAR

The largest sanctioning body of motor sports in the United States is NASCAR, which oversees a number of racing series, the largest among them being the NASCAR Sprint Cup, the NASCAR Nationwide Series, and the Craftsman Truck Series. Once merely a regional diversion in the South, NASCAR has exploded into a nationwide phenomenon, rivaling baseball for the number-two spot behind football for the hearts and viewing hours of American sports fans, though both attendance and television viewership began to slump in 2005, after a decade of impressive growth. By 2010, however, NASCAR had rebounded, as sponsorship revenues increased by 10% over the previous year, according to the article "NASCAR's

Sponsorship Revenue up by 10 Percent" (Sporting News Wire Service, December 8, 2010). Kurt Badenhausen reports in "NASCAR's Most Valuable Teams" (*Forbes*, February 23, 2011) that NASCAR had an estimated 30 million "avid fans" in 2010, making it second only to the National Football League in popularity, with an average race attendance of 100,000 spectators. In all, NASCAR (2011, http://www.nascar.com/guides/about/nascar/) sanctions over 1,200 races per year.

Stock car racing evolved out of bootlegging in the rural South. Alcohol runners would modify their cars to make them faster and more maneuverable. It was natural for these drivers to start racing their souped-up cars against one another.

NASCAR was founded in 1948 by William France Sr. (1909–1992) and Ed Otto (1908–1986) as a way to organize, standardize, and promote racing of unmodified, or stock, cars for entertainment. The first NASCAR Strictly Stock race took place at North Carolina's Charlotte Speedway in June 1949. Over time, modifications were allowed into the sport, and by the mid-1960s only the bodies of the cars looked stock; the innards were specially built for speed.

NASCAR's rapid growth began during the 1970s, when R. J. Reynolds Tobacco Company began to sponsor racing as a way to promote its products after they had been banned from television advertising. The top series, formerly known as the Grand National Series, became the Winston Cup. At about this time, television networks began to occasionally cover stock car racing. Columbia Broadcasting System's broadcast of the 1979 Daytona 500 was the first time a stock car race had been aired nationwide from start to finish.

In 2004 Nextel assumed sponsorship of the series formerly known as the Winston Cup. That year, NASCAR established a new 10-race playoff system called the Chase for the Cup, in which the top-10 drivers (according to NASCAR's point system) after 26 races compete for

TABLE 5.4

Top-10 NASCAR drivers, by earnings, 2010

Driver	Team	Total earnings in 2010*
Dale Earnhardt, Jr.	Hendrick Motorsports	$29.0 million
Jeff Gordon	Hendrick Motorsports	$25.0 million
Jimmie Johnson	Hendrick Motorsports	$24.0 million
Tony Stewart	Stewart-Haas Racing	$18.0 million
Kevin Harvick	Richard Childress Racing	$15.0 million
Carl Edwards	Roush Fenway Racing	$14.0 million
Kyle Busch	Joe Gibbs Racing	$13.0 million
Kasey Kahne	Red Bull Racing Team	$11.5 million
Denny Hamlin	Joe Gibbs Racing	$11.0 million (tie)
Matt Kenseth	Roush Fenway Racing	$11.0 million (tie)

NASCAR = National Association for Stock Car Auto Racing.
*Earnings include merchandise sales, corporate endorsements, driver salary, and race winnings and bonuses.

SOURCE: Adapted from Kurt Badenhausen, "Nascar's Highest-Paid Drivers," *Forbes*, February 23, 2011, http://www.forbes.com/2011/02/23/nascar-highest-paid-drivers-business-sports-nascar-11.html (accessed June 13, 2011)

the series championship. In 2008 the Nextel Cup became the Sprint Cup Series to reflect the merger of Nextel Communications with the phone company Sprint. As of 2011 the Sprint Cup remained the most prominent and lucrative NASCAR racing series.

Table 5.4 shows the top-10 NASCAR drivers of 2010, by earnings.

Open-Wheeled Cars

As millions of fans flocked to stock car racing, the two major open-wheeled series, the IRL and the Champ Car Series, struggled beginning around 2000. The reasons for this are complex, but it is reasonable to attribute the situation in part to the acrimonious relationship between the IRL and Champ Car. Neither was doing well financially, although the success of the rookie Danica Patrick (1982–) breathed some life into the IRL in 2005. When Champ Car was merged into the IRL in 2008, open-wheeled aficionados were hopeful that the merger would help restore the stature of their sport.

Indy Racing League

The IRL was formed in 1994 by a group of drivers breaking away from the Championship Auto Racing Teams (CART; later known as the Champ Car Series), which had coordinated Indy car racing since breaking away from the U.S. Auto Club (USAC) in 1979. The IRL consists of two series: the premier IndyCar Series, which is virtually synonymous with the IRL, and the Firestone Indy Lights Series (formerly known as the Indy Pro Series), which functions as a developmental series for drivers aspiring to join the IndyCar circuit.

Before 1979 the term *IndyCar* was generically used to refer to cars racing in USAC events. By the 1980s IndyCar was a term commonly used to refer to CART,

which by that time was the preeminent sanctioning body for open-wheeled racing in the United States. The name "IndyCar" became the subject of fierce legal battles during the 1990s. The Indianapolis Motor Speedway, home of the Indianapolis 500, trademarked the name in 1992 and licensed it to CART, which in turn renamed its championship the IndyCar World Series. Two years later Tony George (1959–), the president of the speedway, started his own racing series called the Indy Racing League. In 1996 CART sued to protect its right to continue using the IndyCar name. The speedway countered with its own suit. The two groups eventually reached a settlement in which CART agreed to stop using the IndyCar name after the 1996 season, and the IRL could start using it after the 2002 season. The IRL's premier series has been called the IRL IndyCar Series since the beginning of the 2003 season. The 2011 IndyCar Series (http://www.indycar.com/schedule/) featured 17 races from April to October.

Champ Car Series

The USAC was formed in 1956 to take over coordination of the national driving championship from the American Automobile Association, which had launched the championship in 1909. The USAC controlled the championship until 1979, when a group of car owners formed the Championship Auto Racing Teams that they hoped would give them power in negotiations with the USAC over media contracts, race purses, promotion, and other issues. The two entities immediately clashed, and CART soon separated from the USAC to establish its own racing series. Most of the top teams defected from the USAC, and CART quickly became the dominant open-wheeled racing circuit. The USAC held its last National Championship in 1979, before reluctantly handing the reins over to CART.

The IRL's split from CART put open-wheeled racing into a tailspin. The rivalry may have helped pave the way for NASCAR's rise, as both competing organizations struggled for control over the sport's available pot of money. In 2003 CART declared bankruptcy, and its assets were liquidated and put up for sale. A group of CART car owners bought the company and opened the 2004 season under the new name Champ Car Series. Beginning in 2005 Champ Car ran both the Champ Car World Series and the Champ Car Atlantic Championship, which functioned as a developmental circuit for drivers trying to get into Champ Car. In February 2008 the IRL and the Champ Car Series reached an agreement that unified the sport. As a result of the agreement, the Champ Car Series was discontinued.

BOXING

Boxing is unique among professional sports in that there is no nationwide commission that oversees it, no regular schedules, no seasons, and few universal rules.

Every set of matches (called a card) is set up separately, usually by one of a handful of top-level boxing promoters. Each state has its own boxing commission with its own set of rules. Some state boxing commissions regulate the sport more rigorously than others, and the different governing organizations establish their own regulations. For example, variations exist regarding whether a boxer who has been knocked down can be "saved by the bell," whether a referee or a ringside physician has the authority to stop a match, and whether a match should automatically be stopped if a fighter is knocked down three times within one round. In the United States and Canada, state, regional, and tribal boxing commissions are also organized into the Association of State Boxing Commissions, an umbrella organization that helps oversee and regulate professional and amateur fighting in North America.

Boxing matches in the United States consist of a maximum of 12 three-minute rounds with one minute of rest between each round. Opponents in a fight must belong to the same weight class, with competitors being weighed before the fight to ensure that neither holds an unfair weight advantage. Table 5.5 provides a breakdown of boxing weight classes according to the sport's different sanctioning bodies. Three judges at the ringside score the fight according to a 10-point must system; that is,

each judge must award 10 points to the winner of the round and fewer points to the loser of the round. Matches end in one of five ways:

- Knockout—one fighter is unable to return to his feet within 10 seconds of a knockdown

- Technical knockout—a decision is made to stop the fight because one fighter is clearly losing

- Decision—the fight ends without a knockout or technical knockout and is won based on the scoring of the three judges at the ringside

- Draw—the fight ends without a knockout or technical knockout, and the judges award each fighter the same number of points

- Disqualification—the fight is stopped because of a rule infraction on the part of one of the fighters

Unlike other professional sports, boxing does not use a playoff series or a point system to name a champion. In fact, there is not necessarily even a consensus about who is the champion of any given weight class. Different champions are recognized by several competing boxing organizations. The most prominent boxing organizations are the International Boxing Federation, the World Boxing Association, the World Boxing Council, and the World Boxing Organization. A fighter may be recognized as a champion

TABLE 5.5

Men's professional boxing weight classes, by sanctioning body

Weight class	Maximum weight	Sanctioning body
Mini flyweight	105 pounds/47.627 kilograms	Association Boxing Commissions (ABC), International Boxing Federation (IBF), World Boxing Organization (WBO)
Strawweight	105 pounds/47.627 kilograms	World Boxing Council (WBC), International Boxing Organization (IBO)
Minimumweight	105 pounds/47.627 kilograms	World Boxing Association (WBA)
Junior flyweight	108 pounds/48.988 kilograms	IBF, WBO
Light flyweight	108 pounds/48.988 kilograms	ABC, IBO, WBA, WBC
Flyweight	112 pounds/50.802 kilograms	ABC, IBF, IBO, WBA, WBC, WBO
Super flyweight	115 pounds/52.163 kilograms	ABC, IBO, WBA, WBC
Junior bantamweight	115 pounds/52.163 kilograms	IBF, WBO
Bantamweight	118 pounds/53.524 kilograms	ABC, IBF, IBO, WBA, WBC, WBO
Super bantamweight	122 pounds/55.338 kilograms	ABC, IBO, WBA, WBC
Junior featherweight	122 pounds/55.338 kilograms	IBF, WBO
Featherweight	126 pounds/57.153 kilograms	ABC, IBF, IBO, WBA, WBC, WBO
Super featherweight	130 pounds/58.967 kilograms	ABC, IBO, WBA, WBC
Junior lightweight	130 pounds/58.967 kilograms	IBF, WBO
Lightweight	135 pounds/61.235 kilograms	ABC, IBF, IBO, WBA, WBC, WBO
Super lightweight	140 pounds/63.503 kilograms	ABC, WBA, WBC
Junior welterweight	140 pounds/63.503 kilograms	IBF, WBO
Light welterweight	140 pounds/63.503 kilograms	IBO
Welterweight	147 pounds/66.678 kilograms	ABC, IBF, IBO, WBA, WBC, WBO
Super welterweight	154 pounds/69.853 kilograms	ABC, WBA, WBC
Junior middleweight	154 pounds/69.853 kilograms	IBF, WBO
Light middleweight	154 pounds/69.853 kilograms	IBO
Middleweight	160 pounds/72.575 kilograms	ABC, IBF, IBO, WBA, WBC, WBO
Super middleweight	168 pounds/76.204 kilograms	ABC, IBF, IBO, WBA, WBC, WBO
Light heavyweight	175 pounds/79.379 kilograms	ABC, IBF, IBO, WBA, WBC, WBO
Cruiserweight	200 pounds/90.719 kilograms	ABC, IBF, IBO, WBA, WBC
Junior heavyweight	200 pounds/90.719 kilograms	WBO
Heavyweight	Unlimited	ABC, IBF, IBO, WBA, WBC, WBO

SOURCE: Adapted from "Weight Classes or Divisions," in *Ringside by Gus*, 2011, http://www.ringsidebygus.com/boxing-weight-classes.html (accessed June 16, 2011)

in his weight class by more than one of these organizations at a time, or each organization may have a different champion at any given time. Some of the biggest boxing matches are unification bouts between champions who are recognized by two different sanctioning organizations, the winner walking away with both titles.

Because boxing competitions are often international in nature, it is difficult to gauge the size of the boxing industry in the United States. Much of the money comes from cable television, where championship fights are usually broadcast on a pay-per-view basis.

The scoring system for boxing is complex, and the overall rankings can sometimes appear arbitrary. As a result, the sport has long been a tempting target for organized crime and others seeking illicit financial gain. Even in the 21st century bribery is thought to be rampant. Mysterious judging decisions and bizarre rankings are not at all rare. Boxing's reputation also suffers because of the sheer brutality of the sport. Fighters have sometimes died or suffered disabling brain trauma as a result of a particularly violent bout. For example, Mike Tyson (1966–), a former heavyweight champion and convict, once bit off part of Evander Holyfield's ear during a bout.

Over the years, attempts have been made to clean up boxing. Congress has been involved in trying to regulate the sport, and in 1996 it established minimum health and safety standards for professional boxing that were later expanded by the Muhammad Ali Boxing Reform Act of 2000. In 2004 the former boxer Muhammad Ali (1942–) testified in favor of a bill that was introduced by Senator John McCain (1936–; R-AZ) to create a federal boxing commission. The bill was passed by the U.S. Senate, but it failed to pass the U.S. House of Representatives. In 2009 McCain reintroduced the Professional Boxing Amendments Act. Frederic J. Frommer explains in "The Influence Game: Ultimate Fighting Ducks Punch" (Associated Press, February 4, 2009) that "the proposed legislation would establish a U.S. Boxing Commission under the Commerce Department, charged with protecting the health, safety and general interests of boxers. The commission would oversee all professional boxing matches and license boxers, promoters, managers and sanctioning organizations." The bill, according to McCain as quoted by Frommer, would "better protect professional boxing from the fraud, corruption and ineffective regulation that have plagued the sport for far too many years and that have devastated physically and financially many of our nation's professional boxers." The Professional Boxing Amendments Act of 2009 died in committee.

World Boxing Association

The World Boxing Association (WBA; 2011, http://www.wbaonline.com/) was the first sanctioning body of professional boxing. It was formed as the National Boxing Association (NBA) in 1921. The first NBA-sanctioned match was a heavyweight championship fight between Jack Dempsey (1895–1983) and Georges Carpentier (1894–1975). Brilliant and colorful champions such as Joe Louis (1914–1981) carried the WBA through the World War II (1939–1945) era. The dawn of television boosted the popularity of professional boxing during the 1950s. The sport's globalization during this period led the organization to change its name in 1962 to the World Boxing Association, an entity that would usher through future legends such as Ali.

World Boxing Council

The World Boxing Council (WBC; 2011, http://www.wbcboxing.com/) was formed in 1963 by representatives of 11 countries (Argentina, Brazil, Japan, Mexico, Panama, Peru, the Philippines, Spain, the United Kingdom, the United States, and Venezuela) and Puerto Rico (a territory of the United States). Its purpose, according to WBC founders, was to improve the standards of professional boxing, including the safety of fighters. Among the WBC's innovations was the shortening of world championship fights from 15 to 12 rounds in 1983, a move that was eventually adopted by the other sanctioning organizations. In 2003 the WBC filed for bankruptcy in an attempt to avoid paying $30 million in damages from a lawsuit over questionable handling of title fight eligibility. The following year the lawsuit was settled for a lesser amount, allowing the WBC to avoid having to disband and liquidate its assets.

International Boxing Federation

The boxing historian Herb Goldman explains in "Boxing Bodies: A Brief Chronology and Rundown" (*International Boxing Digest*, vol. 40, no. 1, January 1998) that the International Boxing Federation (IBF; 2011, http://www.ibf-usba-boxing.com/) was formed in 1983 by a group of WBA representatives who were upset with the political machinations within the WBA. Its creation was spearheaded by Robert W. Lee, the president of a smaller regional organization called the U.S. Boxing Association (USBA). The new group was originally called the IBF-USBA. During its first year of operation the IBF remained fairly obscure. In 1984, however, the IBF decided to recognize as champions a number of high-profile fighters who were already established title holders within other organizations, including Larry Holmes (1949–) and Marvin Hagler (1952–). When Holmes opted to relinquish his WBC title to accept the IBF's, he lent the IBF instant credibility. The IBF's reputation took a major hit in 1999, however, when Lee was convicted on racketeering and other charges.

World Boxing Organization

The World Boxing Organization (WBO; 2011, http://www.wbo-int.com/) was formed in 1988 by a group of

Puerto Rican and Dominican businessmen who were disenchanted with what they perceived as illegitimate rules and rating systems within the WBA. The WBO's first championship fight was a junior welterweight championship match between Héctor Camacho (1962–) and Ray Mancini (1961–). The WBO achieved a level of legitimacy comparable to that of the WBA, the WBC, and the IBF, largely thanks to its recognition as champions of many of the sport's best-known competitors. The WBO has also tended at times to provide more opportunities for non-U.S.-based fighters than the other organizations. The WBO was formed out of protest against allegedly corrupt practices, but it has certainly exhibited its share of inexplicable decisions that raise questions about the organization's integrity. In "New WBO Division: Dead Weight" (ESPN, February 20, 2001), Tim Graham notes that a particularly embarrassing example took place in 2001, when the WBO twice moved Darrin Morris (1966–2000) up in its super-middleweight rankings, even though Morris had been dead for a year.

Women's Boxing

Women's professional boxing began to gain in popularity during the 1990s. There are three sanctioning bodies that govern women's professional fighting: the International Women's Boxing Federation, the Women's International Boxing Association, and the Women's International Boxing Federation. Part of the sport's popularity can be attributed to the participation of Laila Ali (1977–), daughter of the boxing great Muhammad Ali. Jacqui Frazier-Lyde (1961–), daughter of the legendary boxer Joe Frazier (1944–2011), has also been prominent in the sport. Ali made her professional boxing debut in 1999. In 2001 she and Frazier squared off, with Ali emerging victorious.

The 2004 film *Million Dollar Baby* brought greater attention to the sport of women's boxing, not all of it positive, because the movie highlighted some of the more brutal aspects of the sport. Even though the absence of charismatic new boxers has been an obstacle to the continued growth of professional women's boxing, the amateur version of the sport has been gaining participants. In August 2009 the International Olympic Committee voted unanimously to include women's boxing in the 2012 Olympic Games.

Challenges to Boxing's Future

By 2011 boxing had been declining in popularity for years. A major part of the problem was the lack of big-name, attention-drawing stars, particularly in the heavyweight division. The sport thrives when it is dominated by colorful heavyweights, such as when Ali and Tyson took center stage. Ali was the public face of boxing for decades and was arguably the most recognized athlete in the world. Fans have not been as enthusiastic about plodding champions and contenders with unfamiliar names, such as the Klitschko brothers, Vitali (1971–) and Wladimir (1976–), who were at the top of the heavyweight ranks during the first decade of the 21st century.

The biggest name in boxing since the 1990s has been Oscar De La Hoya (1973–). Nicknamed the "Golden Boy," De La Hoya won an Olympic gold medal in 1992 and went on to capture 10 professional titles in 6 different weight classes. De La Hoya's 2007 match against Floyd Mayweather (1977–), which he lost in a split decision, was the biggest pay-per-view boxing match ever. Robert Cassidy reports in "Boxing Facing Challenge from Mixed Martial Arts" (*Newsday*, August 4, 2007) that the De La Hoya–Mayweather bout generated a record 2.2 million pay-per-view purchases worth $120 million. Another $19.3 million was collected from live spectators. De La Hoya, however, was already past his prime. He announced his retirement in April 2009, a few months after he was badly beaten in a much-hyped match against the rising star Manny Pacquiao (1978–). For most of the 1990s and the first decade of the 21st century, De La Hoya was boxing's only guaranteed big draw. By 2010 Pacquiao had emerged as the sport's top draw, earning fighter of the decade honors from the Boxing Writers Association of America, according to Elie Seckbach, in "Fighter of the Decade: Manny Pacquiao or Floyd Mayweather?" (AOL News, June 3, 2010).

As boxing struggled to regain the allegiance of boxing fans, the sport found itself competing to an increasing degree with the emerging sport of mixed martial arts (MMA), a more brutal sport that allows not only punching but also kicking, wrestling, elbowing, and choking one's opponent into submission. The top MMA circuit, Ultimate Fighting Championship (UFC), has emerged as a serious challenger to boxing for domination of the fight game. As of August 2011, its pay-per-view events did not yet attract as many viewers as those of boxing, but viewership was increasing quickly, and the sport had a large and growing base of loyal, mostly young, fans. It has been suggested that there may also be a racial element to the rise of MMA. Profiled by Steve Cofield in "Mayweather: Whites Needed a Fight Sport, So They Invented MMA" (Yahoo! Sports, July 20, 2009), Mayweather opined that white fans have embraced the sport—many top UFC contenders are white—in response to the dominance of boxing by African-American and Hispanic athletes.

CHAPTER 6
COLLEGE, HIGH SCHOOL, AND YOUTH SPORTS

College athletics function as a minor, or preparatory, league for some professional sports, particularly football and basketball, but there is nothing minor about Americans' passion for them or about the sums of money that intercollegiate sports generate. Just as college sports serve as a feeder system for professional leagues, high schools fill the same role for colleges, and schools often compete for the services of elite teenage athletes. For the most part, high school and college athletes participate in sports for their own rewards. Most of them understand that the chances of striking it rich as a professional athlete are remote. For example, out of 154,345 boys who play on high school basketball teams during their senior year, only 44 (less than 0.03%) will be drafted by professional teams. (See Table 6.1.) Regardless, the money that flows through the sports industry—an industry of which intercollegiate sports are an integral part—is so abundant that its influence can be felt even in U.S. high schools. Even youth sports, such as Little League baseball and youth basketball leagues, have become big business, as industry insiders seek to identify the next generation of superstars at ever-younger ages.

COLLEGE SPORTS

In contrast to professional sports, where turning a profit is the motivating force behind most decisions, college sports must reconcile commercial interests, educational priorities, and a jumble of other influences ranging from alumni pride to institutional prestige. Even though it may make high-minded university officials uncomfortable to admit it, college sports have become big business in the United States.

The most important governing organization of college sports in the United States is the National Collegiate Athletic Association (NCAA), although there are other governing bodies as well.

National Collegiate Athletic Association

The NCAA is a voluntary association whose members consisted of 1,315 institutions, conferences, organizations, and individuals during the 2010–11 school year; 1,062 of them were active member schools. (See Table 6.2.) The NCAA's main purpose, according to its constitution, is to "maintain intercollegiate athletics as an integral part of the educational program and the athlete as an integral part of the study body and, by so doing, retain a clear line of demarcation between intercollegiate athletics and professional sports." In other words, college sports are supposed to be strictly amateur and are supposed to fulfill an educational role.

Organizationally, the NCAA's structure consists of nearly 140 committees, which, since a new governance structure was adopted in 1997, have enjoyed a fair amount of autonomy. Several of these committees are association-wide, including the Executive Committee and committees having to do with ethics, women's opportunities, and minority opportunities. The rest are specific to one of the NCAA's three divisions—Divisions I, II, and III—which classify the schools by the number of sports they sponsor and other factors. NCAA member schools and organizations vote on the rules they will follow. It is then up to the NCAA National Office to implement and enforce the rules and bylaws dictated by the members.

The NCAA's divisions are based on factors such as the number of sports sponsored, attendance at the school's sporting events, and financial support to athletes. Division I is further divided into the Football Bowl Subdivision (FBS, formerly Division I-A) and the Football Championship Subdivision (FCS, formerly Division I-AA). There are also schools that do not offer football, which are sometimes referred to as Division I-AAA, though they may compete against FBS or FCS colleges in other sports. Intercollegiate sports under the auspices of the

TABLE 6.1

Estimated probability of competing in athletics beyond high school

Student-athletes	Men's basketball	Women's basketball	Football	Baseball	Men's ice hockey	Men's soccer
High school student athletes	540,207	439,550	1,109,278	472,644	36,475	391,839
High school senior student athletes	154,345	125,586	316,937	135,041	10,421	111,954
NCAA student athletes	17,008	15,423	66,313	30,365	3,945	21,770
NCAA freshman roster positions	4,859	4,407	18,947	8,676	1,127	6,220
NCAA senior student athletes	3,780	3,427	14,736	6,748	877	4,838
NCAA student athletes drafted	44	32	250	600	33	76
Percent high school to NCAA	3.10%	3.50%	6.00%	6.40%	10.80%	5.60%
Percent NCAA to professional	1.20%	0.90%	1.70%	8.90%	3.80%	1.60%
Percent high school to professional	0.03%	0.03%	0.08%	0.44%	0.32%	0.07%

SOURCE: "Estimated Probability of Competing in Athletics beyond the High School Interscholastic Level," in *Academics and Athletes: Education and Research*, National Collegiate Athletic Association, 2010, http://www.ncaa.org/wps/portal/ncaahome?WCM_GLOBAL_CONTEXT=/ncaa/NCAA/Academics+and+ Athletes/Education+and+Research/Probability+of+Competing/ (accessed June 1, 2011). © National Collegiate Athletic Association. 2011. All rights reserved.

TABLE 6.2

Composition of NCAA Membership, 2010–11

	Division I				Division II	Division III	
	I-FBS	I-FCS	I	Total			Total
Active	120	117	100	337	290	435	1,062
Provisional	0	0	1	1	5	8	14
Candidacy					16		16
Voting conference	11	11	9	31	22	42	95
Nonvoting conference	0	3	18	21	0	21	42
Corresponding							13
Affiliated							73
Total							**1,315**

Notes: NCAA = National Collegiate Athletic Association.
FBS = Football bowl subdivision.
FCS = Football championship subdivision.

SOURCE: "2010–11 Composition," in *Composition and Sports Sponsorship of the NCAA*, National Collegiate Athletic Association, 2011, http://www.ncaa .org/wps/portal/ncaahome?WCM_GLOBAL_CONTEXT=/ncaa/NCAA/ About+The+NCAA/Membership/membership_breakdown.html (accessed June 1, 2011). © National Collegiate Athletic Association. 2011. All rights reserved. Please note: Statistics provided in tables differ from year to year and are subject to change.

NCAA are also divided into conferences, which function like the leagues and divisions in professional sports. The most prominent conferences, often referred to collectively as the Big Six, are shown in Table 6.3. The colleges in these conferences sponsor many sports, have large athletic budgets, and draw many fans. Table 6.4 shows that among both men and women, basketball is the sport sponsored by the greatest number of colleges and universities.

History of the NCAA

Until the mid-19th century there was no governing body that oversaw intercollegiate athletics. Typically, it was students rather than faculty or administrators who ran the programs. Even so, there was already a fair amount of commercialization and illicit professionalism in college sports. For example, James Hogan (1876–1910), the captain of the Yale University football team in 1904, was compensated with, among other things, a suite of rooms in the dorm, free University Club meals, profits from the sale of programs, and a 10-day vacation to Cuba. What ultimately led administrators to the conclusion that formal oversight was necessary was the sheer brutality of college sports, particularly football. According to *The Business of Sports* (2004), edited by Scott R. Rosner and Kenneth L. Shropshire, there were at least 18 deaths and more than 100 major injuries in intercollegiate football in 1905 alone. In response to the growing violence of college football, President Theodore Roosevelt (1858–1919) convened a White House conference of representatives from Harvard, Princeton, and Yale Universities to review the rules of the game. When the deaths and serious injuries continued, Henry M. Mac-Cracken (1840–1918), the chancellor of the University of the City of New York (now New York University), called for a national gathering of representatives from the major football schools. In early December 1905 representatives of 13 schools met with MacCracken and formed a Rules Committee. This group held another meeting on December 28 that was attended by representatives of more than 60 college football programs, during which the Intercollegiate Athletic Association (IAA) was formed. The IAA was a national organization with 62 founding members, including schools in Minnesota, Nebraska, New Hampshire, New York, Ohio, Pennsylvania, and Texas. The IAA became the NCAA in 1910.

Initially, the NCAA's chief role was to make rules to keep sports safe and fair. The organization also served as a discussions forum for other issues, such as the formation of athletic conferences and the transfer of oversight responsibilities from students to faculty. In 1921 the NCAA created its first national title, the National Collegiate Track and Field Championships.

TABLE 6.3

NCAA "Big Six" conferences, 2011

Atlantic Coast Conference (ACC)

Boston College
Clemson University
Duke University
Florida State University
George Tech
University of Maryland
University of Miami
University of North Carolina
North Carolina State University
University of Virginia
Virginia Tech
Wake Forest University

Big East Conference

University of Cincinnati
University of Connecticut
DePaul University
Georgetown University
University of Louisville
Marquette University
University of Notre Dame
University of Pittsburgh
Providence College
Rutgers University
St. John's University
Seton Hall University
University of South Florida
Syracuse University
Villanova University
West Virginia University

Big 10 Conference

University of Illinois
Indiana University
University of Iowa
University of Michigan
Michigan State University
University of Minnesota
University of Nebraska
Northwestern University
Ohio State University
Pennsylvania State University
Purdue University
University of Wisconsin

Big 12 Conference

Baylor University
Iowa State University
University of Kansas
Kansas State University
University of Missouri
University of Oklahoma
Oklahoma State University
University of Texas
Texas A&M University
Texas Tech

Pacific-12 Conference (Pac-12)

University of Arizona
Arizona State University
University of California, Berkeley (Cal)
University of Colorado
University of Oregon
Oregon State University
Stanford University
University of California, Los Angeles (UCLA)
University of Southern California
University of Utah
University of Washington
Washington State University

TABLE 6.3

NCAA "Big Six" conferences, 2011 [CONTINUED]

Southeastern Conference (SEC)

University of Alabama
University of Arkansas
Auburn University
University of Florida
University of Georgia
University of Kentucky
Louisiana State University
University of Mississippi (Ole Miss)
Mississippi State University
University of South Carolina
University of Tennessee
Vanderbilt University

SOURCE: Created by Stephen Meyer for Gale, 2011

commercialism. In 1929 the Carnegie Foundation for the Advancement of Education issued a report on college sports, which stated that "a change of values is needed in a field that is sodden with the commercial and the material and the vested interests that these forces have created. Commercialism in college athletics must be diminished and college sport must rise to a point where it is esteemed primarily and sincerely for the opportunities it affords to mature youth."

In response to the Carnegie report, schools made token attempts to reduce commercial influences on college sports; however, the trend continued. A dramatic increase in access to higher education following World War II (1939–1945) accelerated the commercialization of college athletics. In 1948, in response to a series of gambling scandals and questionable recruiting incidents, the NCAA adopted the Sanity Code, which established guidelines for recruiting and financial aid. In addition, the code set academic standards for players and defined the status of college athletes as amateurs—that is, those "to whom athletics is an avocation." The NCAA also created a Constitutional Compliance Committee to enforce the Sanity Code and investigate possible violations. The Sanity Code did not have much of an impact, however, and was repealed in 1951. The Constitutional Compliance Committee was replaced by the Committee on Infractions, which was given broader authority to sanction institutions that broke the rules. The NCAA also hired its first full-time executive director, Walter Byers (1922–), that same year. A national headquarters was established in Kansas City, Missouri, in 1952. The 1950s also brought the first lucrative television broadcast contracts, which provided the NCAA with the revenue it needed to become more active. Its capacity to enforce rules expanded throughout the 1950s and 1960s. Nevertheless, the influence of money on college sports continued to grow. In 1956 the NCAA moved to regulate athletic scholarships, but the eight schools of the Ivy League—Brown, Columbia, Cornell, Dartmouth, Harvard, Penn, Princeton, and Yale—refused to comply.

By the mid-1920s college athletics had become an integral part of college life, as well as a subject of intense public interest. Along with this interest came creeping

TABLE 6.4

NCAA sports sponsorship, by sport and division, 2010–11

	Men's				Women's				Mixed			
	I	II	III	T	I	II	III	T	I	II	III	T
Baseball	293	251	373	**917**								
Basketball	337	296	413	**1,046**	335	298	436	**1,069**				
Bowling	1	1	0	**2**	34	21	10	**65**				
Cross country	307	250	389	**946**	333	276	411	**1,020**				
Fencing	20	2	12	**34**	23	3	15	**41**	0	0	0	**0**
Field hockey					79	26	158	**263**				
Football	237	164	238	**639**								
(I-FBS 120)												
(I-FCS 117)												
Equestrian					18	5	15	**38**				
Golf	292	218	288	**798**	249	154	174	**577**				
Gymnastics	16	0	1	**17**	63	5	15	**83**				
Ice hockey	58	6	71	**135**	35	2	49	**87**				
Lacrosse	60	41	176	**277**	90	61	205	**356**				
Rifle	3	0	1	**4**	8	1	2	**11**	18	2	6	**24**
Rowing	28	3	29	**60**	85	17	40	**142**				
Rugby					2	1	2	**5**				
Soccer	201	184	404	**789**	315	235	426	**976**				
Softball					283	274	409	**966**				
Squash					10	0	19	**29**				
Swimming	136	67	204	**407**	194	84	243	**521**				
Tennis	256	172	328	**756**	314	227	379	**920**				
Track, indoor	254	126	231	**611**	304	142	236	**682**				
Track, outdoor	274	168	272	**714**	312	182	281	**775**				
Volleyball	23	16	57	**96**	321	286	428	**1,035**				
Water polo	22	6	14	**42**	33	8	19	**60**				
Wrestling	80	53	88	**221**								

Notes: NCAA = National Collegiate Athletic Association.
FBS = Football bowl subdivision.
FCS = Football championship subdivision.

SOURCE: "Current Sport Sponsorship," in *Composition and Sports Sponsorship of the NCAA*, National Collegiate Athletic Association, 2011, http://www.ncaa.org/wps/portal/ncaahome?WCM_GLOBAL_CONTEXT=/ncaa/NCAA/About+The+NCAA/Membership/membership_breakdown.html (accessed June 1, 2011). © National Collegiate Athletic Association. 2011. All rights reserved. Please note: Statistics provided in tables differ from year to year and are subject to change.

In 1973 the NCAA divided its membership into three competitive divisions. Three years later the organization acquired the authority to penalize colleges directly for violating rules. In 1978, in response to the rapid growth in the number of football programs relative to other sports, Division I members voted to break the division solely for football purposes into two subdivisions: I-A and I-AA.

During the 1970s and 1980s major football colleges began to see that they could make more money from broadcast revenue by negotiating their own deals. A group of schools, led by the University of Georgia and the University of Oklahoma, began to challenge the NCAA's monopoly on negotiation of lucrative television contracts. In 1984 the U.S. Supreme Court ruled in *NCAA v. Board of Regents of the University of Oklahoma* (468 U.S. 85) that the NCAA had violated antitrust laws. This ruling allowed colleges to start negotiating broadcast deals directly. Meanwhile, the relationship between sports and the academic performance of athletes remained a matter of intense debate. In 1986 the NCAA implemented Proposition 48, later modified by Proposition 16 (1995), which set down minimum academic standards for athletes

entering college. Among the requirements, student-athletes needed to maintain a 2.0 grade point average (GPA) in academic courses and have a Scholastic Assessment Test (SAT) score of 1010 or a combined American College Test (ACT) score of 86.

SCANDALS AND SANCTIONS IN NCAA SPORTS PROGRAMS. More than a century after Hogan's royal treatment at Yale University, payments and other special perks for student-athletes remain prevalent in college sports, in spite of the NCAA's enforcement efforts. There have been several cases of institutions and their boosters making illicit payments to players. For example, during the early 1980s Southern Methodist University (SMU) became a football powerhouse through a highly organized system of player payments, in blatant violation of NCAA rules. According to Chris DuFresne, in "Life after 'Death'" (*Los Angeles Times*, December 28, 2005), the payoff system, which had been in place for decades, began to unravel in November 1986, when SMU linebacker David Stanley admitted that he had accepted $25,000 from boosters. Within days another player, Albert Reese, confessed that he had been living in a rent-free apartment provided by a booster. After an investigation revealed widespread corruption that went as high as the Texas governor's office, the NCAA hit the university with what became known in college sports as the "death penalty." The sanctions included cancellation of SMU's entire 1987 football season and restriction of the following season to eight games.

The NCAA has not wielded the death penalty again since the SMU scandal, but its threat has not halted corrupt practices in college sports. Another high-profile case involved the National Basketball Association (NBA) star Chris Webber (1973–). In July 2003 Webber pleaded guilty to criminal contempt related to charges that he had received tens of thousands of dollars from the booster Ed Martin (1933?–2003) while a member of the University of Michigan basketball team in 1994. Martin pleaded guilty to money laundering in May 2002. Webber's sentence, a fine of $100,000, was announced in August 2005.

By 2011, in the wake of new money scandals involving players at Auburn University, Ohio State University, and other elite football schools, a fierce debate had emerged concerning the issue of compensation for NCAA athletes. Michael Wilbon argues in "College Athletes Deserve to Be Paid" (ESPN, July 18, 2011) that with the NCAA able to generate billions of dollars in revenue through lucrative media deals, the "people who produce the revenue"—namely, the players—deserve to "share a teeny, tiny slice of it." Wilbon asserts that even if it would be "beyond impractical" to compensate athletes through athletic department funds, the NCAA should have no authority to prohibit elite athletes from earning money through product endorsements, speaking engagements, and other legal means. Wilbon concludes that "the players have become employees of the universities and conferences as much as students—employees with no compensation, which not only violates common decency but perhaps even the law."

Other commentators, however, contend that paying student-athletes loses sight of the true value of a higher education. For example, Jay Paterno of Pennsylvania State University suggests in "Pay Student-Athletes? They're Already Getting a Great Deal" (June 2, 2011, http://www.ncaa.org/) that many elite student-athletes receive full scholarships, worth tens of thousands of dollars, to pursue their athletic passions while also receiving access to a range of educational opportunities. According to Paterno, the core "problem is what society sells to big-time athletes and their families. Society sells lights, camera, the NFL or NBA. Those are sexy products. What isn't being sold is education, studying and a chance to enrich the mind and get rich in the classroom."

Special treatment of student-athletes does not always involve money. In 1999 a University of Minnesota employee told the *St. Paul Pioneer Press* that she had completed course work for at least 20 members of the school's basketball program. Four top sports officials at the university lost their jobs in the resulting scandal. Academics also figured prominently in a scandal that resulted in the NCAA stripping the University of Memphis of its entire 2007–08 season, which included an impressive 38 victories and a trip to the Final Four. The university's star player, Derrick Rose (1988–), now a star for the NBA's Chicago Bulls, allegedly paid another student to take the SAT exams for him, after he failed the ACT three times.

College Sports Participation

In *1981–82–2009–10 NCAA Sports Sponsorship and Participation Rates Report* (November 2010, http://www.ncaapublications.com/productdownloads/PR2011.pdf), Erin Zgonc of the NCAA provides detailed information on participation across the full range of college sports. During the 2009–10 school year there were 430,301 student-athletes participating in championship sports at NCAA schools. The average NCAA institution had approximately 406 student-athletes—232 of them men and 174 women.

Table 6.5 shows participation in women's sports at NCAA schools during the 2008–09 school year. According to Zgonc, 11,433 women participated on NCAA Division I outdoor track and field teams that year, the highest total of any women's sport; nearly as many women (11,324) participated during the indoor track season. NCAA women's Division I soccer teams had a total of 8,117 participants in 2008–09. Including all sports, both championship and emerging, 75,603 women participated in Division I sports that year. Another 37,103 women played at the Division II level and 69,797 women played at the Division III level.

Table 6.6 shows participation in men's collegiate sports during the 2008–09 school year. Zgonc indicates that 91,325 student-athletes participated on 2,927 Division I men's teams that year. The sport with the greatest number of Division I teams was basketball, with 332. However, basketball squads are relatively small, averaging 15.4 members per squad in Division I. By comparison, 26,104 men played football at the Division I level in 2008–09, with an average of 109.7 members per squad. Outdoor track was second, with 10,564 participants, followed by baseball, with 9,710 participants. Division II men's sports included 53,929 participants and Division III had 99,013 participants.

Figure 6.1 and Figure 6.2 put college sports participation in historical perspective. During the 1981–82 school year there were 231,445 student-athletes competing in NCAA championship sports in all divisions; 167,055 of them were men. By the 1994–95 school year the total number of student-athletes had grown to 294,212. About twice as much of this growth was on the women's side as on the men's. The total number of student-athletes had grown to 430,301 by the 2008–09 school year. However, it is important to note a change in

TABLE 6.5

NCAA participation in women's sports, by division, 2008–09

Sport	Division I			Division II			Division III			Overall		
	Teams	Athletes	Avg. squad	Teams	Athletes	Avg. squad	Teams	Athletes	Avg. squad	Teams	Athletes	Avg. squad
Championship sports												
Basketball	331	4,815	14.5	288	4,200	14.6	435	6,366	14.6	1,054	15,381	14.6
Bowling	29	255	8.8	18	162	9.0	8	68	8.5	55	485	8.8
Cross country	327	5,534	16.9	269	3,117	11.6	400	5,450	13.6	996	14,101	14.2
Fencing*	22	369	16.8	4	55	13.8	15	249	16.6	41	673	16.4
Field hockey	76	1,726	22.7	26	589	22.7	158	3,288	20.8	260	5,603	21.6
Golf	243	2,085	8.6	136	1,020	7.5	164	1,203	7.3	543	4,308	7.9
Gymnastics	63	1,070	17.0	5	105	21.0	16	280	17.5	84	1,455	17.3
Ice hockey	35	816	23.3	2	50	25.0	47	1,110	23.6	84	1,976	23.5
Lacrosse	86	2,341	27.2	48	1,058	22.0	185	3,820	20.6	319	7,219	22.6
Rifle*	24	125	5.2	4	24	6.0	7	23	3.3	35	172	4.9
Rowing	87	5,448	62.6	16	467	29.2	43	1,374	32.0	146	7,289	49.9
Skiing*	14	222	15.9	7	77	11.0	20	203	10.2	41	502	12.2
Soccer	310	8,117	26.2	225	5,437	24.2	424	9,803	23.1	959	23,357	24.4
Softball	276	5,400	19.6	268	4,991	18.6	405	7,098	17.5	949	17,489	18.4
Swimming/diving	194	5,298	27.3	73	1,462	20.0	243	4,866	20.0	510	11,626	22.8
Tennis	311	2,913	9.4	220	1,945	8.8	369	3,861	10.5	900	8,719	9.7
Track, indoor	299	11,324	37.9	127	3,514	27.7	235	6,216	26.5	661	21,054	31.9
Track, outdoor	307	11,433	37.2	175	4,529	25.9	276	6,993	25.3	758	22,955	30.3
Volleyball	317	4,685	14.8	276	3,971	14.4	422	6,171	14.6	1,015	14,827	14.6
Water polo	32	709	22.2	7	143	20.4	21	304	14.5	60	1,156	19.3
Subtotal	**3,383**	**74,685**		**2,194**	**36,916**		**3,893**	**68,746**		**9,470**	**180,347**	
Emerging sports												
Archery	1	12	12.0	0		N/A	0		N/A	1	12	12.0
Badminton	0		N/A	0		N/A	2	19	9.5	2	19	9.5
Equestrian	18	707	39.3	5	119	23.8	23	625	27.2	46	1,451	31.5
Rugby	1	23	23.0	1	54	54.0	3	107	35.7	5	184	36.8
Squash	9	117	13.0	0		N/A	19	264	13.9	28	381	13.6
Synchronized swimming	4	59	14.8	1	14	14.0	3	36	12.0	8	109	13.6
Team handball	0		N/A	0		N/A	0		N/A	0	0	N/A
Subtotal	**33**	**918**		**7**	**187**		**50**	**1,051**		**90**	**2,156**	
Total	**3,416**	**75,603**		**2,201**	**37,103**		**3,943**	**69,797**		**9,560**	**182,503**	

*Coed championship.

Notes: Participation totals are adjusted to reflect all institutions sponsoring each sport. Provisional members are included in these numbers. Coed sport teams had coed teams: a) cross country, b) equestrian, c) fencing, d) golf, e) rifle, f) skiing, g) swimming & diving, h) indoor track & field and i) outdoor track & field. The total row contains data from the emerging sports subtotal row added to the championship sports subtotal row. N/A = not applicable.

SOURCE: Erin Zgonc, "2008–09 Participation Study—Women's Sports," in *1981–82–2009–10 NCAA Sports Sponsorship and Participation Rates Report*, National Collegiate Athletic Association, November 2010, http://www.ncaapublications.com/productdownloads/PR2011.pdf (accessed June 1, 2011). © National Collegiate Athletic Association. 2011. All rights reserved.

TABLE 6.6

NCAA participation in men's sports, by division, 2008–09

Sport	Division I			Division II			Division III			Overall		
	Teams	Athletes	Avg. squad	Teams	Athletes	Avg. squad	Teams	Athletes	Avg. squad	Teams	Athletes	Avg. squad
Championship sports												
Baseball	292	9,710	33.3	241	8,412	34.9	372	11,694	31.4	905	29,816	32.9
Basketball	332	5,129	15.4	287	4,644	16.2	411	7,138	17.4	1,030	16,911	16.4
Cross country	302	4,652	15.4	239	2,929	12.3	375	5,434	14.5	916	13,015	14.2
Fencing*	19	349	18.4	3	45	15.0	12	221	18.4	34	615	18.1
Football	238	26,104	109.7	154	15,655	101.7	241	23,120	95.9	633	64,879	102.5
FBS	119	14,146	118.9	N/A	N/A	N/A				N/A	N/A	N/A
FCS	119	11,958	100.5	N/A	N/A	N/A				N/A	N/A	N/A
Golf	291	2,968	10.2	212	2,234	10.5	289	3,097	10.7	792	8,299	10.5
Gymnastics	16	300	18.8	0	0	0.0	2	35	17.5	18	335	18.6
Ice hockey	58	1,609	27.7	7	222	31.7	74	2,270	30.7	139	4,101	29.5
Lacrosse	57	2,598	45.6	35	1,334	38.1	155	5,334	34.4	247	9,266	37.5
Rifle*	19	133	7.0	5	26	5.2	6	61	10.2	30	220	7.3
Skiing*	13	205	15.8	6	71	11.8	19	229	12.1	38	505	13.3
Soccer	197	5,607	28.5	180	4,919	27.3	400	11,075	27.7	777	21,601	27.8
Swimming/diving	139	3,823	27.5	56	1,113	19.9	198	3,932	19.9	393	8,868	22.6
Tennis	258	2,641	10.2	168	1,634	9.7	323	3,685	11.4	749	7,960	10.6
Track, indoor	249	9,565	38.4	114	3,833	33.6	230	7,860	34.2	593	21,258	35.8
Track, outdoor	269	10,564	39.3	162	5,052	31.2	270	8,802	32.6	701	24,418	34.8
Volleyball	22	441	20.0	12	204	17.0	49	674	13.8	83	1,319	15.9
Water polo	22	562	25.5	5	76	15.2	15	276	18.4	42	914	21.8
Wrestling	86	2,668	31.0	46	1,409	30.6	92	2,445	26.6	224	6,522	29.1
Subtotal	**2,879**	**89,628**		**1,932**	**53,812**		**3,533**	**97,382**		**8,344**	**240,822**	
Non-championship sports												
Archery	0	N/A	N/A	0	N A	N A	0	N/A	N/A	0	N/A	N/A
Badminton	0	N/A	N/A	0	N A	N A	0	N/A	N/A	0	N/A	N/A
Bowling	0	0	N/A	1	35	35.0	0	0	N/A	1	35	N/A
Equestrian	0	N/A	N/A	0	N A	N A	3	9	3.0	3	9	3.0
Rowing	28	1,330	47.5	4	76	19.0	31	947	30.5	63	2,353	37.3
Rugby	0	N A	N A	0	N A	N A	1	63	63.0	1	63	63.0
Sailing	11	224	20.4	1	6	6.0	13	290	22.3	25	520	20.8
Squash	9	143	15.9	0	6	N/A	19	322	16.9	28	465	16.6
Subtotal	**48**	**1,697**		**6**	**117**		**67**	**1,631**		**121**	**3,445**	
Total	**2,927**	**91,325**		**1,938**	**53,929**		**3,600**	**99,013**		**8,465**	**244,267**	

*Coed championship.

Notes: Participation totals are adjusted to reflect all institutions sponsoring each sport. Provisional members are included in these numbers.
Coed sport teams from the sports sponsorship database were added to both the men's AND women's team data. The following sports had coed teams: a) cross country, b) equestrian, c) fencing, d) golf, e) rifle, f) sailing, g) skiing, h) swimming & diving, i) indoor track & field and j) outdoor track & field. The total row contains data from the non-championship sports subtotal row added to the championship sports subtotal row. FBS = Football bowl subdivision. FCS = Football championship subdivision.
N/A = not applicable.

SOURCE: Erin Zgonc, "2008–09 Participation Study—Men's Sports," in *1981–82–2009–10 NCAA Sports Sponsorship and Participation Rates Report*, National Collegiate Athletic Association, November 2010, http://www.ncaapublications.com/productdownloads/PR2011.pdf (accessed June 2, 2011). © National Collegiate Athletic Association. 2011. All rights reserved.

FIGURE 6.1

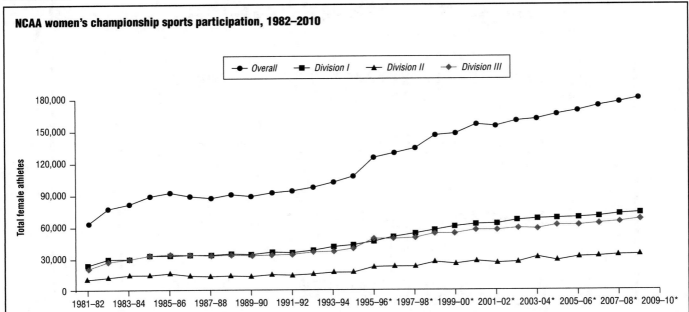

NCAA women's championship sports participation, 1982–2010

FIGURE 6.2

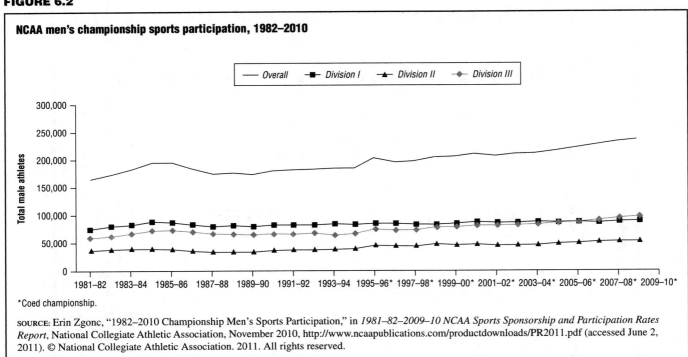

NCAA men's championship sports participation, 1982–2010

*Coed championship.

the way the total is calculated: provisional NCAA members were included in the count beginning in the 1995–96 school year. In addition, the numbers for 1995–96 and 1996–97 were adjusted to comply with the Equity in Athletics Disclosure Act, making it difficult to compare current participation numbers with data from before 1995.

Table 6.7 and Table 6.8 provide a breakdown of championship sports teams sponsored by NCAA member schools for both women and men. During the 2009–10 school year there were 1,059 women's basketball teams, the most of any women's sport. Women's volleyball was second with 1,025 teams, followed by cross-country with

TABLE 6.7

NCAA women's sports teams, by sport, 1981–2010

[Divisions I, II, and III overall number of women's teams]

Year	Archery[a]	Badminton[a]	Basketball	Bowling[a]	Cross country	Equestrian[a]	Fencing	Field hockey	Golf	Gymnastics	Ice hockey[a]	Lacrosse	Rifle[b]	Rowing
1981–82		11	705	11	417		76	268	125	179	17	105	16	43
1982–83			747		464		68	262	119	170	17	113		45
1983–84			746		500		65	257	120	160	15	114		48
1984–85			751		541		62	251	123	150	15	114		51
1985–86			759		611		58	245	141	143	14	113		48
1986–87			757		633		55	233	139	125		114		38
1987–88			756		638		52	231	133	121		114		45
1988–89			764		638		48	225	132	112		118		39
1989–90			761		648		49	219	143	108		118		39
1990–91			786		666		48	217	145	103		118		12
1991–92			810		677		47	213	162	96		122		56
1992–93			827		700		42	211	177	91		126		51
1993–94			855		727		43	214	206	92		133		67
1994–95			869		747		41	221	216	90		144		74
1995–96[c]			952		842		51	231	288	96	21	164	10	90
1996–97[c]			956		834		43	228	303	91	22	183	12	98
1997–98[c]			956		843		44	234	329	91	30	201	11	111
1998–99[c]	6	10	1,001	5	891	41	45	240	364	90	40	213	44	122
1999–00[c]	3	3	1,011	23	882	30	45	239	382	90	50	225	43	129
2000–01[c]	3	3	1,020	25	923	47	46	248	437	90	63	238	45	138
2001–02[c]	3	4	1,017	39	928	46	46	252	451	89	69	249	46	140
2002–03[c]	3	4	1,016	43	930	44	45	253	456	86	70	256	43	141
2003–04[c]	3	3	1,022	42	942	41	44	255	477	86	72	258	39	143
2004–05[c]	3	3	1,025	45	940	39	45	257	483	85	74	264	36	141
2005–06[c]	2	3	1,039	44	958	45	44	258	504	86	75	271	37	142
2006–07[c]	2	2	1,050	49	967	48	45	259	512	86	79	286	36	144
2007–08[c]	1	2	1,057	52	988	45	43	258	516	85	81	301	36	144
2008–09[c]	1	2	1,054	55	996	46	41	260	543	84	84	319	35	146
2009–10[c]	0	0	1,059	57	1,005	47	41	262	557	83	84	334	36	143

Year	Rugby[a]	Skiing	Soccer	Softball	Squash[a]	Synchronized swimming[a]	Swimming/ diving	Team handball[a]	Tennis	Track, indoor	Track, outdoor	Volley ball	Water polo[a]
1981–82		33	80	416	16		348		610	239	427	603	
1982–83		35	103	441	16		361		652	280	462	638	
1983–84		36	133	451	17		370		657	327	472	645	
1984–85		37	165	493	17		374		667	358	482	649	
1985–86		38	201	528	17		390		687	385	520	685	
1986–87		41	230	543			392		690	391	526	701	
1987–88		43	259	543			397		690	416	537	705	
1988–89		39	270	549			397		691	419	540	719	
1989–90		40	294	557			396		694	421	537	722	
1990–91		41	318	580			396		711	447	553	741	
1991–92		44	350	605			394		723	466	561	762	
1992–93		37	387	618	23		391		732	479	574	784	
1993–94		35	446	646	23		393		759	489	582	810	
1994–95		37	515	656	23		400		774	496	593	828	
1995–96[c]		53	631	735	27	7	443		859	533	656	903	20
1996–97[c]		43	694	760	27	6	433		855	529	641	915	23
1997–98[c]		42	724	778	26	6	444		852	540	649	915	32
1998–99[c]		44	790	831	27	7	458	0	877	560	671	960	37
1999–00[c]		42	811	857	28	8	458	0	870	558	662	967	40
2000–01[c]		48	851	877	30	9	470	0	891	593	696	975	50
2001–02[c]		45	868	895	27	9	478	0	898	595	697	974	55
2002–03[c]	2	42	879	899	29	8	481	0	891	611	703	973	56
2003–04[c]	2	42	895	908	27	8	488	0	880	617	701	978	59
2004–05[c]	3	39	913	911	27	8	489	0	876	621	704	982	61
2005–06[c]	4	40	930	932	26	8	497	0	888	630	722	992	61
2006–07[c]	5	44	941	942	27	8	504	0	895	641	732	1,007	61
2007–08[c]	5	42	956	950	28	8	509	0	898	645	745	1,014	60
2008–09[c]	5	41	959	949	28	8	510	0	900	661	758	1,015	60
2009–10[c]	4	38	967	957	28	0	512	0	912	673	767	1,025	59

[a]Empty cells for these sports indicate that the data were not tracked for that year.
[b]Prior to the 1995–96 academic year, women's rifle data were included with the men's rifle data. Rifle is a co-ed championship sport.
[c]Provisional members are included in these numbers.

SOURCE: Erin Zgonc, "NCAA Sports Sponsorship, 1981–82–2009–2010: Divisions I, II and III Overall Number of Women's Teams," in *1981–82–2009–10 NCAA Sports Sponsorship and Participation Rates Report*, National Collegiate Athletic Association, November 2010, http://www.ncaapublications.com/productdownloads/PR2011.pdf (accessed June 2, 2011). © National Collegiate Athletic Association. 2011. All rights reserved.

TABLE 6.8

NCAA men's sports teams, by sport, 1981–2010

[Divisions I, II, and III overall number of men's teams]

Year	Archery[a]	Badminton[a]	Baseball	Basketball	Bowling[a]	Cross country	Equestrian[a]	Fencing	Football	Golf	Gymnastics	Ice hockey[a]	Lacrosse	Rifle[b]
1981–82			642	741	13	650		79	497	590	79	130	138	83
1982–83			650	754		672		72	509	598	71	123	138	92
1983–84			650	749		683		71	507	591	71	122	141	88
1984–85			652	752		694		67	503	595	65	124	144	88
1985–86			657	759	10	682		65	509	591	61	125	144	84
1986–87			662	760		681		58	510	577	56	126	150	65
1987–88			666	759		682		55	510	583	50	128	149	66
1988–89			667	768		670		48	522	570	47	126	150	61
1989–90			672	768		674		48	524	569	45	123	152	55
1990–91			692	795		695		49	534	603	43	123	157	50
1991–92			713	814		706		49	546	610	40	123	160	47
1992–93			730	831		723		47	553	619	40	121	168	50
1993–94			751	854		730		45	561	637	33	123	170	46
1994–95			763	868		736		42	566	652	29	122	172	43
1995–96[c]			827	938		815		47	600	726	39	123	177	59
1996–97[c]			820	941		786		38	600	695	28	127	183	42
1997–98[c]			817	938		790		37	599	696	27	129	186	40
1998–99[c]	6	4	844	980	10	827	33	37	605	716	26	131	197	41
1999–00[c]	1	0	857	989	3	811	0	37	610	719	24	126	203	38
2000–01[c]	1	0	860	991	1	860	10	52	624	750	24	132	208	45
2001–02[c]	1	0	866	990	2	858	8	38	617	754	23	134	211	43
2002–03[c]	1	0	861	987	0	859	5	39	619	748	20	135	214	42
2003–04[c]	1	0	864	994	1	871	4	37	617	758	20	133	211	35
2004–05[c]	1	0	873	1,000	1	865	3	36	614	762	19	133	214	35
2005–06[c]	1	0	890	1,013	2	879	8	36	618	777	19	133	222	36
2006–07[c]	1	0	897	1,022	2	898	8	36	625	782	19	136	226	29
2007–08[c]	0	0	906	1,031	0	912	2	35	629	795	18	138	239	29
2008–09[c]	0	0	905	1,030	1	916	3	34	633	792	18	139	247	30
2009–10[c]	0	0	910	1,038	1	928	5	34	633	798	17	136	262	31

Year	Rowing	Rugby[a]	Sailing[a]	Skiing	Soccer	Squash[a]	Swimming/ diving	Tennis	Track, indoor	Track, outdoor	Volley ball	Water polo[a]	Wrestling
1981–82	48		15	55	521	21	377	690	422	577	63	49	363
1982–83	50		18	50	523	25	380	696	435	587	55	51	351
1983–84	48			46	533	21	378	700	446	580	58	52	342
1984–85	53		20	50	544	22	381	694	453	581	62	52	325
1985–86	46		22	47	550	21	375	691	447	572	58	53	317
1986–87	41		15	47	548	16	375	686	439	569	50	56	300
1987–88	40		19	50	546	17	383	687	446	564	50	58	289
1988–89	35			39	543	18	368	673	440	557	51	58	286
1989–90	36			40	547	18	361	675	434	554	54	55	278
1990–91	43			45	567	23	365	692	456	566	58	54	280
1991–92	51			46	581	24	367	701	476	580	58	48	275
1992–93	51			37	591	22	369	705	489	582	59	47	265
1993–94	60			35	609	24	368	720	493	588	61	39	264
1994–95	59			35	618	25	368	726	490	588	60	37	257
1995–96[c]	55			50	678	25	400	805	527	651	74	44	277
1996–97[c]	90			40	678	31	371	767	509	622	71	42	248
1997–98[c]	90			39	682	31	371	757	512	625	68	43	246
1998–99[c]	70		22	40	717	21	381	769	526	637	79	43	242
1999–00[c]	55		21	38	715	25	374	758	518	635	75	42	234
2000–01[c]	60		25	44	730	26	385	774	553	659	83	46	235
2001–02[c]	57		24	41	734	22	388	770	553	657	81	48	231
2002–03[c]	58	1	29	38	732	25	383	754	557	662	84	46	222
2003–04[c]	55	2	26	39	729	23	387	744	563	657	81	46	223
2004–05[c]	59	1	33	35	737	21	381	742	565	656	79	46	224
2005–06[c]	60	2	24	36	752	25	381	754	567	670	82	45	228
2006–07[c]	63	3	26	40	763	27	390	745	575	678	80	41	229
2007–08[c]	87	2	24	39	775	31	389	754	575	687	82	42	227
2008–09[c]	63	1	25	38	777	28	393	749	593	701	83	42	224
2009–10[c]	61	1	24	34	782	29	399	752	601	706	90	41	217

[a]Empty cells for these sports indicate that the data were not tracked for that year.
[b]Prior to the 1995–96 academic year, women's rifle data were included with the men's rifle data. Rifle is a co-ed championship sport.
[c]Provisional members are included in these numbers.

SOURCE: Erin Zgonc, "NCAA Sports Sponsorship, 1981–82–2009–2010: Divisions I, II and III Overall Number of Men's Teams," in *1981–82–2009–10 NCAA Sports Sponsorship and Participation Rates Report*, National Collegiate Athletic Association, November 2010, http://www.ncaapublications.com/productdownloads/PR2011.pdf (accessed June 2, 2011). © National Collegiate Athletic Association. 2011. All rights reserved.

1,005 squads. Between 1995–96, when women's water polo was introduced as a competitive sport, and 2009–10 the number of NCAA women's water polo teams nearly tripled, from 20 to 59. Basketball was also the leading sport for men, with 1,038 teams in Divisions I, II, and III. Cross-country was second, with 928 teams, and baseball was third, with 910 teams.

Table 6.9 illustrates trends in the average number of sports teams per school. As the table reveals, the gender balance shifted considerably between 1981–82 and 2009–10. For example, in 1981–82 the average number of teams across all divisions was 9.1 for men and 6.4 for women; by 2009–10 the average number of men's teams declined to 7.9, whereas the women's teams increased to 9.

Women's Sports and Gender Equity

Table 6.10 illustrates what has happened to the gender gap in college sports since the 1981–82 school year. The average number of male student-athletes per college across all divisions has remained fairly stable, from 225.8 in 1981–82 to 232.3 in 2009–10, whereas the average number of female student-athletes per college has risen steadily, from 98.7 in 1981–82 to 173.8 in 2009–10. The difference has been most pronounced in Division I sports. Overall, the average number of women athletes per institution grew by 100.6 between 1990–91 and 2009–10, whereas the average number of male athletes dropped slightly.

In *Women in Intercollegiate Sport: A Longitudinal, National Study—Thirty-Three Year Study, 1977–2010* (2010, http://www.acostacarpenter.org/2010pdf%20combined%20final.pdf), R. Vivian Acosta and Linda Jean Carpenter of Brooklyn College examine the status of women's college athletics between 1977 and 2010. The researchers find that nationwide college women have more athletic teams available to them than ever before. Since 1978 (the mandatory compliance date for Title IX, explained below) the number of women's athletic teams per school rose from 5.6 to 8.6 in 2010. There were a total of 9,087 varsity women's intercollegiate teams in the NCAA in 2010.

According to Acosta and Carpenter, the sport most frequently found in women's intercollegiate athletic programs was basketball, which was offered by 99.1% of NCAA schools in 2010. (See Table 6.11.) Basketball was the most popular sport throughout the period covered during the study. It ranked number one in 1977, when it was offered at 90.4% of colleges. Three other sports— cross-country, soccer, and volleyball—were offered for women at more than 90% of colleges in 2010. Like basketball, volleyball has maintained its ranking since 1977, when it was offered at 80.1% of schools.

Title IX

No piece of legislation has had a greater impact on gender equity in sports participation than Title IX of the Education Amendments of 1972 of the Civil Rights Act of 1964, which is usually referred to simply as Title IX. In 1971 the gender disparity in sports participation was overwhelming. According to the Women's Sports Foundation, in *Playing Fair: A Title IX Playbook for Victory* (April 2009, http://www.womenssportsfoundation.org/en/home/advocate/know-your-rights/parent-resources/~/media/PDFs/Educational%20Guides/Play_Fair_Final.ashx), 294,015 girls were participating in interscholastic sports programs that year, compared to 3.6 million boys. Title IX was based on the notion that unequal federal funding between genders was an illegal form of discrimination. Title IX requires institutions receiving federal funding—including both secondary schools and colleges—to provide resources equally to male and female students. In practice, this has meant that schools must attempt to maintain equal facilities, equal coaching staffs, and a gender ratio among athletes similar to the ratio among the student body as a whole. Critics of Title IX have been dismayed by the fact that compliance has sometimes meant cuts in men's sports programs, but the biggest impact has been an explosion in the prevalence and popularity of women's sports. In 2002 President George W. Bush (1946–) officially renamed Title IX the Patsy T. Mink Equal Opportunity in Education Act, after the legislation's author, a congresswoman from Hawaii. It is still, however, generally referred to as Title IX.

Women Coaches in College

One ironic consequence of the increase in the number of women's sports offered in college is a decrease in the percentage of teams that are coached by women. In 1972 women coached more than 90% of women's college sports teams. (See Table 6.12.) By 1978 the percentage had dropped to 58.2%. Acosta and Carpenter suggest that this drop was because of the rapid increase in the number of women's sports teams, which was not accompanied by a comparable growth in the number of qualified female coaches. The percentage, however, has continued to fall since 1978; by 2010 it stood at 42.6%. Acosta and Carpenter argue that this decline in women's representation in college coaching is due in part to discrimination and differences in the way men and women coaches are recruited. The percentage varies substantially from sport to sport. Table 6.13 shows that 57% of women's college basketball teams had female coaches in 2010 and that 55.7% of women's volleyball coaches were female. Men, however, dominated the coaching ranks of women's track and field (where only 15.5% of coaches were female), cross-country (18.6%), and soccer (32.5%).

College Sports and Ethnicity

According to Zgonc, in *1999–2000–2009–10 NCAA Student-Athlete Ethnicity Report* (September 2010, http://www.ncaapublications.com/productdownloads/SAEREP11.pdf),

TABLE 6.9

Average number of men's and women's teams, per college, 1981–2010

Year	Division I			Division II			Division III			Overall		
	Men's	Women's	Overall	Men's	Women's	Overall	Men's	Women's	Overall	Men's	Women's	Overall
1981–82	10.3	7.3	17.5	7.9	5.5	13.4	8.8	6.1	14.8	9.1	6.4	15.5
1982–83	10.2	6.9	17.1	7.4	5.7	13.1	8.3	6.2	14.6	8.8	6.3	15.1
1983–84	10.2	7.1	17.3	7.5	5.9	13.4	8.2	6.3	14.6	8.7	6.5	15.3
1984–85	10.2	7.3	17.4	7.5	6.1	13.6	8.2	6.6	14.8	8.7	6.7	15.5
1985–86	10.1	7.7	17.9	7.3	6.3	13.6	8.2	6.8	15.0	8.7	7.0	15.7
1986–87	9.7	7.8	17.5	7.1	6.2	13.3	8.4	7.0	15.4	8.6	7.1	15.7
1987–88	9.6	7.8	17.4	7.1	6.2	13.3	8.4	7.1	15.6	8.6	7.2	15.7
1988–89	9.4	7.7	17.2	6.9	6.1	13.0	8.3	7.2	15.4	8.4	7.1	15.5
1989–90	9.4	7.8	17.2	6.9	6.2	13.1	8.2	7.2	15.4	8.3	7.2	15.5
1990–91	9.5	7.8	17.3	6.8	6.0	12.8	8.3	7.2	15.4	8.3	7.1	15.4
1991–92	9.6	8.1	17.6	6.7	5.9	12.6	8.2	7.2	15.4	8.3	7.2	15.5
1992–93	9.5	8.2	17.7	6.7	5.9	12.6	8.1	7.3	15.3	8.2	7.2	15.4
1993–94	9.6	8.4	18.0	6.5	5.9	12.4	7.9	7.4	15.3	8.1	7.3	15.4
1994–95	9.5	8.5	18.0	6.1	5.6	11.7	7.3	7.0	14.3	7.7	7.1	14.8
1995–96*	9.6	9.0	18.6	6.5	6.1	12.5	7.8	7.7	15.5	8.0	7.6	15.6
1996–97*	9.4	9.1	18.5	6.3	6.1	12.4	7.6	7.8	15.5	7.8	7.7	15.5
1997–98*	9.3	9.3	18.7	6.4	6.4	12.8	7.7	8.0	15.7	7.8	8.0	15.8
1998–99*	9.4	9.6	19.0	6.3	6.5	12.8	7.6	8.1	15.7	7.8	8.1	15.9
1999–00*	9.1	9.7	18.8	6.1	6.4	12.4	7.5	8.2	15.7	7.8	8.1	15.7
2000–01*	9.2	10.0	19.2	6.4	6.8	13.2	7.9	8.5	16.4	7.9	8.5	16.3
2001–02*	9.2	10.1	19.2	6.5	7.0	13.4	7.9	8.6	16.5	7.9	8.6	16.5
2002–03*	9.0	10.1	19.1	6.4	7.1	13.5	7.9	8.7	16.6	7.9	8.7	16.5
2003–04*	8.9	10.1	19.1	6.5	7.2	13.7	7.8	8.6	16.4	7.8	8.7	16.5
2004–05*	8.9	10.2	19.0	6.4	7.1	13.6	7.8	8.6	16.4	7.8	8.7	16.4
2005–06*	8.9	10.2	19.1	6.5	7.2	13.7	7.8	8.5	16.3	7.8	8.7	16.6
2006–07*	8.8	10.2	19.0	6.6	7.5	14.1	7.9	8.7	16.6	7.8	8.8	16.6
2007–08*	8.6	10.2	18.8	6.8	7.6	14.5	8.6	8.9	17.5	8.1	9.0	17.0
2008–09*	8.8	10.3	19.0	6.6	7.5	14.2	8.1	8.9	17.0	7.9	8.9	16.9
2009–10*	8.8	10.3	19.0	6.7	7.6	14.3	8.2	8.9	17.1	7.9	9.0	16.9

*Provisional members are included in these numbers.

SOURCE: Erin Zgonc, "NCAA Sports Sponsorship, 1981–82–2009–2010: Average Number of Teams per Institution," in *1981–82–2009–10 NCAA Sports Sponsorship and Participation Rates Report*, National Collegiate Athletic Association, November 2010, http://www.ncaapublications.com/productdownloads/PR2011.pdf (accessed June 2, 2011). © National Collegiate Athletic Association. 2011. All rights reserved.

TABLE 6.10

Average number of student-athletes per college, by gender, 1981–2010

Year	Division I			Division II			Division III			Overall		
	Men's	Women's	Overall	Men's	Women's	Overall	Men's	Women's	Overall	Men's	Women's	Overall
1981–82	273.5	114.8	388.3	185.8	81.6	267.4	206.5	94.7	301.1	225.8	98.7	324.5
1982–83	293.3	120.3	413.6	180.2	78.1	258.3	202.8	100.3	303.1	228.7	101.6	330.3
1983–84	301.8	120.3	422.1	194.1	91.2	285.3	213.8	107.5	321.3	239.9	107.9	347.8
1984–85	318.2	127.2	445.4	203.6	97.8	301.4	227.1	116.6	343.7	254.2	115.9	370.1
1985–86	315.2	133.0	448.2	199.5	103.8	303.3	227.0	118.3	345.3	251.9	120.1	372.0
1986–87	290.8	128.7	419.5	186.7	95.3	282.0	224.2	114.0	338.2	239.9	115.0	354.9
1987–88	275.6	125.9	401.5	177.1	94.3	271.4	207.5	112.5	320.0	225.7	113.3	338.9
1988–89	277.9	127.8	405.7	172.2	92.7	264.9	208.2	114.7	322.9	225.2	114.3	339.4
1989–90	275.8	126.0	401.7	168.4	90.1	258.5	202.2	110.5	312.7	220.9	111.2	332.1
1990–91	277.7	128.3	405.9	171.2	87.3	258.6	206.3	113.2	319.4	222.9	112.1	335.0
1991–92	278.7	132.9	411.6	168.6	87.6	256.2	200.1	114.2	314.3	219.7	113.9	333.5
1992–93	277.5	137.8	415.3	164.5	86.2	250.7	197.2	115.4	312.7	216.5	115.6	332.1
1993–94	286.5	147.4	433.8	159.1	85.8	244.9	186.2	116.1	302.3	212.6	118.3	330.9
1994–95	278.8	153.1	431.8	146.6	81.3	227.9	173.7	112.4	286.0	199.7	116.7	316.4
1995–96*	284.9	169.4	454.3	157.3	90.7	248.0	189.5	129.2	318.7	209.4	130.3	339.7
1996–97*	276.8	172.3	449.1	154.3	90.6	244.9	185.0	129.7	314.7	204.4	131.5	335.9
1997–98*	277.7	180.4	458.1	157.4	96.6	254.0	186.6	132.4	319.0	206.8	137.2	344.0
1998–99*	274.1	194.1	468.3	160.0	103.0	263.0	185.6	136.7	322.3	205.0	144.4	349.4
1999–00*	267.3	195.6	463.0	152.5	99.4	251.9	188.9	136.8	325.7	202.7	144.3	346.9
2000–01*	272.3	203.2	473.6	159.4	107.6	266.4	195.5	143.6	338.5	209.0	151.8	359.8
2001–02*	263.9	203.2	467.2	156.6	104.6	261.2	192.4	140.6	333.1	204.8	150.1	354.9
2002–03*	266.1	210.0	476.1	163.4	108.9	272.2	197.9	144.5	342.4	210.0	155.5	365.6
2003–04*	265.5	213.4	478.9	165.5	112.5	278.0	194.9	142.5	337.4	209.2	156.6	365.8
2004–05*	268.5	216.8	485.2	166.8	114.4	281.2	202.0	146.1	348.1	213.2	159.5	372.8
2005–06*	269.3	218.1	487.4	171.0	117.1	288.1	202.7	146.4	349.1	214.4	160.3	374.6
2006–07*	270.6	221.5	492.0	177.6	122.6	300.2	210.5	149.4	359.9	219.8	164.0	383.8
2007–08*	269.4	222.9	492.3	188.1	126.1	314.1	234.0	153.8	387.8	232.3	167.6	399.8
2008–09*	274.2	227.0	501.3	184.7	127.1	311.8	223.0	157.2	380.2	228.5	170.7	399.2
2009–10*	276.2	230.2	506.5	189.9	131.3	321.2	227.2	159.2	386.4	232.3	173.8	406.1

*Provisional members are included in these numbers.

SOURCE: Erin Zgonc, "NCAA Sports Sponsorship, 1981–82–2009–2010: Average Number of Student-Athletes per Institution," in *1981–82–2009–10 NCAA Sports Sponsorship and Participation Rates Report*, National Collegiate Athletic Association, November 2010, http://www.ncaapublications.com/productdownloads/PR2011.pdf (accessed June 2, 2011). © National Collegiate Athletic Association. 2011. All rights reserved.

TABLE 6.11

Most popular intercollegiate women's sports, selected years 1977–2010

Rank in 2010		% offering sport	Rank in 2008		Rank in 2006		Rank in 2004		Rank in 2002		Rank in 1977	
1.	Basketball	99.1	1	98.8	1	98.4	1	98.3	1	98.0	1	90.4
2.	Volleyball	96.8	2	95.7	2	95.2	2	94.6	2	95.4	2	80.1
3.	Soccer	91.2	3	92.0	3	89.4	4	88.6	3	87.9	20	2.8
4.	Cross country	90.9	4	90.8	4	89.2	3	88.8	5	86.5	8	29.4
5.	Softball	88.2	5	89.2	5	87.1	5	86.4	6	86.2	4	48.4
6.	Tennis	85.2	6	84.7	6	85.1	6	85.2	4	87.7	3	80.0
7.	Track & field	71.6	7	70.9	7	67.4	7	67.4	7	67.5	5	46.1
8.	Golf	54.9	8	54.4	8	52.2	8 tie	48.7	9	48.4	10	19.9
9.	Swimming	52.1	9	52.3	9	50.9	9 tie	48.7	8	52.0	6	41.0
10.	Lacrosse	35.8	10	32.6	10	30.6	10	28.5	11	26.7	11	13.0
11.	Field hockey	27.7	11	27.9	11	28.0	11	28.2	10	27.0	7	36.3
12.	Crew/rowing	14.8	12	17.4	12	15.2	12	14.0	12	16.2	13	6.9
13.	Gymnastics	10.6	13	10.7	14	9.5	13	11.0	13	12.0	9	25.9
14.	Ice hockey	9.8	14	9.4	13	9.7	14	8.8	14	8.5	24	1.3
15.	Water polo	6.1	15	6.7	16 tie	5.9	15	6.5	15	6.0	—	—
16.	Squash	4.7	19	4.2	20 tie	3.4	18	3.8	21	3.1	21 tie	2.3
17.	Fencing	4.5 tie	16 tie	5.2	15 tie	5.9	17	4.6	16	5.8	12	9.8
18.	Skiing	4.5 tie	18	4.3	17	5.7	16	5.8	17	5.0	16	3.6
19.	Riding/equest.	3.9	17 tie	5.2	19	3.6	19	3.6	19	3.6	23	2.0
20.	Riflery	3.2	22	2.8	21 tie	3.4	22	2.8	18	3.8	15	3.8
21.	Bowling	3.0	21 tie	3.2	22	3.2	20	3.3	22	2.6	17	3.4
22.	Sailing	2.5	20 tie	3.2	18	3.8	21	3.2	20	3.1	21 tie	2.3
23.	Badminton	0.5	24	0.2	24	0.4	24	0.3	25	0.1	14	5.9
24.	Synch swim	0.4	23	1.2	23	1.3	23	0.5	23	1.0	18	3.3
25.	Archery	0.2	25	0.1	25	0.2	25	0.2	24	0.5	19	3.0

SOURCE: R. Vivian Acosta and Linda Jean Carpenter, "Most Popular Sports in 2010 (Most Frequently Found Sports in Women's Intercollegiate Programs)," in *Women in Intercollegiate Sport: A Longitudinal, National Study—Thirty-Three Year Update, 1977–2010,* http://www.acostacarpenter.org/2010pdf%20combined%20final.pdf (accessed June 2, 2011)

---

the percentage of non-Hispanic African-American male student-athletes increased from 16.3% in 1999–2000 to 18.7% in 2009–10. During this same period the percentage of non-Hispanic African-American female athletes increased from 9.4% to 11.6%.

Table 6.14 breaks down sports participation (all divisions combined) by ethnicity and sport. Some sports, such as lacrosse at a little over 90% for each gender, were overwhelmingly white during the 2009–10 school year. In contrast, a substantial portion of college basketball players—45.6% of men and 32.8% of women—were African-American. The overall ethnic balance across all divisions has remained fairly stable over the last several years, among both male and female athletes. This stability is represented visually in Table 6.15, which traces the ethnicity percentages of student-athletes between the 1999–2000 and 2009–10 school years.

Spending on College Sports

Even in hard economic times, athletic departments demand a substantial share of college budgets. Steve Berkowitz and Jodi Upton report in "Athletic Departments See Surge Financially in Down Economy" (*USA Today,* June 16, 2011) that Division I schools devoted roughly $2 billion in subsidies to athletic departments in 2010, an increase of 28% compared to 2006 figures. These subsidies accounted for nearly one-third of the $6.2 billion spent on college athletics in 2010, and came

at a time when many educational institutions were contending with severe budget cuts to academic programs, teacher layoffs, and tuition and fee increases. In "22 Elite College Sports Programs Turned a Profit in 2010, but Gaps Remain, NCAA Reports Says" (*Chronicle of Higher Education,* June 15, 2011), Libby Sander notes that only 22 out of 120 Division I-FBS athletic departments were profitable in 2010. Meanwhile, the average debt for the remaining 98 athletic departments came to $11.6 million.

As the trend toward university-subsidized sports accelerates, tensions have developed between athletics and academics on the campuses of many top schools. The debate has gotten more fierce as substantial cuts in higher education funding by state governments have led many schools to eliminate jobs, downsize academic programs, increase class sizes, and raise tuition.

In *2004–10 Revenues and Expenses of NCAA Division I Intercollegiate Athletics Programs Report* (August 2011, http://www.ncaapublications.com/productdownloads/2010 RevExp.pdf), Daniel L. Fulks of the NCAA indicates that in 2004 the median (half were higher and half were lower) Division I-FBS athletic program had generated revenues of $22.9 million and expenses of $29 million. By 2010 the median-generated revenues had increased to $35.3 million, whereas the median expenses had swelled to $46.7 million.

TABLE 6.12

Percentage of female coaches in intercollegiate sports, selected years 1972–2010

2010	42.6% of women's teams are coached by women
2008	42.8%
2006	42.4%
2004	44.1%
2003	44.0%
2002	44.0%
2001	44.7%
2000	45.6%
1999	46.3%
1998	47.4%
1997	47.4%
1996	47.7%
1995	48.3%
1994	49.4%
1993	48.1%
1992	48.3%
1991	47.7%
1990	47.3%
1989	47.7%
1988	48.3%
1987	48.8%
1986	50.6%
1985	50.7%
1984	53.8%
1983	56.2%
1982	52.4%
1981	54.6%
1980	54.2%
1979	56.1%
1978	58.2%
1972	**90.0%+ women coaching women's teams**

SOURCE: R. Vivian Acosta and Linda Jean Carpenter, "Percentage of Female Coaches All Division, All Sports, 2010," in *Women in Intercollegiate Sport: A Longitudinal, National Study—Thirty-Three Year Update, 1977–2010*, http://www.acostacarpenter.org/2010pdf%20combined%20final.pdf (accessed June 2, 2011)

TABLE 6.13

Percentage of female coaches, by sport, 1977 and 2010

[All divisions]

	2010	1977
Archery	0.0%	83.4%
Badminton	0.0%	75.0%
Basketball	57.0%	79.4%
Bowling	11.8%	42.9%
Crew/rowing	42.2%	11.9%
Cross country	18.6%	35.2%
Fencing	16.0%	51.7%
Field hockey	96.1%	99.1%
Golf	45.8%	54.6%
Gymnastics	50.8%	69.7%
Ice hockey	32.7%	37.5%
Lacrosse	87.5%	90.7%
Riding	77.3%	75.0%
Riflery	16.7%	17.4%
Sailing	14.3%	7.1%
Skiing	8.0%	22.7%
Soccer	32.5%	29.4%
Softball	63.8%	83.5%
Squash	26.9%	71.4%
Swim/fiving	24.1%	53.6%
Synch. swim	100.0%	85.0%
Tennis	28.2%	72.9%
Track and field	15.5%	52.3%
Volleyball	55.7%	86.6%
Water polo	20.6%	—

SOURCE: R. Vivian Acosta and Linda Jean Carpenter, "Percentage & Number of Female Coaches, All Divisions, 2010 and 1977, Now and Then," in *Women in Intercollegiate Sport: A Longitudinal, National Study—Thirty-Three Year Update, 1977–2010*, http://www.acostacarpenter.org/2010pdf%20combined%20final.pdf (accessed June 2, 2011)

In fiscal year 2010 football ($16.2 million in generated revenues and $12.4 million in expenses) and men's basketball ($4.8 million in generated revenues and $4 million in expenses) accounted for a huge share of both the median spending and median revenue in Division I-FBS college sports, and both produced sizable net financial gains. (See Table 6.16.) Table 6.17 details where Division I-FBS schools' athletics revenue came from in fiscal year 2010. Ticket sales were the biggest source, accounting for a median of $9 million of the total revenue.

Academic Eligibility

Incoming student-athletes must meet a set of academic standards to participate in NCAA-sanctioned sports programs. These standards vary according to the division in which a school competes. According to the NCAA, in *2011–12 Guide for the College-Bound Student-Athlete* (2011, http://www.ncaapublications.com/productdownloads/CBSA.pdf), Division I academic eligibility rules for the 2011–12 school year require that student-athletes:

- Graduate from high school

- Complete 16 core courses: four years of English; three years of math; two years of natural or physical science; one extra year of English, math, or natural or physical science; two years of social science; and four extra core courses of English, math, or science, or foreign language, nondoctrinal religion, or philosophy

- Achieve a minimum required GPA in core courses

- Achieve a combined SAT or ACT score that matches the student's GPA on a special NCAA chart

The requirements for Divisions II and III are similar to those for Division I, though less stringent.

In *Guide for the College-Bound Student-Athlete*, the NCAA also outlines the rules for recruiting high school athletes, which vary somewhat by sport as well as by division. The recruiting rules for Division I are summarized in Table 6.18 and include regulations that pertain to phone contact, campus visits, and other forms of communication between coaches and prospective college athletes.

HIGH SCHOOL SPORTS
Participation

According to the U.S. Census Bureau, 56.3% of U.S. high school students played on a sports team in 2007.

TABLE 6.14

College athletes and ethnicity, 2009–10

[For Divisions I, II, and III overall]

Sport	American Indian/ Alaskan Native Men	Women	Asian Men	Women	Black/ African American Men	Women	Hispanic/Latino Men	Women	Native Hawaiian/ Pacific Islander Men	Women	Other Men	Women	Two or more races Men	Women	White, non-Hispanic Men	Women
Archery	0.0	0.0	N/A	0.0	0.0	0.0	0.0	0.0	N/A	0.0	0.0	0.0	N/A	0.0	0.0	0.0
Badminton	0.0	0.0	N/A	N/A	0.0	0.0	0.0	0.0	N/A	0.0	0.0	0.0	N/A	N/A	0.0	0.0
Baseball	0.4	N/A	1.0	N/A	4.1	N/A	5.6	N/A	0.2	N/A	2.0	N/A	0.7	1.4	86.1	N/A
Basketball	0.3	0.5	0.6	1.0	45.6	32.8	2.5	2.5	0.2	0.3	3.2	2.5	1.1	0.6	46.7	58.9
Bowling	0.0	0.2	2.5	0.8	2.5	40.8	0.0	2.4	0.0	0.4	0.0	2.2	0.0	0.8	95.0	52.7
Cross country	0.4	0.4	1.7	1.5	9.2	9.4	5.4	4.9	0.1	0.1	3.5	3.4	0.7	0.5	79.0	79.5
Equestrian	0.0	0.4	0.0	0.9	0.0	0.7	0.0	1.9	0.6	0.0	0.0	1.8	0.0	1.2	100.0	93.9
Fencing	0.8	0.7	10.4	10.9	5.1	6.1	5.5	8.0	0.6	0.1	9.0	9.4	0.8	0.8	67.8	63.5
Field hockey	N/A	0.1	N/A	1.2	N/A	1.6	N/A	1.8	N/A	0.1	N/A	3.9	N/A	N/A	N/A	90.5
Football	0.4	N/A	0.8	N/A	34.5	N/A	2.9	N/A	0.6	N/A	2.4	N/A	1.0	N/A	57.4	N/A
Golf	0.3	0.5	2.5	5.0	2.3	2.7	2.6	3.9	0.1	0.2	3.6	5.5	0.3	0.6	88.1	81.6
Gymnastics	0.3	0.2	6.3	5.4	4.5	5.4	6.0	2.9	0.9	0.1	6.6	5.3	0.6	1.3	74.8	79.2
Ice hockey	0.2	0.8	1.0	1.4	0.7	0.4	0.8	0.8	0.0	0.1	9.1	7.2	0.3	0.1	87.9	89.4
Lacrosse	0.3	0.1	0.8	1.1	2.2	2.4	1.6	1.8	0.1	0.1	3.3	3.3	0.4	0.6	91.4	90.6
Rifle	0.0	0.5	4.5	7.9	0.8	1.6	4.1	5.3	0.0	0.0	1.2	1.6	0.0	0.5	89.3	82.6
Rowing	0.5	0.4	4.3	3.8	1.5	2.8	3.4	4.2	0.1	0.2	8.7	6.8	0.7	1.2	80.8	80.6
Rugby	0.0	0.0	1.6	2.7	3.2	8.2	6.3	12.3	1.6	1.4	0.0	3.4	0.0	1.4	87.3	70.5
Sailing	0.5	N/A	2.4	N/A	0.3	N/A	3.1	N/A	0.0	N/A	6.0	N/A	0.0	N/A	87.7	N/A
Skiing	0.0	0.0	0.8	0.8	0.4	0.2	0.4	0.0	0.2	0.0	8.9	7.6	0.2	0.2	89.0	91.2
Soccer	0.2	0.3	2.0	1.5	8.0	3.8	9.5	5.0	0.1	0.2	4.7	3.2	0.9	1.1	74.6	84.9
Softball	N/A	0.7	N/A	1.2	N/A	5.8	N/A	5.6	N/A	0.4	N/A	1.8	N/A	1.2	N/A	83.3
Squash	0.2	0.0	8.3	8.4	1.1	2.9	5.0	2.9	0.0	0.0	13.1	14.2	0.7	1.6	71.6	70.0
Swimming/diving	0.2	0.2	3.4	2.9	2.1	1.3	3.9	3.2	0.1	0.2	5.1	4.9	0.8	0.7	84.4	86.6
Sync. swimming	N/A	0.0	N/A	0.0	N/A	0.0	N/A	0.0	N/A	0.0	N/A	0.0	N/A	0.0	N/A	0.0
Team handball	0.0	0.0	N/A	N/A	0.0	0.0	0.0	0.0	N/A	N/A	0.0	0.0	N/A	N/A	N/A	0.0
Tennis	0.2	0.1	5.7	4.9	4.8	7.0	7.8	5.5	0.1	0.3	10.0	7.8	0.6	0.8	70.8	73.6
Track, indoor	0.3	0.4	1.5	1.3	21.2	21.5	3.4	3.3	0.1	0.2	3.6	3.7	0.8	0.9	69.1	68.8
Track, outdoor	0.3	0.4	1.6	1.4	22.0	21.8	4.2	3.9	0.1	0.1	3.4	3.6	0.9	0.9	67.5	67.9
Volleyball	0.5	0.3	4.5	1.6	5.3	9.8	11.7	4.0	1.0	0.6	5.2	2.7	1.1	1.1	70.7	79.9
Water polo	0.3	0.6	3.4	4.6	0.9	1.0	6.1	7.0	0.9	1.0	8.5	5.2	1.5	2.8	78.5	77.6
Wrestling	0.6	N/A	1.7	N/A	5.8	N/A	6.1	N/A	0.0	N/A	3.5	N/A	0.9	N/A	81.3	N/A
All sports	**0.3**	**0.4**	**1.5**	**1.9**	**18.7**	**11.6**	**4.3**	**4.0**	**0.2**	**0.2**	**3.6**	**3.8**	**0.8**	**1.0**	**70.4**	**77.2**

N/A = not applicable.

SOURCE: Erin Zgonc, "2009–10 Student-Athlete Race/Ethnicity Percentages for Divisions I, II and III Overall," in 1999–2000–2009–10 NCAA Student-Athlete Ethnicity Report, National Collegiate Athletic Association, September 2010, http://www.ncaapublications.com/productdownloads/SAEREP11.pdf (accessed June 2, 2011). © National Collegiate Athletic Association. 2011. All rights reserved.

TABLE 6.15

College athlete race and ethnicity percentages, 1999–2010

[For Divisions I, II, and III overall]

Year	American Indian/ Alaskan Native		Asian/Native Hawaiian/Pacific Islander		Black, non-Hispanic		Hispanic		Other		Two or more races		White, non-Hispanic	
	Men	Women	Men	Women	Men	Women	Men	Women	Men	Women	Men	Women	Men	Women
All sports														
1999–00*	0.3	0.3	1.2	1.5	16.3	9.4	3.0	2.4	6.0	6.8			71.6	78.1
2000–01*	0.3	0.4	1.3	1.7	17.2	10.2	3.3	2.7	3.3	3.7			70.4	77.0
2001–02*	0.3	0.3	1.4	1.7	17.7	10.4	3.5	2.8	3.1	3.2			71.6	79.1
2002–03*	0.3	0.3	1.4	1.9	17.9	10.5	3.5	3.0	2.7	2.9			71.6	78.9
2003–04*	0.4	0.3	1.4	2.0	18.1	10.6	3.5	3.2	2.5	2.8			71.4	78.2
2004–05*	0.3	0.3	1.5	2.1	18.0	10.9	3.8	3.3	2.7	3.0			71.1	77.5
2005–06*	0.4	0.4	1.5	2.0	18.1	10.7	3.7	3.5	2.7	2.7			70.6	77.4
2006–07*	0.3	0.4	1.6	2.1	18.3	11.2	3.9	3.6	3.7	3.9			72.2	78.8
2007–08*	0.3	0.4	1.7	2.2	18.5	11.3	4.4	3.8	4.3	3.6	0.3	0.4	72.2	78.9
2008–09*	0.3	0.3	1.7	2.2	18.4	11.4	4.2	3.9	3.4	3.7	0.5	0.7	71.4	77.8
2009–10*	0.3	0.4	1.8	2.1	18.7	11.6	4.3	4.0	3.6	3.8	0.8	1.0	70.4	77.2

*Provisional members are included in these numbers.

Notes: N/A = not applicable. Beginning in 2006–07 resident alien status is collected separate from ethnicity and reported in a separate table. Empty cells indicate the data are unavailable. In 2007–08 the categories of Asian and Hawaiian Native/Pacific Islander have been combined.

SOURCE: Erin Zgonc, "Student-Athlete Race and Ethnicity Percentages for Divisions I, II and III Overall—All Sports," in *1999–2000–2009–10 NCAA Student-Athlete Ethnicity Report*, National Collegiate Athletic Association, September 2010, http://www.ncaapublications.com/productdownloads/SAEREP11.pdf (accessed June 2, 2011). © National Collegiate Athletic Association. 2011. All rights reserved.

TABLE 6.16

Division I—FBS (Football Bowl Subdivision) revenue and expenses, by sport, fiscal year 2010

[Median values]

Sport	Men's programs			Women's programs		
	Generated revenues	Expenses	Net revenue	Generated revenues	Expenses	Net revenue
Baseball	338,000	1,292,000	(588,000)	277,000	2,168,000	(1,168,000)
Basketball	4,776,000	4,003,000	788,000	105,000	1,104,000	(860,000)
Crew	N/A	N/A	N/A	79,000	910,000	(854,000)
Equestrian	N/A	N/A	N/A	45,000	244,000	(96,000)
Fencing	30,000	175,000	(80,000)	68,000	817,000	(714,000)
Field hockey	N/A	N/A	N/A	N/A	N/A	N/A
Football	16,210,000	12,367,000	3,148,000	48,000	427,000	(274,000)
Golf	68,000	382,000	(228,000)	70,000	824,000	(547,000)
Gymnastics	61,000	573,000	(290,000)	120,000	1,174,000	(1,016,000)
Ice hockey	919,000	2,155,000	(333,000)	157,000	814,000	(390,000)
Lacrosse	548,000	1,161,000	(460,000)	31,000	41,000	(9,000)
Rifle		28,000	(28,000)	43,000	311,000	(173,000)
Skiing	43,000	379,000	(190,000)	67,000	873,000	(529,000)
Soccer	132,000	811,000	(510,000)	66,000	819,000	(582,000)
Softball	N/A	N/A	N/A	47,000	742,000	(463,000)
Swimming	58,000	625,000	(448,000)	27,000	479,000	(337,000)
Tennis	45,000	448,000	(290,000)	52,000	941,000	(596,000)
Track and field/cross country	70,000	798,000	(485,000)	78,000	927,000	(595,000)
Volleyball	162,000	628,000	(350,000)	35,000	611,000	(485,000)
Water polo	168,000	539,000	(335,000)	N/A	N/A	N/A
Wrestling	140,000	719,000	(373,000)	14,000	121,000	(74,000)
Other	231,000	365,000	(273,000)			

Notes: Revenues are reported excluding all allocated revenues. Expenses are reported excluding third party support. Medians shown represent only those institutions reporting some amount for revenues or expenses.

SOURCE: Daniel L. Fulks, "Table 3.11. Total Generated Revenues and Expenses by Sport, Division I—FBS, Fiscal Year 2010," in *2004–10 Revenues and Expenses of NCAA Division I Intercollegiate Athletics Programs Report*, National Collegiate Athletic Association, August 2011, http://www.ncaapublications.com/productdownloads/2010RevExp.pdf (accessed June 9, 2011). © National Collegiate Athletic Association. 2011. All rights reserved.

(See Table 6.19.) The percentage was higher among boys (62.1%) than girls (50.4%). Nearly 59% of white students played on a sports team. Minority students participated in team athletics in slightly lesser proportions, as 54.9% of non-Hispanic African-American students and 50% of Hispanic students played on sports teams. Female Hispanic high school students were the least likely to play on a sports team, at 41.8%.

Since 1971 the National Federation of State High School Associations (NFHS) has compiled data on sports participation from its member associations. The most recent data are published in *2009–10 High School Athletics Participation Survey* (2011, http://www.nfhs.org/WorkArea/linkit.aspx?LinkIdentifier=id&ItemID=4198). Table 6.20 summarizes these NFHS data between 1971 and 2010. During the 2009–10 school year the number of participants in high school sports reached 7.6 million. At nearly 3.2 million, participation among girls reached an all-time high in 2009–10. The total for boys, at nearly 4.5 million, was also a new high.

Table 6.21 shows the most popular high school sports for boys. Over 1.1 million boys participated in football during the 2009–10 school year. Boys' track and field had 572,123 participants, about half as many participants as football. Basketball (540,207), baseball (472,644), and soccer (391,839) were the third-, fourth-, and fifth-most popular boys' sports, respectively. Nationwide, 17,969 schools supported boys' basketball programs, the most of any team sport. Among high school girls, outdoor track and field was the most popular sport, with 469,177 participants, followed by basketball (439,550), volleyball (403,985), fast-pitch softball (378,211), and soccer (356,116). (See Table 6.22.) As with boys' basketball, girls' basketball was the most prevalent high school athletic program in the United States, with 17,711 schools supporting girls' basketball programs.

According to the NFHS, the state with the largest number of high school athletes during the 2009–10 school year was Texas, with 780,721. Other leading states included California (771,465), New York (379,677), Illinois (344,257), and Ohio (334,797).

The national advocacy group Child Trends analyzes data on school sports participation in the United States. Table 6.23 offers an overview of participation levels between 1991 and 2008. The table shows that participation in athletics among eighth-grade boys decreased from 73.4% in 1991 to 66% in 2008. Participation among eighth-grade girls also decreased slightly during this same period, from 66.2% in 1991 to 62.6% in 2008. Child Trends finds that since 1991 the gender gap in high

TABLE 6.17

Sources of revenue, NCAA Division I—FBS, fiscal year 2010

[Median values]

	Public	Private	Total
Total ticket sales	9,526,000	8,270,000	9,015,000
NCAA and conference distributions	6,243,000	8,097,000	7,387,000
Guarantees and options	737,000	650,000	733,000
Cash contributions from alumni and others	6,755,000	7,357,000	6,961,000
Third party support	0	0	0
Other			
Concessions/programs/novelties	829,000	607,000	744,000
Broadcast rights	44,000	10,000	40,000
Royalties/advertising/sponsorship	2,618,000	1,703,000	2,308,000
Sports camps	102,000	28,000	71,000
Endowment/investment income	195,000	1,821,000	275,000
Miscellaneous	688,000	618,000	668,000
Total generated revenues	34,897,000	35,775,000	35,336,000
Allocated revenues			
Direct institutional support	2,233,000	11,075,000	3,030,000
Indirect institutional support	21,000	1,041,000	38,000
Student fees	2,146,000	0	1,815,000
Direct government support	0	0	0
Total allocated revenues	8,678,000	13,884,000	9,762,000
Total all revenues	45,738,000	50,831,000	48,298,000

NCAA = National Collegiate Athletic Assocation.

SOURCE: Daniel L. Fulks, "Table 3.7. Sources of Revenue, Division I—FBS, Fiscal Year 2010," in *2004–10 Revenues and Expenses of NCAA Division I Intercollegiate Athletics Programs Report*, National Collegiate Athletic Association, August 2011, http://www.ncaapublications.com/productdownloads/2010RevExp.pdf (accessed June 9, 2011). © National Collegiate Athletic Association. 2011. All rights reserved.

school sports participation has decreased substantially. Among 10th graders the difference between boys and girls declined from 17 percentage points in 1991 (boys, 69%, and girls, 52%) to seven percentage points in 2008 (boys, 64%, and girls, 57%). (See Figure 6.3.) Likewise, the gap for 12th graders declined from 18 percentage points in 1991 (boys, 65%, and girls, 47%) to 14 percentage points in 2008 (boys, 63%, and girls, 49%).

Child Trends also finds a correlation between parents' education and students' participation in school athletics. Youth whose parents were better educated were more likely to participate than their peers whose parents had fewer years of education. In 2008, 74% of eighth graders with a parent who had attended graduate school participated in school sports, whereas only 47% of eighth graders whose parents did not finish high school participated in school sports. (See Figure 6.4.)

Benefits of High School Sports Participation

In September 2005 the National Center for Education Statistics (NCES) published the report *What Is the Status of High School Athletes 8 Years after Their Senior Year?* (http://nces.ed.gov/pubs2005/2005303.pdf), which analyzes the status of former high school athletes in their mid-20s. The report was part of the National Education Longitudinal Study of 1988, which tracked a large sample of students who were seniors in 1992. The report examined their educational achievement, employment success, and health status as of 2000. The NCES finds that elite (those who were team captains or most valuable players) and varsity-level athletes were more likely than nonathletes to have received some postsecondary education and more likely to have earned a bachelor's degree. It also finds that elite and varsity-level athletes were more likely than nonathletes to be employed and employed full time in 2000. Elite and varsity-level athletes had higher incomes on average than those who did not participate in high school sports. In addition, the NCES finds that high school athletes were more likely than nonathletes to participate in fitness activities and group sports eight years after their senior year. Elite and varsity-level athletes were less likely to be daily smokers than their nonathletic peers. The only negative impact the NCES notes is that elite and varsity-level athletes were more likely than nonathletes to binge drink (i.e., these survey respondents reported having five or more alcoholic drinks on at least one occasion during the two weeks before the survey).

Money and High School Athletics

The vast sums of money involved in college sports have sometimes led schools to engage in unethical recruiting methods to attract elite high school athletes. In 2011, shortly after playing in the Bowl Championship Series title game, the University of Oregon came under investigation by the NCAA amid allegations that the school had paid a recruiting service to influence certain high school players to join its football program. Anne M. Peterson reports in "Ducks Mum on Recruiting Scandal, but for How Long?" (Associated Press, July 16, 2011) that in March 2010 Willie Lyles, a recruiting agent with the Houston-based Complete Scouting Services, had received $25,000 from the university to persuade the running back Lache Seastrunk to sign with the team. During the summer of 2011 Lyles went public with his side of the story, telling media outlets that Oregon had "paid for what they saw as my access and influence with recruits." Admitting that his recruiting services "went beyond what a scouting service should," Lyles also revealed that two other schools, the University of California and Louisiana State University, had previously paid him for access to top athletes. In response to the allegations, the University of Oregon hired Michael Glazier, a former NCAA violations enforcement official who now oversees the Collegiate Sports Practice Group of the law firm Bond, Schoeneck & King, to help with its defense.

YOUTH SPORTS

As noted in Chapter 2, participation in youth sports has generally been declining in the United States over the last several years. However, that trend has been accompanied by another phenomenon: a growing intensity as youth leagues are increasingly seen as a feeder system

TABLE 6.18

Summary of NCAA Division I recruiting rules, 2010–11

Recruiting method	Men's basketball	Women's basketball	Football	Other sports
Sophomore years				
Recruiting materials	• You may receive brochures for camps and questionnaires. • You may begin receiving recruiting materials June 15 after your sophomore year.	• You may receive brochures for camps and questionnaires.	• You may receive brochures for camps and questionnaires.	• You may receive brochures for camps and questionnaires. • Men's ice hockey—You may begin receiving recruiting materials June 15 after your sophomore year.
Telephone calls	• You may make calls to the coach at your expense only. • College may accept collect calls from you at end of your sophomore year. • College coach cannot call you.	• You may make calls to the coach at your expense only. • College coach cannot call you.	• You may make calls to the coach at your expense only. • College coach cannot call you.	• You may make calls to the coach at your expense only. • College coach cannot call you. • Women's ice hockey—A college coach may call international prospects once on or after July 7 through July 31 after sophomore year.
Off-campus contact Official visit Unofficial visit	• None allowed. • None allowed. • You may make an unlimited number of unofficial visits.	• None allowed. • None allowed. • You may make an unlimited number of unofficial visits.	• None allowed. • None allowed. • You may make an unlimited number of unofficial visits.	• None allowed. • None allowed. • You may make an unlimited number of unofficial visits.
Junior year				
Recruiting materials	• Allowed. • You may begin receiving recruiting materials June 15 after your sophomore year.	• You may begin receiving September 1 of junior year.	• You may begin receiving September 1 of junior year.	• You may begin receiving September 1 of junior year. • Men's ice hockey—You may begin receiving recruiting materials June 15 after your sophomore year.
Telephone calls	• You may make calls to the coach at your expense.	• You may make calls to the coach at your expense.	• You may make calls to the coach at your expense.	• You may make calls to the coach at your expense.
College coaches may call you	• Once per month beginning June 15, before your junior year, through July 31 after your junior year.	• Once per month in April (on or after the Thursday following the Women's Final Four) and May. • Once between June 1 and June 20 after your junior year. • Once between June 21 and June 30 after your junior year. • Three times in July after your junior year (maximum of one call per week).	• Once from April 15 to May 31 of your junior year.	• Once per week starting July 1 after your junior year. • Men's ice hockey—Once per month beginning June 15, before your junior year, through July 31 after your junior year. • Women's ice hockey—Once per week beginning July 7 after your junior year.
Off-campus contact	• None allowed.	• None allowed.	• None allowed.	• Allowed starting July 1 after your junior year. • Gymnastics—allowed beginning July 15 after your junior year. • Women's ice hockey—Allowed beginning July 7 after your junior year.
Official visit	• None allowed.	• None allowed.	• None allowed.	• None allowed.
Unofficial visit	• You may make an unlimited number of unofficial visits.	• You may make an unlimited number of unofficial visits.	• You may make an unlimited number of unofficial visits.	• You may make an unlimited number of unofficial visits.

SOURCE: "Summary of Recruiting Rules for Each Sport—Division I," in *2010–11 Guide for the College–Bound Student-Athlete*, National Collegiate Athletic Association, 2010, http://www.ncaapublications.com/productdownloads/CB11.pdf (accessed June 2, 2011). © National Collegiate Athletic Association. 2011.

for the big money college and professional systems. The well-documented health benefits of participation in youth sports are outlined in Chapter 8. However, the adult-driven pressure on young athletes has drawbacks. It has resulted in greater pressure on young athletes to perform, specialization on a single sport at earlier ages, year-round play, and more travel in top-level youth leagues.

In *Until It Hurts: America's Obsession with Youth Sports and How It Harms Our Kids* (2009), Mark Hyman cites numerous examples of children being injured because coaches, who were eager to win at all costs, ignored clear warning signs that their star players were damaging their bodies. In particular, Hyman notes that young baseball pitchers risk serious, permanent arm injuries from overuse,

TABLE 6.19

High school students engaged in organized physical activity, by sex, race, and Hispanic origin, 2007

[In percent. For students in grades 9 to 12. Subject to sampling error.]

Characteristic	Met currently recommended levels of physical activity[a]	Did not participate in 60+ min. of physical activity on any day[b]	Attended physical education class Total[c]	Attended physical education class Attended daily[d]	Played on at least one sports team[e]	Injured while exercising or playing sports[f]	Used computers 3 or more hours/day[g]	Watched three or more hours/day of TV[h]
All students	34.7	24.9	53.6	30.3	56.3	21.9	24.9	35.4
White, non-Hispanic	37.0	22.4	50.4	28.9	58.9	21.8	22.6	27.2
Male	46.1	16.7	54.0	32.2	63.0	23.6	26.9	30.4
Female	27.9	28.2	46.8	25.6	54.8	19.9	18.2	24.0
Black, non-Hispanic	31.1	32.0	55.9	31.9	54.9	23.4	30.5	62.7
Male	41.3	21.8	61.0	35.8	65.1	26.7	34.0	64.6
Female	21.0	42.1	50.6	27.8	44.7	19.3	26.7	60.6
Hispanic	30.2	27.1	61.0	36.0	50.0	22.0	26.3	43.0
Male	38.6	18.8	64.7	36.4	58.1	24.7	30.7	42.4
Female	21.9	35.2	57.3	35.5	41.8	18.7	21.8	43.6
Male	43.7	18.0	57.7	33.2	62.1	24.1	29.1	37.5
Grade 9	44.4	17.1	68.3	39.7	63.4	26.0	30.5	42.0
Grade 10	45.1	16.3	62.3	35.7	64.7	24.5	30.0	38.1
Grade 11	45.2	18.0	51.4	27.9	63.0	23.8	29.5	35.4
Grade 12	38.7	21.5	44.6	27.5	56.2	20.9	25.6	32.8
Female	25.6	31.8	49.4	27.3	50.4	19.3	20.6	33.2
Grade 9	31.5	26.1	65.1	40.4	54.7	21.7	24.9	37.2
Grade 10	24.4	31.7	51.2	26.1	50.8	20.8	22.6	35.9
Grade 11	24.6	34.3	38.8	19.8	52.5	18.2	17.9	29.6
Grade 12	20.6	36.2	38.5	20.2	41.9	14.8	14.8	28.9

[a]Were physically active doing any kind of physical activity that increased their heart rate and made them breathe hard some of the time for a total of at least 60 minutes/day for at least 5 or more days out of the 7 days preceding the survey.
[b]Did not participate in 60 or more minutes of any kind of physical activity that increased their heart rate and made them breathe hard some of the time on at least 1 day during the 7 days before the survey.
[c]On one or more days in an average week when they were in school.
[d]Five days in an average week when they were in school.
[e]Run by their school or community groups during the 12 months before the survey.
[f]Students who saw a doctor or nurse for an injury that happened while exercising or playing sports during the 30 days before the survey, among 79.6% of students
[g]For something that was not school work.
[h]On an average school day.

SOURCE: "Table 209. High School Students Engaged in Organized Physical Activity by Sex, Race, and Hispanic Origin: 2007," in *Statistical Abstract of the United States: 2011*, 130th ed., U.S. Census Bureau, 2010, http://www.census.gov/compendia/statab/2011/tables/11s0209.xls (accessed June 2, 2011)

---

as evidenced by the sharp rise in the number of adolescents needing elbow surgery. Hyman points to, among other things, a growing reliance on the curveball, which exerts a great deal of strain on still-developing arms.

Brooke de Lench argues in "Early Travel Team Play Fosters Elitism" (2008, http://www.momsteam.com/successful-parenting/parenting-elite-athletes/specialization/early-travel-team-play-fosters-elitism) that the rise of top-level teams that travel long distances to play other elite squads has harmed less-talented kids by excluding them. Furthermore, these travel teams offer little benefit to those highly skilled children who are forced into a demanding travel schedule that resembles professional play more than the recreational, community-based play that has been shown to yield the most beneficial effects. Travel teams also disadvantage players from lower-income families because of the high financial cost of participation.

In this article and in a series of others on the website MomsTeam (http://www.momsteam.com/), de Lench and others make a compelling case against early specialization in a single sport, including debunking the myth that a strenuous travel schedule and specialization—pushed mostly by adults who are looking for scholarships and professional careers—contribute to the development of top-notch professional sports talent. Hyman concurs, noting that there is a surprising lack of former Little League superstar pitchers performing in Major League Baseball.

TABLE 6.20

Participation in high school athletic programs, by sex, 1971–2010

Year	Boys participants	Girls participants	Total
1971–72	3,666,917	294,015	3,960,932
1972–73	3,770,621	817,073	4,587,694
1973–74	4,070,125	1,300,169	5,370,294
1975–76	4,109,021	1,645,039	5,754,060
1977–78	4,367,442	2,083,040	6,450,482
1978–79	3,709,512	1,854,400	5,563,912
1979–80	3,517,829	1,750,264	5,268,093
1980–81	3,503,124	1,853,789	5,356,913
1981–82	3,409,081	1,810,671	5,219,752
1982–83	3,355,558	1,779,972	5,135,530
1983–84	3,303,599	1,747,346	5,050,945
1984–85	3,354,284	1,757,884	5,112,168
1985–86	3,344,275	1,807,121	5,151,396
1986–87	3,364,082	1,836,356	5,200,438
1987–88	3,425,777	1,849,684	5,275,461
1988–89	3,416,844	1,839,352	5,256,196
1989–90	3,398,192	1,858,659	5,256,851
1990–91	3,406,355	1,892,316	5,298,671
1991–92	3,429,853	1,940,801	5,370,654
1992–93	3,416,389	1,997,489	5,413,878
1993–94	3,472,967	2,130,315	5,603,282
1994–95	3,536,359	2,240,461	5,776,820
1995–96	3,634,052	2,367,936	6,001,988
1996–97	3,706,225	2,474,043	6,180,268
1997–98	3,763,120	2,570,333	6,333,453
1998–99	3,832,352	2,652,726	6,485,078
1999–00	3,861,749	2,675,874	6,537,623
2000–01	3,921,069	2,784,154	6,705,223
2001–02	3,960,517	2,806,998	6,767,515
2002–03	3,988,738	2,856,358	6,845,096
2003–04	4,038,253	2,865,299	6,903,552
2004–05	4,110,319	2,908,390	7,018,709
2005–06	4,206,549	2,953,355	7,159,904
2006–07	4,321,103	3,021,807	7,342,910
2007–08	4,372,115	3,057,266	7,429,381
2008–09	4,422,662	3,114,091	7,536,753
2009–10	4,455,740	3,172,637	7,628,377

SOURCE: "Athletic Participation Survey Totals," in *2009–10 High School Athletics Participation Survey*, National Federation of State High School Associations, 2011, http://www.nfhs.org/WorkArea/linkit.aspx?Link Identifier=id&ItemID=4198 (accessed June 2, 2011). Reprinted with permission of the National Federation of State High School Associations.

TABLE 6.21

Most popular high school sports for boys, by number of schools and number of participants, 2009–10

	Schools			Participants	
1.	Basketball	17,969	1.	Football—11-player	1,109,278
2.	Track and field—outdoor	16,011	2.	Track and Field—outdoor	572,123
3.	Baseball	15,786	3.	Basketball	540,207
4.	Football—11-player	14,226	4.	Baseball	472,644
5.	Cross country	13,942	5.	Soccer	391,839
6.	Golf	13,693	6.	Wrestling	272,890
7.	Soccer	11,375	7.	Cross country	239,608
8.	Wrestling	10,363	8.	Tennis	162,755
9.	Tennis	9,916	9.	Golf	157,756
10.	Swimming and diving	6,820	10.	Swimming and diving	131,376

SOURCE: "Ten Most Popular Boys Programs," in *2009–10 High School Athletics Participation Survey*, National Federation of State High School Associations, 2011, http://www.nfhs.org/WorkArea/linkit.aspx? LinkIdentifier=id&ItemID=4198 (accessed June 2, 2011). Reprinted with permission of the National Federation of State High School Associations.

TABLE 6.22

Most popular high school sports for girls, by number of schools and number of participants, 2009–10

	Schools			Participants	
1.	Basketball	17,711	1.	Track and field—outdoor	469,177
2.	Track and field—outdoor	15,923	2.	Basketball	439,550
3.	Volleyball	15,382	3.	Volleyball	403,985
4.	Softball—fast pitch	15,298	4.	Softball—fast pitch	378,211
5.	Cross country	13,809	5.	Soccer	356,116
6.	Soccer	10,901	6.	Cross country	201,968
7.	Tennis	10,166	7.	Tennis	182,395
8.	Golf	9,651	8.	Swimming and diving	158,419
9.	Swimming and diving	7,171	9.	Competitive spirit squads	123,644
10.	Competitive spirit squads	4,879	10.	Golf	70,872

SOURCE: "Ten Most Popular Girls Programs," in *2009–10 High School Athletics Participation Survey*, National Federation of State High School Associations, 2011, http://www.nfhs.org/WorkArea/linkit.aspx? LinkIdentifier=id&ItemID=4198 (accessed June 2, 2011). Reprinted with permission of the National Federation of State High School Associations.

TABLE 6.23

Participation in school athletics, 1991–2008

	1991	1992	1993	1994	1995	1996	1997	1998	1999	2000	2001	2002	2003	2004	2005	2006	2007	2008
Eighth grade	**69.6**	**67.3**	**66.6**	**66.5**	**68.1**	**67.4**	**66.7**	**68.7**	**67.7**	**67.3**	**69.1**	**67.2**	**65.3**	**65.7**	**64.1**	**63.4**	**62.4**	**64.0**
Gender																		
Male	73.4	71.0	71.1	70.2	72.5	69.8	68.0	71.7	69.0	69.2	70.8	68.3	68.0	66.6	66.0	65.4	64.7	66.0
Female	66.2	64.0	62.7	63.2	64.3	65.6	65.5	65.8	66.6	65.8	67.5	66.1	62.9	64.9	62.6	62.0	60.5	62.6
Race																		
White	71.1	68.7	70.0	69.8	69.5	70.7	70.1	71.2	70.0	70.2	72.6	71.9	67.5	68.0	67.4	66.1	65.5	69.4
Black	73.8	68.4	61.8	62.4	69.7	64.5	63.0	64.9	69.5	63.4	67.3	65.9	67.2	64.5	60.6	60.5	62.2	61.8
Parental education*																		
Less than high school	54.3	47.7	49.9	51.0	50.5	53.4	52.3	53.0	55.0	47.5	53.3	55.5	51.3	48.8	45.3	46.7	45.9	47.3
Completed high school	66.1	63.7	62.5	63.9	64.8	64.2	61.5	63.0	63.3	64.3	64.1	63.0	64.4	58.1	57.9	58.8	57.1	58.4
Some college	73.3	67.6	69.7	69.5	73.8	69.4	70.5	70.2	69.6	69.8	69.1	66.8	65.0	67.0	63.8	66.0	66.4	64.4
Completed college	73.6	75.5	72.7	72.3	71.3	75.3	71.6	74.0	74.1	74.0	77.0	72.5	69.7	74.0	72.9	69.8	68.2	71.1
Graduate school	76.6	76.7	76.3	74.4	74.9	77.7	74.8	76.6	75.4	75.8	78.7	76.9	76.2	74.8	76.5	73.2	73.9	74.2
College plans																		
None or under 4 years	49.9	46.9	47.9	51.0	51.3	50.5	50.2	49.4	46.8	46.8	46.5	49.0	41.4	45.7	39.3	43.8	40.0	42.9
Complete four years	72.7	70.4	69.0	68.7	70.3	70.0	68.9	70.9	70.2	69.5	71.6	68.7	67.8	67.9	66.8	65.4	64.2	65.9
Tenth grade	**60.2**	**62.9**	**62.0**	**61.8**	**62.6**	**61.5**	**61.7**	**61.6**	**62.2**	**61.5**	**62.9**	**61.1**	**60.2**	**61.1**	**60.4**	**62.7**	**64.0**	**60.3**
Gender																		
Male	68.7	69.8	68.0	69.2	68.2	65.5	66.0	67.8	68.1	65.5	66.3	64.3	63.4	65.5	65.5	67.4	64.2	64.3
Female	51.9	56.6	56.5	54.9	57.5	57.7	57.5	56.1	57.4	58.3	60.0	57.8	57.0	57.2	55.6	58.3	55.8	56.7
Race																		
White	61.8	64.6	64.1	64.0	63.6	63.5	63.3	63.6	65.4	63.8	65.2	62.8	62.8	64.3	63.3	65.6	69.4	63.3
Black	55.7	62.8	59.9	57.2	62.3	56.5	62.5	58.8	57.2	55.7	60.9	64.8	58.5	57.0	59.1	56.5	61.8	62.5
Parental education*																		
Less than high school	44.5	40.1	42.5	42.7	40.9	42.7	44.2	46.7	44.0	45.9	48.3	40.2	44.0	42.0	42.9	43.1	47.3	43.7
Completed high school	54.4	56.8	58.2	53.2	54.3	53.7	56.3	53.6	54.0	51.7	56.5	54.7	50.9	54.2	53.5	52.5	58.4	53.5
Some college	59.8	63.6	62.9	62.0	62.6	62.4	60.5	64.7	65.2	61.4	63.0	60.9	61.8	60.8	59.6	62.2	64.4	60.7
Completed college	67.2	72.6	67.3	70.3	71.8	68.3	68.8	68.1	70.0	69.9	68.9	70.6	66.4	67.7	66.8	70.9	71.1	66.7
Graduate school	70.9	74.6	75.1	74.0	74.9	73.5	72.7	72.9	71.9	75.9	75.5	72.0	74.4	73.0	72.5	74.4	74.2	71.7
College plans																		
None or under 4 years	38.9	42.7	41.3	39.9	39.9	40.3	42.0	45.5	39.0	39.4	41.1	37.5	40.6	38.6	37.6	38.8	42.9	36.7
Complete four years	64.6	66.9	66.0	66.5	66.2	65.1	64.8	64.4	66.0	65.0	66.4	64.9	63.1	64.0	63.4	65.7	65.9	62.9
Twelth grade	**56.2**	**55.6**	**55.7**	**56.3**	**55.1**	**55.1**	**55.5**	**55.9**	**54.3**	**55.0**	**55.0**	**54.0**	**53.3**	**54.8**	**56.3**	**54.3**	**53.8**	**55.3**
Gender																		
Male	64.9	63.8	65.5	66.1	62.4	62.7	63.4	63.0	62.3	64.2	61.9	60.2	58.9	59.5	61.7	58.7	57.5	62.5
Female	47.0	48.0	46.2	47.5	48.1	48.0	48.4	48.7	47.3	46.9	48.6	48.7	48.0	51.3	51.0	50.1	50.2	48.8
Race																		
White	57.0	57.3	56.7	57.7	54.9	56.8	56.3	57.7	56.5	57.4	57.5	56.3	55.4	56.5	56.9	55.4	55.3	58.0
Black	56.2	50.9	52.9	59.7	56.7	53.1	52.9	54.1	50.1	55.4	57.9	48.4	50.5	53.2	64.1	59.2	57.9	56.6
Parental education*																		
Less than high school	41.3	46.7	44.4	41.7	38.7	35.3	37.2	41.3	43.5	33.2	38.0	39.7	42.6	41.9	45.2	48.4	39.5	40.7
Completed high school	50.3	49.1	52.8	51.2	48.4	50.1	50.2	52.5	49.5	53.5	50.1	47.0	49.1	48.5	52.7	49.7	48.0	48.4
Some college	60.3	54.9	55.8	57.1	53.2	54.3	55.5	57.4	54.6	56.8	56.1	53.3	51.5	55.0	55.6	52.3	52.5	56.4
Completed college	61.7	63.8	60.8	61.8	62.2	62.1	60.6	59.1	57.3	58.6	62.1	62.1	57.8	60.8	59.6	58.9	60.6	60.5
Graduate school	66.4	67.5	66.4	68.4	68.0	64.6	66.7	66.2	65.8	63.0	63.5	62.6	66.7	63.8	63.4	64.0	64.2	67.4
College plans																		
None or under 4 years	42.6	41.0	40.0	44.0	41.2	41.6	39.8	42.2	43.3	42.0	40.7	41.6	40.9	40.2	43.6	44.0	40.1	42.7
Complete four years	61.5	60.7	60.4	60.0	58.8	59.0	60.3	59.9	57.8	58.4	58.8	57.7	56.2	58.8	59.0	56.8	56.9	58.1

*Parental education is calculated by the Institute of Social Research as the average of the mother's and father's education. Child Trends has recalculated these results to reflect the education level of the most educated parent. In those circumstances where the gap between mothers' and fathers' education is more than one level, this results in an underestimate of the most educated parent's education level.

SOURCE: "Table 1. Participation in School Athletics, 1991–2008," in *Participation in School Athletics*, Child Trends, June 2010, http://www.childtrendsdatabank .org/sites/default/files/37_Tab01.pdf (accessed June 6, 2011)

FIGURE 6.3

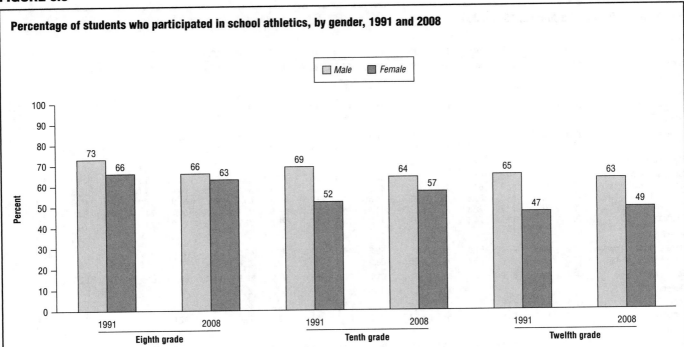

Percentage of students who participated in school athletics, by gender, 1991 and 2008

☐ Male ☐ Female

Note: Participation in school athletics includes all students who have participated to any degree in school athletic teams during the current school year.

SOURCE: "Figure 1. Percentage of Students in Grades 8, 10 and 12 Who Participate in School Athletics, by Gender, 1991 and 2008," in *Participation in School Athletics*, Child Trends, June 2010, http://www.childtrendsdatabank.org/sites/default/files/37_fig01.jpg (accessed June 6, 2011)

FIGURE 6.4

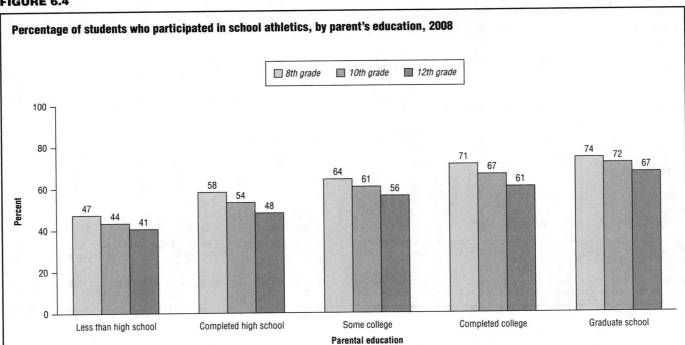

Percentage of students who participated in school athletics, by parent's education, 2008

☐ 8th grade ☐ 10th grade ☐ 12th grade

Notes: Participation in school athletics includes all students who have participated to any degree in school athletic teams during the current school year. Parental education is calculated by the Institute of Social Research as the average of the mother's and father's education. Child Trends has recalculated these results to reflect the education level of the most educated parent. In those circumstances where the gap between mothers' and fathers' education is more than one level, this results in an underestimate of the most educated parent's education level.

SOURCE: "Percentage of Students in Grades 8, 10 and 12 Who Participated in School Athletics, by Parent's Education, 2008," in *Participation in School Athletics*, Child Trends, June 2010, http://www.childtrendsdatabank.org/sites/default/files/37_fig02.jpg (accessed June 6, 2011)

CHAPTER 7
THE OLYMPICS

If professional team sports in the United States epitomize the corporatization of athletics, the Olympics, at least in theory, exemplify the opposite: global goodwill and celebration that surround the pursuit of athletic excellence for its own sake. This spirit of goodwill does not, however, diminish the fact that vast sums of money change hands via the Olympics. Nor does it prevent the pursuit of these vast sums, or political grandstanding, from sometimes overshadowing the Olympic ideal.

The Olympics are divided into the Summer and Winter Olympiads. Table 7.1 lists the sports that will be included in the 2012 summer games in London, England. In October 2009 the International Olympic Committee (IOC) agreed to add two new sports, golf and rugby, to the 2016 summer games in Rio de Janeiro, Brazil. The winter Olympic Games are much smaller than the summer games. Table 7.2 shows the list of winter Olympic sports.

The IOC regularly reviews which sports are to be included in the Olympic Games. A number of factors are taken into consideration, most prominently popularity and cost. For example, beach volleyball made its Olympic debut in 1996, and snowboarding was added to the winter games program in 1998. In contrast, baseball and softball were eliminated following the 2008 games. The Olympic Charter limits the number of sports that can take place at the Olympics; therefore, sports must be cut to accommodate the addition of new ones.

Before the 1996 games the Olympics sometimes included demonstration sports, the purpose of which was to showcase an emerging or locally popular sport before a global audience. Winners in these sports were not officially recognized as Olympic champions. Some of these sports, such as flat-water canoeing and kayaking, were later added as regular Olympic events at subsequent games. Winter demonstration sports that later became regular events include curling and freestyle aerial skiing.

Throughout the history of the Olympic Games, American athletes have excelled on the world stage. Table 7.3 lists the top U.S. Olympic medal winners of all time.

HISTORY OF THE OLYMPICS

In *The Olympic Games in Antiquity* (2007, http://multimedia.olympic.org/pdf/en_report_658.pdf), the IOC explains that the roots of the Olympic Games are in ancient Greece. Exactly when the ancient Olympics started is unknown, but the first recorded games took place in the city of Olympia in 776 BC. The games grew in importance over the next few centuries, reaching their peak during the sixth and fifth centuries BC. By that time, they had grown from a single event—a 200-yard (183 m) foot race called the stadion—to 20 events that were spread over several days. The Greek Olympic Games were held every four years.

As the Roman Empire rose to power in the region and subsequently adopted Christianity as its official religion, the Olympic Games declined in stature. The games, which had always been a religious as much as an athletic celebration, were eventually outlawed in AD 393 by the emperor Theodosius I (347–395).

Interest in the Olympics was revived during the mid-19th century, when modern archaeologists began to unearth the ruins of ancient Olympia. In 1890 the French historian and educator Pierre de Coubertin (1862–1937) developed the idea of holding an international competition of young athletes as a way to promote peace and cooperation among nations. He presented his ideas at Sorbonne University in Paris, France, in 1894, and two years later the first modern Olympic Games were held in Athens, Greece.

According to the IOC, in "Athens 1896" (2011, http://www.olympic.org/athens-1896-summer-olympics), the inaugural Olympic Games of 1896 featured 241 athletes from 14 countries competing in 43 events—the largest international sporting event ever held up to that time. The event was repeated in Paris in 1900 and again in St. Louis, Missouri, in 1904. Other summer Olympic Games sites over the years are shown in Table 7.4.

TABLE 7.1

Summer Olympic sports

Aquatics	Hockey
Archery	Judo
Athletics	Modern pentathlon
Badminton	Rowing
Basketball	Sailing
Boxing	Shooting
Canoe/kayak	Table tennis
Cycling	Taekwondo
Equestrian	Tennis
Fencing	Triathlon
Football	Volleyball
Gymnastics	Weightlifting
Handball	Wrestling

Note: Rugby and golf will be added for 2016 games in Rio de Janeiro.

SOURCE: Created by Robert Jacobson for Gale, 2011

TABLE 7.2

Winter Olympic sports

Biathlon
Bobsleigh
Curling
Ice hockey
Luge
Skating
Skiing

SOURCE: Created by Robert Jacobson for Gale, 2011

Winter Olympics History

By 1908, movement toward establishing a winter version of the Olympics had begun. That year, figure skating was introduced during the summer games in London. A cluster of winter events was scheduled to be added for 1916, but the games were canceled because of the outbreak of World War I (1914–1918). In 1924 several nations participated in the International Winter Sports Week in Chamonix, France. Two years later the IOC retroactively renamed the event the first Olympic Winter Games, according to the IOC, in "Factsheet: Olympic Winter Games" (December 2010, http://www.olympic .org/Documents/Reference_documents_Factsheets/The _Olympic_Winter_Games.pdf). The winter games took place during regular Olympic years until 1992. Beginning with the 1994 games in Lillehammer, Norway, the winter games have been held every four years, alternating with the summer games. Table 7.5 shows the sites at which all the Winter Olympics have been held.

Politics and the Olympics

Wars and other political complications affected the Olympic movement at several points during the 20th century. The 1916 games were a casualty of World War I, and World War II (1939–1945) claimed the 1940 and 1944 Olympics.

Twice the Olympics have been the scene of violent acts of terrorism. At the 1972 summer games in Munich, West Germany, members of the Palestinian terrorist group Black September took members of the Israeli team hostage on September 5. A rescue attempt was unsuccessful, and by the end of the ordeal the militants had killed 11 Israeli athletes and coaches, as well as a West German police officer. During the crisis Mark Spitz (1950–), a Jewish-American swimmer who had finished

TABLE 7.3

Top U.S. Olympic medal winners, all-time

Athlete	Sport	Dates	Gold	Silver	Bronze	Total
Michael Phelps	Swimming	2004–2008	14	0	2	16
Jenny Thompson	Swimming	1992–2004	8	3	1	12
Dara Torres	Swimming	1984–2008	4	4	4	12
Natalie Coughlin	Swimming	2004–2008	3	4	4	11
Matt Biondi	Swimming	1984–1992	8	2	1	11
Mark Spitz	Swimming	1968–1972	9	1	1	11
Carl Osburn	Shooting	1912–1924	5	4	2	11
Gary Hall, Jr.	Swimming	1996–2004	5	3	2	10
Carl Lewis	Athletics	1984–1996	9	1	0	10
Ray Ewry	Athletics	1900–1908	10	0	0	10
Shirley Babashoff	Swimming	1972–1976	3	6	0	9
Martin Sheridan	Athletics	1904–1908	5	3	1	9
Apolo Anton Ohno	Short Track Speed Skating	2002–2010	2	2	4	8
Don Schollander	Swimming	1964–1968	7	1	0	8
Charlie Daniels	Swimming	1904–1908	5	1	2	8

SOURCE: Adapted from "Medal Finder," in *Olympics at Sports-Reference.com*, Sports Reference LLC., 2011, http://www.sports-reference.com/olympics/friv/medal_finder.cgi (accessed June 22, 2011)

TABLE 7.4

Summer Olympic games sites

1896 Athens, Greece

Dates: From 6 to 15 April 1896.

Participants: 14 National Olympic Committees (NOCs), 43 events, 241 athletes (men only).

Officially opened by: King George I. The Games of the Olympiad in Athens were financed by a donation of approximately one million drachmas from a rich businessman, Georges Averof, and by the sale of souvenir stamps and medals. The Greek spectators were rewarded for their enthusiasm and sportsmanship as the star event, the marathon, a new event organized for the first time, was won by a Greek peasant, Spyridon Louis. American James Connolly became the first Olympic champion of the modern era, winning the triple jump on 6 April 1896 (13.71 meters).

1900 Paris, France

Dates: From 14 May to 28 October 1900.

Participants: 24 NOCs, 95 events, 997 athletes (975 men, 22 women).

In 1900, Paris hosted the International Universal Exhibition, and the Games were organized in the framework of this Exhibition. The Games were spread over five months and there were no real opening and closing ceremonies. Women made their Olympic debut in tennis and golf. British tennis player Charlotte Cooper was the first woman to earn the title of Olympic champion.

1904 St. Louis, USA

Dates: From 1 July to 23 November 1904.

Other candidate city: Chicago (USA).

Chicago was chosen initially but the IOC decided to transfer the Games to St. Louis in 1902, because of the Universal Exhibition that took place in this city.

Participants: 12 NOCs, 91 events, 651 athletes (645 men, 6 women).

Officially opened by: David Francis, President of the Louisiana Purchase Exposition (1904 Universal Exhibition). The Games were very similar to those of 1900 and lasted almost five months. Numerous events were not labeled "Olympic," but had the status of sporting championships only in the framework of the world fair. The athletes often competed as individuals who were not really linked to an international team. After 1904, Coubertin swore never again to organize the Olympic Games alongside a fair.

1908 London, Great Britain

Dates: From 27 April to 31 October 1908.

Other candidate cities: Berlin (Germany), Milan (Italy) and Rome (Italy). Rome was chosen initially, but the Games were then awarded to London because Vesuvius erupted in 1906.

Participants: 22 NOCs, 110 events, 2,008 athletes (1,971 men, 37 women).

Officially opened by: King Edward VII.

This edition of the Olympic Games was one of the best organized thus far. The Games were starting to become known throughout the world, and athletes the world over wanted to compete. On the first Sunday of the Games, a religious service took place in St Paul's Cathedral. The Bishop of Pennsylvania gave a sermon here that remained famous, containing the words: The important thing in these Olympiads is not to win, but to take part.

1912 Stockholm, Sweden

Dates: From 5 May to 27 July 1912.

Participants: 28 NOCs, 102 events, 2,407 athletes (2,359 men, 48 women). For the first time, competitors in the Games came from all five continents.

Officially opened by: King Gustav V.

The Swedish hosts unofficially introduced the use of electronic timekeeping for the athletics races, as well as the first loudspeaker system. Sweden totally refused to allow boxing tournaments to take place on its territory, which made the International Olympic Committee (IOC) decide, after the Games, to limit the power of the host city insofar as choosing the Olympic program was concerned.

Games of the VI Olympiad

Did not take place because of WWI. Planned location: Berlin (Germany). Other candidate cities: Alexandria (Egypt) and Budapest (Hungary).

1920 Antwerp, Belgium

Location: Antwerp, Belgium.

Dates: From 20 April to 12 September 1920.

Participants: 29 NOCs, 154 events, 2,626 athletes (2,561 men, 65 women).

Olympic oath (athletes): Victor Boin, fencing.

Officially opened by: King Albert I.

The Opening Ceremony stood out for various reasons: first use of the Olympic flag; first time that a competitor took the Olympic oath; and first pigeon release.

1924 Paris, France

Location: Paris, France.

Dates: From 4 May to 27 July 1924.

Other candidate cities: Amsterdam (Netherlands), Barcelona (Spain), Los Angeles (USA), Prague (Czechoslovakia) and Rome (Italy).

Participants: 44 NOCs, 126 events, 3,089 athletes (2,954 men, 135 women).

Olympic oath (athletes): Georges André, athletics.

Officially opened by: President Gaston Doumergue.

Emblem: Emblem of the City of Paris. At the Closing Ceremony, the practice of raising three flags (one for the IOC, one for the host country and one for the host country of the next edition of the Games) was introduced.

1928 Amsterdam, The Netherlands

Dates: From 17 May to 12 August 1928.

Participants: 46 NOCs, 109 events, 2,883 Athletes (2,606 men, 277 women).

Olympic oath (athletes): Henri Denis, football.

Officially opened by: Prince Hendrik.

For the first time, the Olympic flame was lit at the top of a tower within the stadium. It remained lit throughout the Games. At this period, the Olympic Torch Relay had not yet been invented. The program contained athletics events for women for the first time. The presentation of medals took place on the final day of the Games for the last time.

his events after winning a then record seven gold medals, was evacuated out of fear that he was a target for the terrorists. In the aftermath of the attack, the games were temporarily suspended, and a large memorial ceremony was held in the Olympic stadium.

On July 27, 1996, one person was killed, another died of a heart attack running to the scene, and 111 were injured when a bomb exploded in the Centennial Olympic Park at the 1996 summer games in Atlanta, Georgia. The perpetrator, Eric Robert Rudolph (1967–)—a member of a

TABLE 7.4

Summer Olympic games sites [CONTINUED]

1932 Los Angeles, USA

Dates: From 30 July to 14 August 1932.
Participants: 37 NOCs, 117 events, 1,332 athletes (1,206 men, 126 women).
Olympic oath (athletes): George Calnan, fencing.
Officially opened by: Vice-President Charles Curtis.
Emblem: Arms in the colors of the United States, with, in the foreground, the Olympic rings and motto.
The 1932 Olympic Games were the first to take place over 16 days. For the first time, male athletes were accommodated in a single Olympic village (the women stayed in a hotel). At the medal presentation ceremonies, the winners stepped onto podiums and their countries' flags were raised. Automatic timing was introduced for the athletics events, as was the photo finish.

1936 Berlin, Germany

Location: Berlin, Germany.
Dates: From 1 to 16 August 1936.
Other candidate city: Barcelona (Spain).
Participants: 49 NOCs, 129 events, 3,963 athletes (3,632 men, 331 women).
Olympic oath (athletes): Rudolf Ismayr, weightlifting.
Olympic cauldron lit by: Fritz Schilgen.
Officially opened by: Chancellor Adolf Hitler.
Emblem: A bell with the Olympic rings under the German eagle. The 1936 Olympic Games put paid to Adolf Hitler's attempt to prove his theories on the superiority of the Aryan race. These Games witnessed the introduction of the Olympic Torch Relay. The flame is carried from Olympia to the site of the Games. The 1936 Games were also the first to be broadcast on television.

Games of the XII Olympiad

Did not take place because of WWII. Planned location: initially Tokyo (Japan) but, because of the Sino-Japanese conflict, the Games were reassigned to Helsinki (Finland).

Games of the XIII Olympiad

Did not take place because of WWII. Planned location: London (Great Britain). Other candidate cities: Detroit (USA), Lausanne (Switzerland) and Rome (Italy).

1948 London, Great Britain

Location: London, Great Britain.
Dates: From 29 July to 14 August 1948.
Other candidate cities: Baltimore (USA), Lausanne (Switzerland), Los Angeles (USA), Minneapolis (USA) and Philadelphia (USA).
Participants: 59 NOCs, 136 events, 4,104 athletes (3,714 men, 390 women).There were no athletes from Japan or Germany.
Olympic oath (athletes): Donald Finlay, athletics.
Olympic cauldron lit by: John Mark.
Officially opened by: King George VI.
Emblem: Big Ben with the Olympic rings in the foreground.

1952 Helsinki, Finland

Dates: From 19 July to 3 August 1952.
Other candidate cities: Los Angeles (USA), Amsterdam (Netherlands), Minneapolis (USA), Detroit (USA), Chicago (USA) and Philadelphia (USA).
Participants: 69 NOCs, 149 events, 4,955 athletes (4,436 men, 519 women).
Olympic oath (athletes): Heikki Savolainen, artistic gymnastics.
Olympic cauldron lit by: Paavo Nurmi and Hannes Kolehmainen: after having lit a first cauldron in the stadium, Nurmi passed the torch to Kolehmainen, who lit a second cauldron at the top of the stadium tower, in honor of the 1940 Games which did not take place.
Officially opened by: President Juho Paasikivi.
Emblem: The stadium tower with the Olympic rings at the top. The Soviet Union took part in the Games for the first time. One of the first women authorized to compete against the men in dressage was Denmark's Lis Hartel, who won a silver medal

1956 Melbourne, Australia

Dates: From 22 November to 8 December 1956.
Other candidate cities: Buenos Aires (Argentina), Los Angeles (USA), Detroit (USA), Mexico City (Mexico), Chicago (USA), Minneapolis (USA), Philadelphia (USA) and San Francisco (USA).
Participants: 67 NOCs, 145 events, 3,155 athletes (2,791 men, 364 women).
Olympic oath (athletes): John Landy, athletics.
Olympic cauldron lit by: Ron Clarke
Officially opened by: The Duke of Edinburgh.
Emblem: Drawing of Australia, under an Olympic torch and rings. In the lower part, the inscription "MELBOURNE 1956," extended at both ends by laurel branches.

Equestrian games, Stockholm, Sweden

Dates: From 10 to 17 June 1956.
Other candidate cities: Paris (France), Rio de Janeiro (Brazil), Berlin (Germany) and Los Angeles (USA).
Participants: 29 NOCs, 6 events, 159 athletes (147 men, 12 women).
Olympic oath (athletes): Henri Saint Cyr.
Olympic cauldron lit by: Hans Wikne.
Officially opened by: King Gustaf VI Adolf.
Emblem: The Olympic rings under an ancient horseman. For the first time, the competitions took place in two countries. As the equine quarantine law was too strict to allow the entry of foreign horses into Australia, the equestrian events took place in Stockholm. The two Germanys (west and east) took part as a combined team. This practice continued for the following two editions of the Games. For the first time, the athletes paraded together, rather than by country, as a symbol of world unity.

radical Christian group violently opposed to abortion and homosexuality—was not arrested until 2003. In 2005 he pleaded guilty to the Olympic bombing, as well as to a string of other bombings that occurred between 1996 and 1998, and was sentenced to four consecutive life sentences without parole.

TABLE 7.4

Summer Olympic games sites [CONTINUED]

1960 Rome, Italy

Dates: From 25 August to 11 September 1960.
Other candidate cities: Lausanne (Switzerland), Detroit (USA), Budapest (Hungary), Brussels (Belgium), Mexico City (Mexico) and Tokyo (Japan).
Participants: 83 NOCs, 150 events, 5,338 athletes, (4,727 men, 611 women).
Olympic oath (athletes): Adolfo Consolini, athletics.
Olympic cauldron lit by: Giancarlo Peris.
Officially opened by: President Giovanni Gronchi.
Emblem: The Olympic rings under the Roman shewolf, suckling Romulus and Remus.
Rome organized the competitions on several ancient sites (the ruins of the Basilica of Maxence, the
   Caracalla Baths and the Arch of Constantine [finish line of the marathon]). These Games were broadcast live in 18 European countries; they were also broadcast with a time delay of a
   few hours in the USA and Canada.

1964 Tokyo, Japan

Dates: From 10 to 24 October 1964.
Other candidate cities: Detroit (USA), Vienna (Austria) and Brussels (Belgium).
Participants: 93 NOCs, 163 events, 5,151 athletes (4,473 men, 678 women).
Olympic oath (athletes): Takashi Ono, artistic gymnastics.
Olympic cauldron lit by: Yoshinori Sakaï.
Officially opened by: Emperor Hirohito.
Emblem: Rising sun juxtaposed with the Olympic rings.
The 1964 Tokyo Games were the first ones organized in Asia. The Japanese highlighted their success in reconstructing their country after WWII by choosing as the last torchbearer
   Yashinori Sakaï, who was born in Hiroshima on the same day that the city was destroyed by an atomic bomb.

1968 Mexico City, Mexico

Dates: From 12 to 27 October 1968.
Other candidate cities: Detroit (USA), Lyon (France) and Buenos Aires (Argentina).
Participants: 112 NOCs, 172 events, 5,516 athletes (4,735 men, 781 women).
Olympic oath (athletes): Pablo Lugo Garrido, athletics.
Olympic cauldron lit by: Norma Enriqueta Basilio de Sotelo.
Officially opened by: President Gustavo Diaz Ordaz.
Emblem: Composed of a combination of the five rings and the Olympic year.
There were a few "firsts": the Games were held in Latin America; a woman lit the Olympic flame; the winners had to undergo doping controls (narcotics and stimulants); and a synthetic
   material (Tartan) was used for the athletics track.

1972 Munich, Germany

Dates: From 26 August to 11 September 1972. Other candidate cities: Montreal (Canada), Madrid (Spain) and Detroit (USA).
Participants: 121 NOCs, 195 events, 7,134 athletes (6,075 men, 1,059 women).
Olympic oath (athletes): Heidi Schüller, athletics.
Olympic oath (officials): Heinz Pollay, equestrian sports.
Olympic cauldron lit by: Günter Zahn.
Officially opened by: President Gustave Heinemann.
Emblem: Crown of rays of light.
Mascot: Waldi (a dachshund).
On the morning of 5 September, the Games were interrupted when eight Palestinian terrorists, representing the militant group Black September, broke into the Olympic Village, taking as
   hostages, then killing, 11 members of the Israeli Olympic team. The Olympic Games were suspended for 34 hours and a memorial service for the victims held in the main stadium. The
   flags of all the nations flew at half-mast.

1976 Montreal, Canada

Dates: From 17 July to 1 August 1976.
Other candidate cities: Moscow (USSR) and Los Angeles (USA).
Participants: 92 NOCs, 198 events, 6,084 athletes (4,824 men, 1,260 women).
Olympic oath (athletes): Pierre Saint-Jean, weightlifting.
Olympic oath (officials): Maurice Forget, athletics.
Olympic cauldron lit by: Stéphane Préfontaine and Sandra Henderson.
Officially opened by: Queen Elizabeth II.
Emblem: Olympic rings under an Olympic podium, also representing the letter "M" for Montreal.
Mascot: Amik (a beaver).
The 1976 Montreal Olympic Games fell victim to a boycott by the African nations, in protest at the New Zealand national rugby team's tour of South Africa, and because the New Zealand
   team had been authorized to take part in the Olympic Games.

1980 Moscow, USSR

Dates: From 19 July to 3 August 1980.
Other candidate city: Los Angeles (USA).
Participants: 80 NOCs, 203 events, 5,179 athletes (4,064 men, 1,115 women).
Olympic oath (athletes): Nikolay Andrianov, artistic gymnastics.
Olympic oath (officials): Aleksandr Medved, wrestling.
Olympic cauldron lit by: Sergei Belov.
Officially opened by: President of the Supreme Soviet Leonid Brezhnev.
Emblem: Olympic rings under parallel lines in a pyramid shape, crowned by a star representing the stars of the Kremlin.
Mascot: Misha (a bear).
Further to a boycott launched by the USA, only 80 countries (the fewest since 1956) took part in the Moscow Games.

BOYCOTTS. The Olympics have also been used to make political statements. In "Long History of Olympics Protests" (BBC News, April 7, 2008), Paul Reynolds provides an overview of notable boycotts throughout Olympics history. The first boycott occurred in 1908, when Irish athletes refused to participate in the London games, in protest against British political oppression. The 1956 games in Melbourne, Australia, were the scene of two different

TABLE 7.4
Summer Olympic games sites [CONTINUED]

1984 Los Angeles, USA

Dates: From 28 July to 12 August 1984.
Participants: 140 NOCs, 221 events, 6,829 athletes (5,263 men, 1,566 women).
Olympic oath (athletes): Edwin Moses, athletics.
Olympic oath (officials): Sharon Weber, artistic gymnastics.
Olympic cauldron lit by: Rafer Johnson.
Officially opened by: President Ronald Reagan.
Emblem: "Stars in movement": three stars (red, white and blue) crossed by 13 horizontal, parallel lines representing movement and the 13 original colonies.
Mascot: Sam (an eagle).
Although a boycott, called by the USSR in response to the 1980 one, left some sports venues rather empty, a record 140 countries took part in these Games. They were the first since 1896 to be organized without government funding.

1988 Seoul, Korea

Dates: From 17 September to 2 October 1988.
Other candidate city: Nagoya (Japan).
Participants: 159 NOCs, 237 events, 8,391 athletes (6,197 men, 2,194 women).
Olympic oath (athletes): Hur Jae (basketball), Son Mi-Ha (handball).
Olympic oath (officials): Lee Hak-Rae, judo.
Olympic cauldron lit by: Chung Sun-Man, Kim Won-Tak and Sohn Mi-Chung.
Officially opened by: President Roh Tae-Woo.
Emblem: Traditional Korean motif, three swirls representing the meeting of peoples and progression towards world peace.
Mascot: Hodori (a tiger).
Despite a boycott by North Korea, which had wanted to co-host the Games, this edition had the most participants in Olympic history, with the greatest number of countries represented.

1992 Barcelona, Spain

Dates: From 25 July to 9 August 1992.
Other candidate cities: Paris (France), Brisbane (Australia), Belgrade (Yugoslavia), Birmingham (Great Britain) and Amsterdam (Netherlands).
Participants: 169 NOCs, 257 events, 9,356 athletes (6,652 men, 2,704 women).
Olympic oath (athletes): Luis Doreste Blanco, sailing.
Olympic oath (officials): Eugenio Asensio, football.
Olympic cauldron lit by: Antonio Rebollo (Paralympic archer).
Officially opened by: King Juan Carlos I.
Emblem: A stylized athlete in the throes of action, flying above an obstacle (the Olympic rings).
Mascot: Cobi (a dog).
Since Seoul in 1988, the face of the world had changed. The Soviet Union no longer existed; Estonia, Latvia and Lithuania were once again independent countries; Germany was reunified; Yugoslavia was divided into several republics; and North and South Yemen had become one. All these new national groupings appeared in Barcelona. South Africa took part in the Games for the first time since 1960.

1996 Atlanta, USA

Dates: From 19 July to 4 August 1996.
Other candidate cities: Athens (Greece), Toronto (Canada), Melbourne (Australia), Manchester (Great Britain) and Belgrade (Yugoslavia).
Participants: 197 NOCs, 10,318 athletes, 271 events (6,806 men, 3,512 women).
Olympic oath (athletes): Teresa Edwards, basketball.
Olympic oath (officials): Hobie Billingsly, diving.
Olympic cauldron lit by: Muhammad Ali.
Officially opened by: President Bill Clinton.
Emblem: The logo represented a flame composed of the five Olympic rings with the number 100 (centennial) at their base, and a whimsical flame ending in four stars.
Mascot: Izzy (original name "Whatizit") A computer-generated, blue cartoon character.
For the first time in Olympic history, all the recognized National Olympic Committees were represented at the Games. A record number of 79 countries won medals, and 53 won gold.

2000 Sydney, Australia

Dates: From 15 September to 1 October 2000.
Other candidate cities: Berlin (Germany), Manchester (Great Britain), Beijing (China) and Istanbul (Turkey).
Participants: 200 NOCs, 10,651 athletes, 300 events (6,582 men, 4,069 women).
Olympic oath (athletes): Rechelle Hawkes, hockey.
Olympic oath (officials): Peter Kerr, water polo.
Olympic cauldron lit by: Cathy Freeman.
Officially opened by: The Governor General of Australia, Sir William Deane.
Emblem: The emblem represented all the elements of Australian culture: Australian colors, boomerangs, Sydney harbor, beaches, red earth and the indigenous inhabitants.
Mascots: "Syd," a duck-billed platypus, "Millie," an echidnea, and "Olly," a kookaburra.
These Games were the biggest in history: 10,651 athletes competed in 300 events. North and South Korea paraded together under the same flag. Four athletes from Timor Leste took part individually under the Olympic flag.

boycotts: by the Netherlands, Spain, and Switzerland in response to the Soviet Union's brutal handling of the Hungarian uprising that year; and by Egypt, Lebanon, and Iraq in protest of British and French involvement in the Suez crisis in the Middle East. Several African nations threatened to boycott the Olympics in 1968, 1972, and 1976 in protest of South African and Rhodesian racial policies; the IOC ultimately banned South Africa and Rhodesia from participating in the 1968 and 1972 Olympics. In 1980 and 1984 the two major cold war powers traded boycotts: the United States and 61 other Western nations stayed home from the 1980 Olympics in Moscow in protest of the Soviet invasion of Afghanistan; four years later the Soviet Union and 14 of its allied nations retaliated by boycotting the Los Angeles games of 1984, on the grounds that the American hosts could not guarantee their safety. In 1988 North Korea boycotted the Olympics in South Korea, arguing that the two countries should have been named cohosts.

TABLE 7.4

Summer Olympic games sites [CONTINUED]

2004 Athens, Greece

Dates: From 12 to 28 August 2004.
Other candidate cities: Buenos Aires (Argentina), Cape Town (South Africa), Rome (Italy) and Stockholm (Sweden).
Participants: 201 NOCs, 10,625 athletes, 301 events (6,296 men, 4,329 women).
Olympic oath (athletes): Zoï Dimoschaki, swimming.
Olympic oath (officials): Lazaros Voreaadis, basketball.
Olympic cauldron lit by: Nikolaos Kaklamanakis.
Officially opened by: The President of the Republic, Konstantinos Stephanopoulos.
Emblem: A crown made of an olive branch. It represented through a characteristic Hellenic shape the four values of the 2004 Games: legacy, participation, celebration and the human dimension.
Mascots: "Phivos," who bore the name of a mythical god of Olympia, Apollon-Phoebos, and his sister "Athina," goddess of wisdom. These two mascots were inspired from dolls from Ancient Greece.
The shot put competition was held in the ancient stadium in Olympia, while the marathon was staged on the historic route. The Olympic Torch Relay, which started in Olympia, was the first relay in the history of the Games to cross the five continents, before returning to Greece.

2008 Beijing, China

Dates: From 8 to 24 August 2008.
Other candidate cities: Istanbul (Turkey), Osaka (Japan), Paris (France), Toronto (Canada).
Participation: 204 NOCs, 10,5001 athletes, 302 events. 11 Preliminary figures.
Olympic oath (athletes): Yining Zhang, table tennis.
Olympic oath (officials): Liping Huang, gymnastics.
Olympic cauldron lit by: Ning Li.
Officially opened by: The President of the Peoples Republic of China, Jintao Hu.
Emblem: The emblem, entitled "Dancing Beijing," combined the art of calligraphy and sport, the latter being represented by a human silhouette running to celebrate victory.
Mascots: There were five mascots representing the Beijing Games: four animals: Beibei the fish, Jingjing the panda, Yingying the Tibetan antelope, and Nini the swallow; the fifth being Huanhuan the Olympic flame. When the first syllables of the mascots are put together, it creates: Bei Jing Huan Ying Nin, which means "Welcome to Beijing" in Chinese.

2012 London, Great Britain

Dates: From 27 July to 12 August 2012.
Other candidate cities: Paris (France), Madrid (Spain), Moscow (Russian Federation) and New York (USA).

2016 Rio de Janeiro, Brazil

Dates: From 5 August to 21 August 2016.
Other candidate cities: Chicago (USA), Tokyo (Japan), Madrid (Spain).

SOURCE: Adapted from "Factsheet: The Olympic Summer Games," in *Reference Documents—Factsheets*, International Olympic Committee, January 2010, http://www.olympic.org/Documents/Reference_documents_Factsheets/The_Olympic_Summer_Games.pdf (accessed June 13, 2011)

TABLE 7.5

Winter Olympic games sites

1924: Chamonix, France
1928: St. Moritz, Switzerland
1932: Lake Placid, New York, United States
1936: Garmisch-Partenkirchen, Germany
1940: Games not held due to World War II
1944: Games not held due to World War II
1948: St. Moritz, Switzerland
1952: Oslo, Norway
1956: Cortina d'Ampezzo, Italy
1960: Squaw Valley, California, United States
1964: Innsbruck, Austria
1968: Grenoble, France
1972: Sapporo, Japan
1976: Innsbruck, Austria
1980: Lake Placid, New York, United States
1984: Sarajevo, Yugoslavia
1988: Calgary, Alberta, Canada
1992: Albertville, France
1994: Lillehammer, Norway
1998: Nagano, Japan
2002: Salt Lake City, Utah, United States
2006: Torino (Turin), Italy
2010: Vancouver, Canada
2014: Sochi, Russia
2018: Pyeongchang, South Korea

SOURCE: Adapted from "Factsheet: The Olympic Winter Games," in *Reference Documents: Factsheets*, International Olympic Committee, December 2010, http://www.olympic.org/Documents/Reference_documents_Factsheets/The_Olympic_Winter_Games.pdf (accessed June 13, 2011)

SCANDAL. In 1998 it emerged that several members of the IOC had accepted gifts from the 2002 Salt Lake City Winter Olympics organizing committee in exchange for their site selection votes. Ten IOC members were forced off the committee, and the process for selecting host cities subsequently underwent a dramatic transformation. Still, questions remain whether the reforms have actually eliminated the potential for bribery in the Olympic site selection process. The BBC documentary *Panorama: Buying the Games* (August 2004, http://news.bbc.co.uk/1/hi/programmes/panorama/3937425.stm) reveals that agents with IOC connections accepted money from undercover reporters who posed as consultants for London business interests; in exchange, the agents promised to help obtain votes for the city's bid for the 2012 summer games.

More controversy occurred during the 2002 winter games, when Russia's Elena Berezhnaya (1977–) and Anton Sikharulidze (1976–) received high marks in the pairs figure skating competition, in spite of committing a noticeable error. Meanwhile, the Canadian skaters, Jamie Salé (1977–) and David Pelletier (1974–), delivered a seemingly flawless performance, convincing the event's announcers that they had earned the gold medal. When the scores were revealed, however, the Russians had been awarded the top prize. Later, the National Broadcasting Corporation (NBC) commentator Sandra Bezic was quoted in the article "NBC Commentators Surprised, Shocked by Judges" (Associated Press, February 11, 2002) as saying, "My heart breaks, and I'm embarrassed for our sport right now." In the subsequent investigation, the French judge said she was pressured to vote for the Russians. The scandal resulted in a second gold medal being awarded to the Canadian pair, and the IOC and the International Skating Union decided to declare both pairs as Olympic cochampions. New scoring rules, including anonymous judging, were adopted afterward.

A different controversy emerged six years later during the 2008 summer games, when questions arose regarding the ages of some members of the Chinese gymnastics squad. Allegations surfaced that some of the Chinese tumblers were younger than 16, the minimum age that is dictated by Olympic rules for the sport. The suspicions went beyond the obvious fact that some of the girls, particularly the stars He Kexin and Jiang Yuyuan, were very small and had youthful features and body shapes. Jeré Longman and Juliet Macur report in "Records Say Chinese Gymnasts May Be under Age" (*New York Times*, July 27, 2008) that information on official Chinese media news websites contradicted the girls' passports, which indicated that they were 16 years old.

STRUCTURE OF THE OLYMPIC MOVEMENT
International Olympic Committee

The Olympics are run by a complex array of organizations that are known primarily by their initials. At the center of the structure is the IOC (2011, http://www .olympic.org/), which is based in Lausanne, Switzerland. In *Structure of the Olympic Movement* (January 31, 2002, http://www.olympic.org/Documents/Reports/EN/en_report _269.pdf), the IOC defines itself as the "supreme authority of the Olympic Movement. Its role is to promote top-level sport as well as sport for all in accordance with the Olympic Charter. It ensures the regular celebration of the Olympic Games and strongly encourages, by appropriate means, the promotion of women in sport, that of sports ethics and the protection of athletes."

The IOC was created by the International Athletic Congress of Paris in June 1894 and convened by Coubertin, who is generally considered the father of the modern Olympic movement. The IOC was charged with the control and development of the modern Olympic Games. Membership in the IOC is limited to one member from most countries, and two members from the largest and most active member countries, or countries that have hosted the Olympics. Members must speak French or English and be citizens and residents of a country with a recognized national Olympic committee (NOC).

The IOC runs the Olympic movement according to the terms of the Olympic Charter (July 7, 2007, http://multi media.olympic.org/pdf/en_report_122.pdf). The charter outlines the six Fundamental Principles of Olympism. These principles, as written in the charter, are:

1. Olympism is a philosophy of life, exalting and combining in a balanced whole the qualities of body, will and mind. Blending sport with culture and education, Olympism seeks to create a way of life based on the joy of effort, the educational value of good example and respect for universal fundamental ethical principles.

2. The goal of Olympism is to place sport at the service of the harmonious development of man, with a view to promoting a peaceful society concerned with the preservation of human dignity.

3. The Olympic Movement is the concerted, organised, universal and permanent action, carried out under the supreme authority of the IOC, of all individuals and entities who are inspired by the values of Olympism. It covers the five continents. It reaches its peak with the bringing together of the world's athletes at the great sports festival, the Olympic Games. Its symbol is five interlaced rings.

4. The practice of sport is a human right. Every individual must have the possibility of practising sport, without discrimination of any kind and in the Olympic spirit, which requires mutual understanding with a spirit of friendship, solidarity and fair play. The organisation, administration and management of sport must be controlled by independent sports organisations.

5. Any form of discrimination with regard to a country or a person on grounds of race, religion, politics, gender or otherwise is incompatible with belonging to the Olympic Movement.

6. Belonging to the Olympic Movement requires compliance with the Olympic Charter and recognition by the IOC.

The next level of Olympic oversight, the International Federations (IFs), coordinates international competition within a particular sport. These federations make all the rules that pertain to their sport and run the world championships and other international competitions within their realm. Each country that competes in a sport at the international level has a national governing body (NGB), which coordinates the sport domestically.

U.S. Olympic Committee

In the United States, building a team to represent the nation at the Olympics is the responsibility of the U.S. Olympic Committee (USOC). The USOC consists of 72 member organizations. Thirty-nine of them are NGBs—such as USA Gymnastics and USA Track and Field—each of which supports a particular sport. In the United States the NGBs are responsible for selecting the athletes who will represent their country in their sport at the Olympics. Other USOC members include community- and education-based multisport organizations, U.S. Armed Forces sports, and organizations that are involved in sports for people with disabilities. Besides the Olympics, the USOC also oversees U.S. participation in the Pan American Games, an international goodwill sports competition that features athletes from the Americas and that takes place every four years in the year preceding the Summer Olympics.

Besides its role in developing the U.S. Olympic team, the USOC is instrumental in U.S. cities' bids to host the Winter or Summer Olympics or the Pan American Games. The USOC may vote on and endorse a particular city's bid to serve as host. All U.S. Olympic Trial site selections also go through the USOC. The USOC gets much of its money from the IOC. According to Ray Lilley, in "IOC, USOC Reach Deal for Fresh Funding 'Tier,'" (Associated Press, March 30, 2009), the USOC receives "20 percent of the IOC's top sponsorship program and 12.75 percent of its TV revenue." Lilley notes that even though other national committees have complained about the huge share of Olympic revenue that ends up in USOC coffers, USOC officials counter that the majority of the money that is pumped into the Olympic system comes from American companies, including the $894 million paid by NBC to televise the games in Beijing, China.

As of August 2011, the USOC operated three training centers that were located in Colorado Springs, Colorado; Lake Placid, New York; and Chula Vista, California. The USOC also maintains an Olympic Education Center in Marquette, Michigan, where athletes can pursue an academic degree without interrupting their training.

The USOC is a nonprofit organization, but it must constantly monitor its flow of dollars. Unlike most NOCs around the world, the USOC does not receive direct financial support from the government, but it nevertheless manages to provide millions of dollars per year in direct support to athletes, as well as assistance to NGBs. Tripp Mickle reports in "Beijing Olympics a Financial Boon for USOC" (*SportsBusiness Journal*, June 1, 2009) that the USOC spent $71.4 million on athletes and NGBs in 2008, while earning record revenues of $280.6 million through its participation in the Beijing games.

THE FLOW OF OLYMPIC MONEY

All the symbols, images, phrases, and other intellectual property that are associated with the Olympics belong to the IOC. In *Olympic Marketing Fact File: 2011 Edition* (February 2011, http://www.olympic.org/ Documents/IOC_Marketing/OLYMPIC_MARKETING _FACT_FILE_2011.pdf), the IOC indicates that it generates marketing revenue through six major channels:

broadcasting, The Olympic Partners international sponsorships, IOC licensing, host-country licensing, ticketing, and domestic sponsorships. The IOC manages the first three; the others are managed by the Organizing Committees for the Olympic Games (OCOGs) within the host country, under the IOC's direction.

As with the major professional sports in the United States, the biggest financial driver of the Olympics is television. Since the 1990s television broadcasts of the Olympics have brought in a tremendous amount of revenue to the IOC. In *IOC Marketing Media Guide: Beijing 2008* (July 9, 2009, http://multimedia.olympic.org/pdf/ en_report_1329.pdf), the IOC reports that for the 2005–08 Olympic cycle, $2.6 billion was generated in broadcasting revenue. Of this sum, $851 million went to the OCOG for the Beijing games, according to the IOC, in *Olympic Marketing Fact File*. This amount was nearly double the $441 million in broadcasting revenues that was received by the OCOG for the 1992 Barcelona games.

Nielsen Media Research reports in "Beijing Games Most-Watched Olympics Ever" (August 25, 2008, http:// blog.nielsen.com/nielsenwire/media_entertainment/beijing-games-most-watched-olympics-ever/) that the first 10 days of the Beijing games attracted a cumulative television audience of 4.4 billion viewers, nearly two-thirds of the world population. This was about a half billion more than the number of viewers who watched the 2004 Athens Olympics. All told, a record of more than 5,000 hours of live broadcast feed of the 2008 Olympics was offered worldwide, according to the IOC, in *Marketing Report: Beijing 2008* (November 16, 2009, http://www.olympic .org/Documents/Reports/EN/en_report_1428.pdf). The Beijing games were also the first fully digital Olympics, with comprehensive coverage available via the Internet and other digital media. More than 6 million Americans watched coverage of the games on their mobile phones. In *Marketing Report: Vancouver 2010* (July 6, 2010, http:// www.olympic.org/Documents/IOC_Marketing/Marketing _Report_Vancouver_2010_eng.pdf), the IOC indicates that the winter games in Vancouver attracted approximately 1.8 billion viewers worldwide. Overall, the Vancouver games had 190 million American viewers, which was the second-largest U.S. viewing audience after the 1994 games in Lillehammer.

A second key revenue source is the IOC's corporate sponsorship program, known officially as The Olympic Partners (TOP) program. In *Olympic Marketing Fact File*, the IOC notes that for the 2009–12 cycle the TOP program consisted of 11 international corporations, which in return for their money are ensured exclusive sponsorship in their business category. As with broadcast rights, the United States dominates the TOP program; six of the TOP sponsors are U.S. based.

Ticket sales represent another major source of revenue for the IOC. In *Marketing Report: Beijing 2008*, the IOC indicates that of the 6.8 million tickets that were available during the Beijing games 6.5 million (95.6%) were sold, at an average price of $23 per ticket. According to the IOC, in *Marketing Report: Vancouver 2010*, ticket sales for the 2010 winter games in Vancouver generated $244 million (CAD 257 million), and another $54 million (CAD 57 million) came from licensing royalties. The other major revenue source, the sale of licensed merchandise bearing Olympic logos and other trademarks, including Olympic coins and stamps, generated the remainder of the IOC's revenue.

Slightly more than 90% of the IOC's revenue is subsequently distributed to the other organizations that collectively make up the Olympic movement, including the OCOGs, which are the committees that run the Olympics within the country that has been selected to host the games; the NOCs, whose main role within each of the approximately 200 countries in the Olympic family is to field their country's Olympic team; and the IFs, which coordinate and monitor international competition within their specific sport or family of sports. The IOC retains just under 10% of its overall revenue. These funds are used to cover the organization's operating and administrative costs.

The vast commercial activity that fuels the Olympic flame would seem to conflict with the philosophical groundings of the Olympic movement, which value the noble spirit of competition above financial matters. The Olympic Charter acknowledges this apparent contradiction, and the IOC has implemented policies designed to address it. No advertising is allowed in the venues where events take place or on the uniforms of athletes, coaches, or officials. The TOP program is designed to generate the maximum amount of support with a minimum number of corporate sponsors, and images of Olympic events are not allowed to be used for commercial purposes.

SELECTION OF OLYMPIC SITES

One of the IOC's chief responsibilities is to select the cities that will host the Olympics. Olympic site selection is a two-phase procedure. The first phase is called Applicant Cities. Applicant cities must be proposed to the IOC by their NOC. They must then complete a questionnaire that outlines how they plan to carry out the monumental task of hosting the games. The IOC assesses the applications with regard to the cities' ability to organize the games. Criteria include technical capacity, government support, public opinion, general infrastructure, security, venues, accommodations, and transportation. The IOC then accepts a handful of these applicants for the next phase, called Candidate Cities.

In the second phase, candidate cities must provide the IOC with a candidature file. These files are analyzed by the IOC Evaluation Commission, which consists of IOC members, representatives of the IFs, the NOCs, the IOC Athletes' Commission, the International Paralympics Committee, and other experts. The Evaluation Commission also physically inspects the candidate cities. It then issues a report, on whose basis the IOC Executive Board prepares a list of final candidates. This list is submitted to the IOC session for a vote. The IOC vote to determine the location of the 2016 summer games drew widespread media attention during the fall of 2009, when President Barack Obama (1961–) joined the campaign to promote his hometown of Chicago, Illinois, which was in the running against Madrid, Spain; Tokyo, Japan; and Rio de Janeiro, as an Olympic host city. Obama went so far as to make an appearance at the location of the voting in Copenhagen, Denmark, speaking on behalf of Chicago in efforts to sway the votes of the IOC members. His efforts, however, were in vain; Chicago lost by a wide margin during the first of the three rounds of voting, receiving only 18 of 94 votes. Rio de Janeiro was eventually chosen to host the 2016 summer games.

DOPING

Almost from the beginning, the use of performance-enhancing substances, known as doping, has plagued the Olympics. An early example was Thomas J. Hicks (1875–1963), winner of the 1904 marathon, who was given strychnine and brandy. Doping methods improved over time, sometimes with disastrous results. The Danish cyclist Knut Jensen (1936–1960) died after falling from his bicycle during the 1960 games. He was found to have taken amphetamines. The international sports federations and the IOC banned doping during the 1960s, but for most of the time since then officials have lacked the tools to adequately police the use of illicit substances. The highest-profile Olympic athlete to be disqualified for doping in the 20th century was the Canadian sprinter Ben Johnson (1961–), winner of the 100-meter race in 1988. A few years later, it was reported that East German sports officials had doped female athletes for years without the IOC's knowledge. The PBS documentary *Doping for Gold* (June 15, 2011, http://www.pbs.org/wnet/secrets/episodes/doping-for-gold-2/42/) reveals that it was the largest state-sponsored doping program in history. As the problem of doping grew out of control during the 1990s, the international sports community responded by forming the World Anti-Doping Agency (WADA) in 1999. WADA oversees the monitoring and enforcing of doping regulations at the Olympics.

WADA's creation did not, however, solve the problem entirely. Olympic athletes from every era have been found to be in violation of antidoping rules. For the 2008 summer games, new methods were put in place that allowed blood samples to be stored for up to eight years, in case new tests were developed in that time. In "Backup

Samples Positive for 5 Olympians" (Associated Press, July 8, 2009), Stephen Wilson reports that 15 athletes tested positive for drug-related violations during the Beijing Olympics. Six of the cases were detected months after the close of the Olympics, thanks to newly available tests on the preserved samples. The only American athlete on the list did not actually use a substance herself—rather, one was given to the horse she rode in an equestrian event. The last U.S. competitors to test positive for banned substances in their own bodies during competition at the Olympics were the shot-putter Bonnie Dasse (1959–) and the hammer thrower Jud Logan (1959–), both in 1992.

Since then, however, it was discovered after the fact that several Americans had been doping during the Olympics and were stripped of their medals or barred from the Olympics. Others, who appeared headed for the Olympics, fell under a cloud of suspicion and were also barred. In the wake of the BALCO scandal (see Chapter 9 for more information), the sprinter Kelli White (1977–) received a two-year ban that kept her out of the 2004 Olympics. The sprinter Tim Montgomery (1975–), who was also implicated in the BALCO affair, failed to qualify for the 2004 games, but in 2005 he received a two-year ban from competing and was stripped of a number of his past medals and results, including a former world-record performance in the 100-meter dash. Perhaps the highest-profile Olympic athlete embroiled in BALCO was the sprinter Marion Jones (1975–). Jones proclaimed her innocence through several years of investigation, but in October 2007 she admitted to having used illegal performance-enhancing drugs during the 2000 Olympics in Sydney, Australia, in which she won three gold medals and two bronze. Facing pressure from the USOC, she surrendered her Olympic medals and was retroactively disqualified from all events dating back to September 1, 2000. The IOC also banned her from the Beijing Olympics. In 2008 the sprinter Antonio Pettigrew (1967–2010) admitted to using performance-enhancing drugs between 1997 and 2003, a span that included the 2000 Sydney Olympics in which he won a gold medal in the 4x400 relay event. At the time of his confession, Pettigrew volunteered to return his medal, as did teammate Michael Johnson (1967–), who claimed that he felt sullied by Pettigrew's admission. In August 2008 the IOC decided to strip the medals from all the members of Pettigrew's relay team. Like Montgomery and Jones, Pettigrew also received a ban from competing and was stripped of a number of his past awards and results.

OTHER OLYMPIC GAMES
Special Olympics

Special Olympics is a global nonprofit organization that provides opportunities for athletic training and competition for people with developmental disabilities. The organization reports in "Facts & Figures" (2011, http://www.athens2011.org/en/games_info.asp) that the 2011 Special Olympics summer games in Athens, Greece, saw 7,000 athletes compete in 21 different sports.

The Special Olympics movement began during the summer of 1968, when the First International Special Olympics were held at Soldier Field in Chicago, home of the National Football League's Chicago Bears. The roots of the Special Olympics go back to 1962, when Eunice Kennedy Shriver (1921–2009), the sister of President John F. Kennedy (1917–1963), started a day camp for developmentally disabled children. In June of that year Shriver invited 35 boys and girls to Camp Shriver at Timberlawn, her home in Rockville, Maryland. Her idea was that children who were cognitively impaired were capable of accomplishing much more than was generally believed at the time, if they were given opportunities to do so. Building on Camp Shriver, Shriver began to actively promote the notion of involving people with disabilities in physical activities and competition. Through the Kennedy Foundation, she targeted grants to universities, community centers, and recreation departments that created such opportunities. The foundation helped fund 11 camps similar to Camp Shriver across the country in 1963. By 1969, 32 camps serving 10,000 children were being supported by the foundation.

In 1967 the Kennedy Foundation worked with the Chicago Park District to organize a citywide track meet for mentally disabled people that was modeled on the Olympics. According to the Special Olympics, in "The History of Special Olympics" (2011, http://www.special olympics.org/history.aspx), the first Special Olympics at Soldier Field attracted 1,000 athletes from 26 states and Canada, who competed in track and field, floor hockey, and aquatics. Three years later the Special Olympics were granted special status by the USOC, becoming one of only two national organizations (along with the U.S. Olympic Committee) with the right to use the "Olympics" name. In February 1977 the first Special Olympics Winter Games were held, with about 500 athletes competing in skating and skiing events at Steamboat Springs, Colorado.

The Special Olympics movement grew substantially during the 1980s and 1990s. In 1981 the organization launched the Law Enforcement Torch Run, a fund-raiser that was aimed at increasing awareness of the Special Olympics throughout the United States. The run soon became the most successful Special Olympics fund-raising event, earning $30 million per year during the first decade of the 21st century. By the latter part of the decade the movement had truly become international in scope. In 1988 the IOC officially sanctioned the Special Olympics. In 1995 the first Special Olympics Winter Games to take place outside of North America were held in Austria. The first Special Olympics Summer Games to occur outside the United States followed in 2003, when Ireland hosted 5,500 athletes, in what became the largest international sporting event of the year. By 2006 the Special Olympics had grown to 2.5 million competitors, representing 165 nations worldwide. Within two years, the number of athletes had grown to 3 million and the number of participating countries had increased to 180. In 2009 a portrait of the movement's founder, Eunice Shriver, was unveiled at the National Portrait Gallery in Washington, D.C. Shriver died three months later.

Paralympics

While the Special Olympics serves people with mental disabilities, athletes with physical disabilities, including mobility limitations, amputees, and people with visual disabilities and cerebral palsy, may compete in the Paralympics. The International Paralympic Committee (IPC; 2011, http://www.paralympic.org/Paralympic_Games/) notes that the concept for the Paralympics grew out of a 1948 event in Stoke Mandeville, England, a competition for World War II veterans with spinal cord injuries. The first Olympic-style competition for people with physical disabilities took place in 1960 in Rome, Italy. These became the Paralympic games. The Winter Paralympics were added in 1976.

Unlike the Special Olympics, the Paralympics (2011, http://www.paralympic.org/Paralympic_Games/Past_Games/) have always been held during the same year as the Olympic Games. Since the 1988 summer games in Seoul, South Korea, and the 1992 winter games in Albertville, France, the Paralympics have been held during the same venues as well. This arrangement was cemented in place by an agreement with the IOC in 2001. Since the 2002 games in Salt Lake City, both the Olympic and Paralympic games have been set up by the same organizing committee. Paralympic athletes live in the same Olympic village with the same food and medical facilities as their Olympic counterparts, and the ticketing, technology, and transportation systems are shared. A total of 3,951 athletes representing 146 countries competed in the 2008 Summer Paralympics in Beijing. In the 2010 Winter Paralympics in Vancouver, 502 athletes competed; of these, 121, or nearly a quarter, were women. There were 64 medal events in the sports of alpine skiing, ice sledge hockey, Nordic skiing, and wheelchair curling. The IPC oversees the Paralympics, performing much the same role as the IOC does for the Olympics. The IPC (2011, http://www.paralympic.org/IPC/) consists of 170 national Paralympic committees and four disability-specific international sports federations, which are similar to the IFs that oversee specific Olympic sports. The national Paralympics organization for the United States is U.S. Paralympics, which is a division of the USOC.

Deaflympics

Besides the Special Olympics and the Paralympics, the IOC also sanctions the Deaflympics, which have existed since 1924—almost as long as the Olympics themselves. The first Deaflympics, which were organized by the International Committee of Sports for the Deaf (ICSD; 2011, http://www.deaflympics.com/about/), were held in Paris that year. The winter games were added in 1949.

The ICSD (2011, http://www.deaflympics.com/athletes/?ID=239) explains that athletes must have a hearing loss of at least 55 decibels in their better ear to qualify for the Deaflympics. To ensure a level playing field, hearing aids, cochlear implants, and other devices that augment hearing are not used during the competition.

According to the ICSD (2011, http://www.deaflympics.com/games/index.asp?GamesID=37), 2,493 deaf athletes from 77 countries participated in the 21st summer games, which were held in Taipei, Taiwan, in September 2009. Of the competitors at the Taiwan games, 1,514 athletes, or just over 60%, were participating in the Deaflympics for the first time. In all, the Taiwan games consisted of 177 separate events in 17 sports.

The 17th Winter Deaflympics were originally scheduled to take place in High Tatras, Slovakia, in 2011. However, as the Slovak games approached, the organizing committee for the event found itself facing a severe shortfall in funding. Malcolm Kelly notes in "Winter Deaf Games Cancellation Met with Anger" (CBC Sports, February 12, 2011) that in May 2010 the ICSD announced that the 2011 Winter Deaflympics had been canceled due to a lack of preparedness. The following December the games were once again scheduled to take place, after Jaromír Ruda, the head organizer, convinced the ICSD that the necessary finances had been secured. Within two months, however, it became clear that Ruda had misled the ICSD about his committee's ability to host the event, and in early February the Slovak games were definitively canceled. According to the article "Deaflympic Organiser in Slovakia Charged with Fraud" (*Slovak Spectator* [Bratislava, Slovakia], February 22, 2011), in late February 2011 the Slovak Office for the Fight against Corruption initiated formal charges against Ruda, accusing him of obtaining illegal loans to finance the games. In June 2011 Ruda was found guilty and sentenced to 13 years in prison.

CHAPTER 8
SPORTS AND HEALTH

Sport is a preserver of health.

—Hippocrates

The truth of Hippocrates's assertion has been nearly universally accepted for centuries, but only since the 20th century have researchers worked to quantify the impact of physical activity, or the lack thereof, on physical and mental well-being. In 1990 the U.S. Department of Health and Human Services (HHS) created the Healthy People initiative, a program aimed at providing Americans with guidance and resources to help them lead longer, healthier lives. The HHS launches a new Healthy People project every 10 years. According to Healthy People 2020 (2011, http://healthypeople.gov/2020/topicsobjectives2020/overview.aspx?topicid=33), the initiative's exercise goals "reflect the strong state of the science supporting the health benefits of regular physical activity among youth and adults." At the core of the project's objectives is the promotion of "regular physical activity" among Americans, which by definition "includes participation in moderate and vigorous physical activities and muscle-strengthening activities."

Hippocrates may not have appreciated as fully the other side of the sports-health nexus. As sports become a bigger business and as the pressure to perform becomes increasingly intense, greater attention is being given to the potential negative health impact of sports participation, especially on children and youth.

BENEFITS OF PHYSICAL ACTIVITY

In October 2008 the HHS released *2008 Physical Activity Guidelines for Americans* (http://www.health.gov/PAGuidelines/pdf/paguide.pdf), the first comprehensive attempt to provide a standardized set of guidelines for physical exercise. The report provides a list of basic health benefits that are associated with physical activity. For children, these benefits include improved cardiovascular, bone, and muscle fitness. At the same time, the report's findings suggest that there is some evidence that physical activity has the potential to reduce depression in adolescents. The health benefits for adults who engage in physical activity are numerous, and include lowering the risk of heart disease, stroke, breast and colon cancer, and early death, while also alleviating depression and promoting improved cognitive functioning.

The specific health benefits of sports participation depend on the sport. Speed walking, jogging, cycling, swimming, and skiing have been shown to build cardiovascular endurance. Sports that involve gentle bending or stretching, including bowling, golf, and tai chi, are identified as promoting flexibility, which in turn may reduce the risk of injury. Other sports, such as those involving weightlifting or throwing, build strength. One important result of building strong muscles and, especially, bones is that it helps stave off osteoporosis by increasing the mineral content of bones.

Coronary heart disease, diabetes, colon cancer, and high blood pressure can all be prevented or improved through regular physical activity. In "Obesity: Halting the Epidemic by Making Health Easier" (May 26, 2011, http://www.cdc.gov/chronicdisease/resources/publications/AAG/obesity.htm), the Centers for Disease Control and Prevention (CDC) points to an obesity epidemic as the key factor in these chronic health problems. According to the CDC, obesity levels among adults doubled between 1980 and 2008; during this same period obesity rates tripled among children. According to the CDC, obesity-related health problems cost Americans $147 billion in 2008. By 2011 more than one-third of American adults and 17% of American children were obese. Youfa Wang and May A. Beydoun of the Johns Hopkins Bloomberg School of Public Health project in "The Obesity Epidemic in the United States—Gender, Age, Socioeconomic, Racial/Ethnic, and Geographic Characteristics: A Systematic Review and Meta-regression Analysis"

TABLE 8.1

Calories burned through selected sports and other physical activities

	Approximate calories used by a 154-pound person	
	In 1 hour	In 30 minutes
Moderate physical activities		
Hiking	370	185
Light gardening/yard work	330	165
Dancing	330	165
Bicycling (less than 10 miles per hour)	290	145
Walking (3½ miles per hour)	280	140
Weight lifting (general light workout)	220	110
Stretching	180	90
Vigorous physical activities		
Running/jogging (5 miles per hour)	590	295
Bicycling (greater than 10 miles per hour)	590	295
Swimming (slow freestyle laps)	510	255
Aerobics	480	240
Walking (4½ miles per hour)	460	230
Heavy yard work (chopping wood)	440	220
Weight lifting (vigorous effort)	440	220
Basketball (vigorous)	440	220

SOURCE: "Calorie Burner Chart," in *Tools to Help You*, U.S. Department of Agriculture, undated, http://www.fns.usda.gov/eatsmartplayhardhealthy lifestyle/tools/calorieburnerchart.htm (accessed June 3, 2011)

FIGURE 8.1

The link between physical education participation and youth sports activities

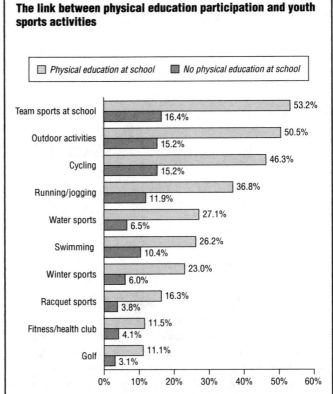

SOURCE: "Regular Activities during School Years," in *Sports, Fitness & Recreational Activities: Topline Participation Report, 2011*, Sporting Goods Manufacturers Association, 2011, http://www.sgma.com/reports/276_2011-SPORTS,-FITNESS-AND-RECREATIONAL-ACTIVITIES-TOPLINE-PARTICIPATION-REPORT----NEW-RELEASE (accessed July 7, 2011)

(*Epidemiologic Reviews*, vol. 29, no. 1, August 2007) that by 2015, 41% of American adults will be obese.

Sports participation helps control weight by burning calories that would otherwise be stored as fat. The more vigorous the sport and the more frequent the participation, the more calories are burned. Table 8.1 shows the approximate number of calories that a 154-pound individual would burn in various moderate and vigorous physical activities in 30 minutes and in one hour.

In *2011 SGMA Sports, Fitness, & Recreational Activities Topline Participation Report* (2011), the Sporting Goods Manufacturers Association examines the relationship between school physical education programs and athletic participation among American children. As Figure 8.1 shows, students who received physical education at school were over three times more likely to belong to a school sports team than students who received no physical education. Among students aged six to 12 years, more than 40% of those who did not receive physical education at school reported engaging in no athletic activities whatsoever. (See Figure 8.2.) By comparison, less than 5% of students aged six to 12 years who received at least some physical education at school reported that they had not participated in any physical activity. These statistics show no fundamental change among students aged 13 to 17 years. (See Figure 8.3.)

Sports Participation and Mental Health

Besides the obvious physical benefits of sports participation, there are psychological benefits as well. Anna Campbell and Heather A. Hausenblas of the University of Florida find in "Effects of Exercise Interventions on Body Image: A Meta-Analysis" (*Journal of Health Psychology*, vol. 14, no. 6, September 2009) that physical exercise has a noticeably positive effect on an individual's body image. According to the article "Exercise Improves Body Image for Fit and Unfit Alike" (*Science Daily*, October 9, 2009), Hausenblas explains that even less athletic individuals develop improved perceptions of their body through sports participation, suggesting that the mental health benefits of physical exercise are distinct from the physiological benefits of exercise. Hausenblas states, "It may be that the requirements to receive the psychological benefits of exercise, including those relating to body image, differ substantially from the physical benefits."

The idea that sports participation can help improve one's mood is well supported by other scientific research. The Mayo Clinic indicates in "Depression and Anxiety: Exercise Eases Symptoms" (October 23, 2009, http://www.mayo clinic.com/health/depression-and-exercise/MH00043) that physical exercise releases endorphins and neurotransmitters, chemicals in the brain that have the potential to alleviate anxiety and depression. At the same time, exercise

FIGURE 8.2

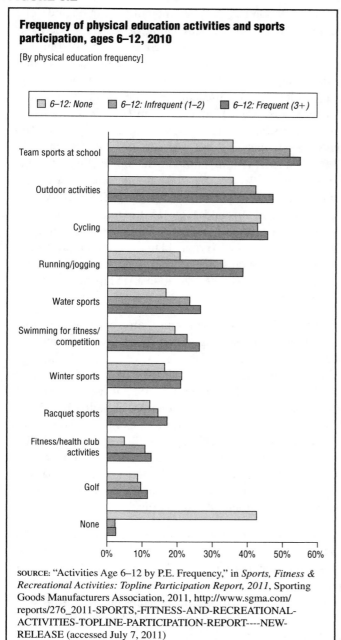

Frequency of physical education activities and sports participation, ages 6–12, 2010

[By physical education frequency]

SOURCE: "Activities Age 6–12 by P.E. Frequency," in *Sports, Fitness & Recreational Activities: Topline Participation Report, 2011*, Sporting Goods Manufacturers Association, 2011, http://www.sgma.com/reports/276_2011-SPORTS,-FITNESS-AND-RECREATIONAL-ACTIVITIES-TOPLINE-PARTICIPATION-REPORT----NEW-RELEASE (accessed July 7, 2011)

FIGURE 8.3

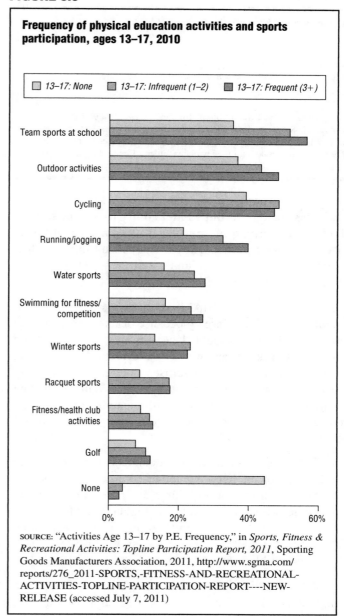

Frequency of physical education activities and sports participation, ages 13–17, 2010

SOURCE: "Activities Age 13–17 by P.E. Frequency," in *Sports, Fitness & Recreational Activities: Topline Participation Report, 2011*, Sporting Goods Manufacturers Association, 2011, http://www.sgma.com/reports/276_2011-SPORTS,-FITNESS-AND-RECREATIONAL-ACTIVITIES-TOPLINE-PARTICIPATION-REPORT----NEW-RELEASE (accessed July 7, 2011)

promotes self-confidence and social interaction, while also providing a distraction from stress that is related to daily life. In "Adolescent Women's Sports Involvement and Sexual Behavior/Health: A Process-Level Investigation" (*Journal of Youth and Adolescence*, vol. 33, no. 5, October 2004), Stephanie Jacobs Lehman and Susan Silverberg Koerner find evidence of a link between girls' involvement in organized sports and positive sexual health and behavior. This study links participation in organized sports with positive behavior that is related to sexual risk-taking, sexual/reproductive health, and sexual/reproductive health-seeking behavior. This effect is connected to self-empowerment and a positive view of one's own body.

HEALTH RISKS OF SPORTS PARTICIPATION
Injuries

TYPES OF INJURIES. The National Institute of Arthritis and Musculoskeletal and Skin Diseases (NIAMS) details in *Sports Injuries* (April 2009, http://www.niams.nih.gov/Health_Info/Sports_Injuries/default.asp) the kinds of injuries that athletes are likely to sustain and the activities in which they sustain them. The NIAMS lists muscle sprains and strains, ligament and tendon tears, dislocated joints, and bone fractures as the most common types of sports injuries. (See Table 8.2.)

The NIAMS divides all sports injuries into two broad categories: acute and chronic. Acute injuries are those that occur suddenly during an activity. They are characterized

TABLE 8.2

Common types of sports injuries

- Muscle sprains and strains
- Tears of the ligaments that hold joints together
- Tears of the tendons that support joints and allow them to move
- Dislocated joints
- Fractured bones, including vertebrae

SOURCE: "Common Types of Sports Injuries," in *Handout on Health: Sports Injuries*, U.S. Department of Health and Human Services, National Institutes of Health, National Institute of Arthritis and Musculoskeletal and Skin Diseases, April 2009, http://www.niams.nih.gov/Health_Info/Sports_Injuries/default.asp (accessed June 3, 2011)

by severe pain, swelling, and inability to use the injured body part. Chronic injuries usually occur through overuse over a long period. They usually result in pain when engaging in the activity, and a dull ache when at rest. There may also be swelling.

According to the NIAMS, the knee is the most commonly injured joint, largely because of its complexity and its role in bearing weight. Knee injuries can result from twisting the knee awkwardly, a direct blow, landing badly after a jump, or overuse. Injuries can range in severity from a minor bruise to serious damage to one or more of the four ligaments—the anterior cruciate, the posterior cruciate, the medial collateral, and the lateral collateral—that stabilize the joint.

The Achilles tendon, which connects the calf muscle to the back of the heel, is another common site of sports injuries. Achilles tendon injures are especially common in people who do not exercise regularly and may not bother to stretch adequately before a game or session. This makes middle-aged "weekend warriors" particularly susceptible, according to the NIAMS.

A fracture is a break in a bone. It can come from a single event, in which case it is called an acute fracture; or it can be caused by repetitive impact, which is called a stress fracture. Stress fractures usually occur in the feet or legs, the result of the pounding these bones take from long periods of running and jumping. When the bones that come together to form a joint get separated, it is called a dislocation. The NIAMS notes that the joints of the hand are the most common points of dislocation, followed by the shoulder.

According to Maureen Haggerty, Teresa G. Odle, and Rebecca J. Frey, in "Sports Injuries" (Jacqueline L. Longe, ed., *Gale Encyclopedia of Medicine*, 2006), the vast majority (95%) of sports injuries are minor soft-tissue traumas. Bruises (or contusions) occur when blood collects at the point of the injury, causing a discoloration of the skin. Sprains involve a partial or complete tear of a ligament and account for about one-third of sports injuries. Strains are similar to sprains, except that a strain involves a tear in

a muscle or tendon rather than in a ligament. Other soft-tissue sports injuries include tendonitis (inflammation of a tendon) and bursitis (inflammation of the fluid-filled sacs that allow tendons to glide over bones). These two injuries usually result from repeated stress on the tissue, rather than from a single traumatic event. The kinds of sports injuries that result from overuse appear to be on the rise among young people. Mark Hyman notes in *Until It Hurts: America's Obsession with Youth Sports and How It Harms Our Kids* (2009) that in 1989 overuse injuries accounted for 20% of patients visiting the sports medicine clinic of Children's Hospital Boston. By 2004 the percentage was 70% and on the rise. Hyman states that "in 2003 more than 3.5 million children under age 15 suffered a sports injury that required medical treatment—about one attended injury for every 10 players." Hyman blames increased pressure to perform from parents and coaches, who seek to turn every promising young athlete into a scholarship recipient or a potential superstar.

Skeletal injuries from sports are less common than soft-tissue injuries. Haggerty, Odle, and Frey indicate that fractures account for 5% to 6% of sports injuries, with arms and legs being the most common sites of a break. Repeated foot pounding that is associated with sports such as long-distance running, basketball, and volleyball, and the stress fractures that can result, sometimes cause an injury called shin splints. Shin splints, according to Haggerty, Odle, and Frey, "are characterized by soreness and slight swelling of the front, inside, and back of the lower leg, and by sharp pain that develops while exercising and gradually intensifies."

The most dangerous class of sports injuries are those to the brain. While fractures of the skull or spine are rare in sports, concussions have become increasingly common. Concussions are caused by a violent jarring of the brain from a blow to the head. They often cause loss of consciousness and may also affect balance, coordination, hearing, memory, and vision.

The early 21st century has seen an increase in awareness of the damaging effects of concussions on professional athletes, notably football players. The article "Head Injuries in Football" (*New York Times*, October 21, 2010) reports that a 2000 survey of more than 1,000 former National Football League (NFL) players revealed that over 60% had suffered at least one concussion during their professional career; another quarter (26%) had incurred three or more concussions. In 2009 the NFL commissioned the Institute for Social Research at the University of Michigan to research cases of Alzheimer's and other memory-related diseases in retired NFL players. The study revealed that former professional football players aged 30 to 49 years were nearly 20 times more likely to be diagnosed with brain diseases than men of the same age who had not played football. In response to these developments, the NFL began to consider more stringent rules regarding head injuries. In December 2009 the league implemented a ban prohibiting players who had demonstrated symptoms of concussions from returning to action the same day. The following summer the NFL launched a campaign aimed at increasing awareness among NFL teams concerning the health risks that are related to head injuries.

Concussions have also been linked to other mental disorders in former football players, including degenerative brain diseases. This disturbing trend received national attention in February 2011, after the former Chicago Bears safety Dave Duerson (1960–2011) committed suicide by shooting himself in the chest. Alan Schwarz reports in "Duerson's Brain Trauma Diagnosed" (*New York Times*, May 2, 2011) that a subsequent medical examination revealed that Duerson had suffered from chronic traumatic encephalopathy (CTE), an incurable degenerative brain disorder that is linked to dementia, memory loss, and depression. According to Schwarz, CTE can currently only be detected through a brain autopsy. In a suicide note to his family, Duerson wrote, "Please, see that my brain is given to the N.F.L.'s brain bank." In "What Will Happen to Former NFL Player's Brain?" (CNN.com, February 26, 2011), Stephanie Smith indicates that Duerson's brain was donated to the Boston University School of Medicine Center for the Study of Traumatic Encephalopathy so that it could be studied.

One of the most alarming aspects of sports-related concussions is that they often produce no immediate symptoms in the affected player. Shankar Vedantam indicates in "The National Brain-Damage League: The Epidemic of Head Injuries in Football Is Even Worse Than You Thought" (January 18, 2011, http://www.slate.com/id/2281515/) that researchers at Purdue University discovered that many concussions suffered by professional football players go undetected. When these players received brain scans soon after the NFL season commenced, however, researchers were able to detect long-ranging changes to the players' brains. The researchers also found that, out of 1 million high school students who play football annually, 67,000 suffer concussions; the researchers also estimate that a comparable number of concussions go undetected. Vedantam suggests that these injuries often "go unreported because fans, coaches, and parents don't want a star athlete pulled from a game." The article "NFL Urging States to Pass Youth Football Concussion Laws" (Associated Press, February 23, 2011) notes that in response to the rise of head injuries among young players, in early 2011 the NFL began urging state legislatures to pass laws requiring more stringent safety measures in high school football.

Since 2000 professional hockey has also witnessed a dramatic increase in the number of concussions that are suffered by players. In April 2011 researchers at the University of Calgary published a comprehensive study of concussions in the National Hockey League (NHL). According to the article "Study: Games Lost to Concussions Rises" (Associated Press, April 18, 2011), the researchers found that of the 559 concussions reported by the NHL between 1997 and 2004, 529 caused players to lose playing time. Of these, 31% resulted in a player losing 10 or more days on the ice. In March 2011, after concussions had forced high-profile players such as Sidney Crosby (1987–) and Marc Savard (1977–) to miss the remainder of the 2010–11 season, the NHL announced strict new rules concerning the treatment of head injuries. The article "NHL Announces Plan to Limit Concussions" (Fox Sports, March 14, 2011) reveals the new guidelines, which include improved in-game medical attention for players, as well as the implementation of higher safety standards at NHL hockey rinks.

STATISTICS ON FREQUENCY AND INJURY RATES. In "Epidemiology of Severe Injuries among United States High School Athletes: 2005–2007" (*American Journal of Sports Medicine*, vol. 37, no. 9, September 2009), Cory J. Darrow et al. analyze sports injuries among American high school athletes between 2005 and 2007. The researchers find that high school athletes suffered an estimated 446,715 severe injuries—that is, injuries resulting in 21 or more days of missed playing time—during this period. Football players accounted for approximately 170,252, or nearly 40%, of all severe injuries. Girls' soccer players reported the second-highest number of severe injuries, with 67,178. By comparison, boys' soccer players recorded 46,755 severe injuries, or 30% fewer severe injuries than girls' soccer players. Overall, female high school athletes accounted for 141,362 severe injuries, whereas boys accounted for 305,353.

PHYSICAL INJURIES AMONG YOUNG ATHLETES. In March 2011 the child safety advocacy group Safe Kids USA surveyed parents of child athletes between the ages of 5 and 14 years. In *A National Survey of Parents' Knowledge, Attitudes, and Self-Reported Behaviors Concerning Sports Safety* (April 2011, http://www.safekids.org/assets/docs/ourwork/research/sports-safety-report-2011.pdf), the organization reports that the percentage of young athletes who had suffered injuries while participating in sports rose from 31% in 2000 to 34% in 2011. The largest increase was among girls between the ages of 10 and 14 years. In 2000, 28% of girls in this age group had suffered a sports-related injury, compared to 44% of boys aged 10 to 14 years. By 2011 the percentage for girls had risen to 43%, whereas injuries among boys in the same age group rose only slightly during the same period, to 45%. The proportion of young athletes who had been injured more than once also rose, from 15% in 2000 to

21% in 2011. In 2011, 5% of young athletes suffered four or more sports-related injuries, compared to 3% in 2000.

In its 2011 study, Safe Kids USA also evaluates parents' knowledge concerning child injuries. The organization reveals that children are more likely than adults to suffer injuries while participating in sports; however, fewer than half (46%) of parents recognized this fact in 2011. Safe Kids USA also finds that even though 71% of parents believed it is "very important" that their child's coach is knowledgeable about sports injuries, only 29% actually believed that coaches are "very knowledgeable and well trained" to deal with injuries. This so-called knowledge gap widens further when it comes to understanding concussions. An overwhelming percentage (94%) of parents said it is very important for youth coaches to be able to recognize concussion symptoms; however, only 29% felt confident that their child's coach can actually detect signs of a concussion. Moreover, even though nearly half (49%) of parents had children who played multiple sports in 2011, only 13% felt serious concern about the potential for injury through overuse or stress.

FACTORS AFFECTING INJURY RATES. Besides children and adolescents, the NIAMS notes that middle-aged people and women of all ages are also particularly vulnerable to sports injuries. Middle-aged people are susceptible to injury because they are not as agile and resilient as when they were younger. Some people expect their bodies to perform as well at the age of 50 as they remember their bodies performing at age 20 or 30. As a result, they put themselves at risk of injury. The risk is highest when an individual tries to make too quick a transition from an inactive lifestyle to an active one.

Studies reveal that women are more likely to suffer certain kinds of injuries than men. Allison Aubrey states in "Training May Curb Some Sports Injuries in Women" (September 4, 2008, http://www.npr.org/templates/story/story.php?storyId=93309486) that "women are more prone than their male counterparts to specific injuries—namely knee injuries like tears of the ACL, or anterior cruciate ligament." Aubrey explains that the muscles in women's legs develop unevenly because women mostly use their front quadriceps. "This means that women's bodies [unlike men's] don't fully activate the muscles on the back side, namely the hamstrings and the glutes," so the imbalance places increased stress on the knee. As a result, strength training techniques have been implemented for women athletes to help them avoid this painful anterior cruciate ligament tear, an injury that requires surgery and long rehabilitation.

PSYCHOLOGICAL IMPACT OF YOUTH SPORTS PARTICIPATION. Frank Brady states in "Children's Organized Sports: A Developmental Perspective" (*Journal of Physical Education, Recreation, and Dance*, vol. 75, no. 2, February 2004) that the "positive effect of sports participation for some youths appears to be offset by the negative experiences of others." The biggest culprit in the negative psychological impact of youth sports participation is an overemphasis on competition, which Brady attributes to misplaced priorities on the part of the adults in supervisory roles.

As a result, there is a high rate of burnout and subsequent dropout in youth sports. Brady explains that sports participation peaks at age 11 and steadily declines through the teenage years. He singles out a subset of the dropout group under the category of "burnout." Burnout refers to young athletes who have been successful in their sport(s) and have participated intensively over a number of years; concentrated training at the expense of other activities can result in diminished enjoyment, competitive anxiety, and ultimately real psychological and emotional damage.

Brady also points to conflicts between heavy sports participation and cognitive development in young children. Most children are not capable of fully grasping the competitive process until about the age of 12 years and have trouble understanding the complex interrelationships that form a team. Some adult coaches get angry and frustrated when, for example, young soccer players swarm to the ball rather than play their positions properly, when in fact many players at age seven or eight are cognitively incapable of absorbing the concept of a position.

In the face of increased pressure to perform, young athletes are burning out at an earlier age. Roger Seay and Sheila Gray examine in "Parents and Kids Work Together to Avoid Sports Burnout" (Fox News, November 3, 2010) the impact of overly competitive sports environments on child athletes. Citing data from the National Alliance for Youth Sports, Seay and Gray reveal that nearly three-quarters (73%) of young athletes drop out of competitive sports by the time they reach the age of 13 years. In many cases, children abandon athletics because of stress, which can manifest itself in "physical and emotional symptoms." Part of the problem lies in a fundamental disconnect between parents and their children. Seay and Gray report that adults tend to have a highly competitive attitude toward sports, whereas children are more inclined to view athletics as an opportunity for enjoyment and socializing with their peers. Furthermore, because only 5% of high school varsity athletes earn scholarships to play at the college level, an undue emphasis on competition can create unrealistic expectations in a number of young athletes. Seay and Gray conclude that by teaching children to place less importance on the outcome of athletic participation, parents can help relieve the pressure that is associated with competition.

SPORTS AND HEALTH: THE OUTLOOK

Are Americans heeding all the advice that is coming from their doctors and the government about the importance of physical activity? Data from the *Early Release of*

Selected Estimates Based on Data from the January–September 2010 National Health Interview Survey (March 23, 2011, http://www.cdc.gov/nchs/data/nhis/earlyrelease/earlyrelease201103.pdf) by the CDC indicate that, in general, the answer seems to be "not really." Figure 8.4 shows that the percentage of adults who engaged in regular leisure-time physical activity between 1997 and 2010 hovered somewhere between 30% and 35%, in spite of the aggressive promotion of exercise by the federal government and others. As shown in Figure 8.5, people tend to exercise less as they age, and this pattern holds true for both genders, with men more likely to be physically active than women in every age category. Non-Hispanic white adults (38.3%) were more likely to engage in regular leisure-time physical activity than either Hispanics (26.9%) or non-Hispanic African-Americans (27.3%). (See Figure 8.6.)

Vigorous physical activity among adolescents seems to be slightly higher. The nonprofit research agency Child Trends reports in *Vigorous Physical Activity by Youth* (July 2010, http://www.childtrendsdatabank.org/?q=node/266) that 40% of all high school students participated in vigorous physical exercise on a regular basis in 2009. (See Figure 8.7.) "Vigorous physical activity" is defined as physical activity for at least 20 minutes that made the person sweat and breathe hard, such as basketball, soccer, running, swimming laps, fast bicycling, fast dancing, or similar aerobic activities, on at least three of the seven days preceding the interview. Figure 8.7 also reveals that in 2009 non-Hispanic African-American and Hispanic students were equally likely to have engaged in physical activity, at 33% each, and that non-Hispanic white students, at 40%, were somewhat more likely to be physically active. As shown in Figure 8.8, 48% of ninth-grade boys in 2009 reported engaging in physical activity, whereas 31% of ninth-grade girls reported such activity. Even though the percentages for both genders declined from ninth to 12th grade, boys were consistently more active than girls, with the gap between the genders the widest in 11th grade.

In the face of an obesity epidemic in the United States, the federal government has taken an active role in promoting fitness among Americans. In 1996 the National Center for Chronic Disease Prevention and Health Promotion published *Physical Activity and Health: A Report of the Surgeon General* (http://www.cdc.gov/nccdphp/sgr/pdf/sgrfull.pdf), a blueprint for improving the physical condition of the U.S. population. Among the report's major conclusions were that people of all ages and genders benefit from regular physical activity and that significant health benefits can be obtained by engaging in a moderate amount of physical activity, such

FIGURE 8.4

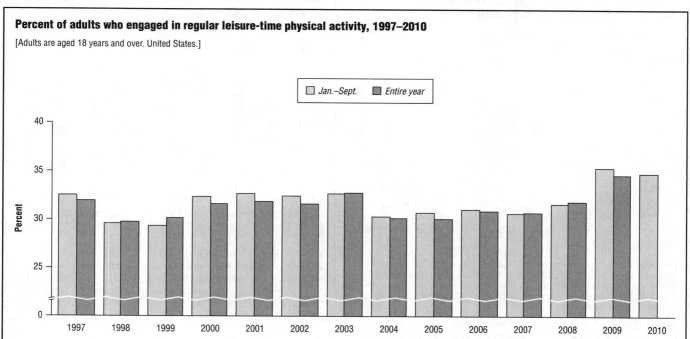

Percent of adults who engaged in regular leisure-time physical activity, 1997–2010

[Adults are aged 18 years and over. United States.]

☐ Jan.–Sept.   ■ Entire year

Notes: Regular leisure-time physical activity is defined as engaging in light-moderate leisure-time physical activity for greater than or equal to 30 minutes at a frequency greater than or equal to five times per week or engaging in vigorous leisure-time physical activity for greater than or equal to 20 minutes at a frequency greater than or equal to three times per week.

SOURCE: "Figure 7.1. Percentage of Adults Aged 18 Years and over Who Engaged in Regular Leisure-Time Physical Activity: United States, 1997–September 2010," in *Early Release of Selected Estimates Based on Data from the January–September 2010 National Health Interview Survey*, U.S. Department of Health and Human Services, Centers for Disease Control and Prevention, National Center for Health Statistics, March 23, 2011, http://www.cdc.gov/nchs/data/nhis/earlyrelease/earlyrelease201103.pdf (accessed June 3, 2011)

FIGURE 8.5

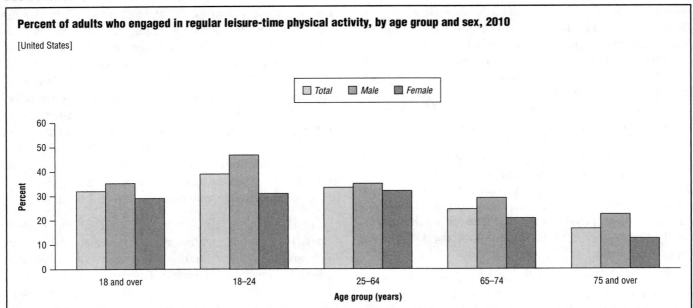

Percent of adults who engaged in regular leisure-time physical activity, by age group and sex, 2010

[United States]

Note: Regular leisure-time physical activity is defined as engaging in light-moderate leisure-time physical activity for greater than or equal to 30 minutes at a frequency greater than or equal to five times per week or engaging in vigorous leisure-time physical activity for greater than or equal to 20 minutes at a frequency greater than or equal to three times per week.

SOURCE: "Figure 7.2. Percentage of Adults Aged 18 Years and over Who Engaged in Regular Leisure-Time Physical Activity, by Age Group and Sex: United States, January–September 2010," in *Early Release of Selected Estimates Based on Data from the January–September 2010 National Health Interview Survey*, U.S. Department of Health and Human Services, Centers for Disease Control and Prevention, National Center for Health Statistics, March 23, 2011, http://www.cdc.gov/nchs/data/nhis/earlyrelease/earlyrelease201103.pdf (accessed June 3, 2011)

FIGURE 8.6

Percent of adults who engaged in regular leisure-time physical activity, by race/ethnicity, 2010

[Adults aged 18 years and over. United States.]

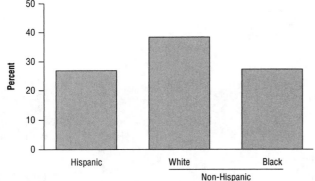

Note: Regular leisure-time physical activity is defined as engaging in light-moderate leisure-time physical activity for greater than or equal to 30 minutes at a frequency greater than or equal to five times per week or engaging in vigorous leisure-time physical activity for greater than or equal to 20 minutes at a frequency greater than or equal to three times per week.

SOURCE: "Figure 7.3. Age-Sex-Adjusted Percentage of Adults Aged 18 Years and over Who Engaged in Regular Leisure-Time Physical Activity, by Race/Ethnicity: United States, January–September 2010," in *Early Release of Selected Estimates Based on Data from the January–September 2010 National Health Interview Survey*, U.S. Department of Health and Human Services, Centers for Disease Control and Prevention, National Center for Health Statistics, March 23, 2011, http://www.cdc.gov/nchs/data/nhis/earlyrelease/earlyrelease201103.pdf (accessed June 3, 2011)

FIGURE 8.7

Vigorous physical activity among adolescents, by race/ethnicity, 2009

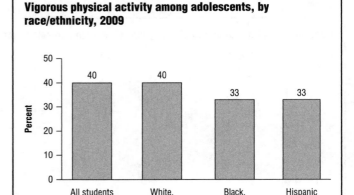

Note: Activities that increased heart rate and caused heavy breathing some of the time for a total of 80 minutes a day on at least 5 of the previous 7 days preceding the survey.

SOURCE: "Figure 3. Physical Activity: The Percentage of Students in Grades 9 through 12 Who Participated in Vigorous Physical Activity, by Race and Hispanic Origin, 2009," in *Vigorous Physical Activity by Youth*, Child Trends, July 2010, http://www.childtrendsdatabank.org/sites/default/files/16_Fig02.jpg (accessed June 6, 2011)

as 45 minutes of volleyball, 30 minutes of brisk walking, or 15 minutes of running. The report noted that additional benefits can be gained through more vigorous and greater amounts of activity. Since then, the federal government has continued its efforts to promote physical fitness

FIGURE 8.8

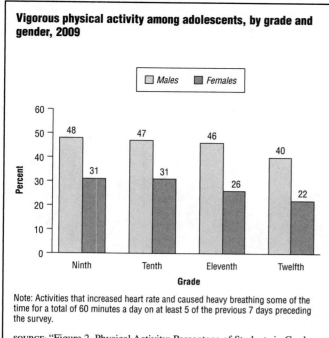

Vigorous physical activity among adolescents, by grade and gender, 2009

Note: Activities that increased heart rate and caused heavy breathing some of the time for a total of 60 minutes a day on at least 5 of the previous 7 days preceding the survey.

SOURCE: "Figure 2. Physical Activity: Percentage of Students in Grades 9 through 12 Who Participated in Regular Vigorous Physical Activity, by Grade and Gender, 2009," in *Vigorous Physical Activity by Youth*, Child Trends, July 2010, http://www.childtrendsdatabank.org/sites/default/files/16_Fig01.jpg (accessed June 6, 2011)

through a variety of programs, including Healthy People 2020 and the HealthierUS initiative (http://georgewbush whitehouse.archives.gov/infocus/fitness/), promoted by

President George W. Bush (1946–), and the President's Challenge, a fitness initiative of the President's Council on Physical Fitness and Sports. The President's Challenge, a six-week competition to determine the nation's most active state, was renewed in May 2009 by President Barack Obama (1961–), who also declared that month National Physical Fitness and Sports Month.

Television has taken on the obesity epidemic as well. Cable television, a longtime source of fitness programming, featured FitTV. Launched in 1993 and owned by Discovery Communications, in February 2011 FitTV merged with the Discovery Health Channel to become Discovery Fit and Health. In recent years network television has also gotten into the fitness game. The National Broadcasting Corporation's *The Biggest Loser* is a reality show in which obese contestants compete in various contests that are designed to help them slim down. The contestant who sheds the most weight (the "biggest loser") is the winner at the end of the season. The show's 12th season was launched in September 2011. During the first decade of the 21st century professional sports leagues also began to play a more active role in promoting fitness among young people. In October 2007 the NFL launched the NFL PLAY 60 project (2011, http://www.nfl.com/play60), an initiative that is aimed at promoting fitness in schools and communities. In its first four years of existence, NFL PLAY 60 donated more than $200 million to health and wellness programs nationwide.

CHAPTER 9
PERFORMANCE-ENHANCING DRUGS

The spirit of sport is the celebration of the human spirit, the body and the mind. Doping is contrary to the spirit of sport, erodes public confidence and jeopardizes the health and well-being of athletes.

—World Anti-Doping Agency

The word *doping* is often used to refer to any practice that involves prohibited substances or other methods to give an athlete an unfair advantage over other competitors. The article "Doping in Sports: Steroids and Supplements" (*World Almanac and Book of Facts*, 2007) notes that the word *dope* probably comes from the Dutch word *dop*, an alcoholic beverage made from grape skins that traditional Zulu warriors believed enhanced their fighting ability.

A BRIEF HISTORY OF DOPING

For as long as people have been engaging in athletic competition, they have been seeking ways to gain an edge on their opponents. There is evidence that doping took place during the ancient Olympics, whose competitions were held from 776 BC until AD 393. For example, Will Carroll notes in *The Juice: The Real Story of Baseball's Drug Problems* (2005) that Greece's Spartan coaches fed their athletes special herb and mushroom concoctions—during a period in which they were supposed to be consuming nothing but cheese and water—that were believed to render them oblivious to pain.

The first known case of an athlete dying as a result of doping occurred in 1886, when the Welsh cyclist Andrew Linton died during a race from Paris to Bordeaux, France. The substance he ingested was thought to be trimethyl, an alcohol-based product that was used by distance racers to ease pain and increase stamina.

According to Carroll, the modern era of doping began with the development of injectable testosterone in 1935. Testosterone is a male hormone that is produced naturally by the body. Injecting additional testosterone into the system increases muscle mass and strength. Originally introduced by Nazi doctors to make soldiers more aggressive, laboratory-produced testosterone did not take long to make its way from the battlefield to the athletic field. German athletes dominated the medals during the 1936 Olympics, possibly with the assistance of these newly developed synthetic drugs.

The father of anabolic steroids (chemical variants of testosterone) in the United States was John Benjamin Ziegler (1917–2000), a physician for the U.S. weightlifting team during the mid-20th century. Ziegler learned from his Russian counterparts that the Soviet weightlifting team's success was in part attributable to its use of performance-enhancing drugs, the formulas for which had been brought east by German scientists who defected to the Soviet Union after World War II (1939–1945). Deciding that U.S. athletes needed chemical assistance to remain competitive, Ziegler worked with the CIBA Pharmaceutical Company to develop an oral anabolic steroid. These efforts resulted in the creation of methandrostenolone, which appeared on the market in 1960. During the Olympics that year, the Danish cyclist Knut Jensen (1936–1960) collapsed and died while competing in the 62-mile (100-km) race. An autopsy revealed the presence of amphetamines and a drug called nicotinyl tartrade in his system.

Drug testing was introduced at the Olympics in 1968. By this time the International Olympic Committee (IOC) had developed a list of officially banned substances; however, because no test had yet been invented that could distinguish between anabolic steroids and naturally occurring testosterone in the body, the testing was largely ineffective. Only one athlete was found to be in violation of the new drug policy in 1968: the Swedish pentathlete Hans-Gunnar Liljenwall (1941–), who was found to have too much alcohol in his blood after drinking a few beers before the shooting portion of his event.

Steroids found their way into professional football during the late 1960s, as teams began hiring strength and conditioning coaches, who were charged with the task of growing a new breed of bigger, bulkier players. Taking their cue from the weightlifting world, these coaches turned to steroids as the fastest way of accomplishing this goal.

By the 1970s the use of performance-enhancing drugs had reached epidemic proportions among elite athletes. The East Germans showed up at the 1976 Olympics in Montreal, Canada, with a team of women swimmers sporting man-sized muscles and deep voices. They won most of the medals. However, even though there was much talk about the likelihood that they were using banned substances, not a single one of these athletes tested positive. It later became clear that the athletes themselves were the victims of a mandatory doping program that was overseen by East German Olympic officials, who injected the swimmers with steroids without their informed consent. Several East German swimmers of that era, as reported by the article "10 Drug Scandals" (CBC Sports, January 19, 2003), have indicated that they began receiving steroid injections at age 13 and have suffered serious long-term health consequences—ranging from liver damage to infertility—as a result of doping.

As doping became more prevalent, methods for detecting it improved. A breakthrough took place in 1983, when a new technology for analyzing blood for banned substances was implemented at the Pan American Games in Caracas, Venezuela. The article "Inquiry Set on Pan Am" (Associated Press, September 14, 1983) reported at that time that 16 athletes from several countries were caught with performance-enhancing drugs in their system. Many other athletes, including 12 members of the U.S. track and field team, withdrew from the event rather than risk the embarrassment of being caught.

The first major Olympic disqualification due to steroids occurred in 1988, when the Canadian sprinter Ben Johnson (1961–) was stripped of both his gold medal and his world record in the 100-meter sprint after testing positive for the banned steroid stanozolol. Years later, it was revealed that a number of U.S. track competitors had also tested positive for illicit drugs prior to the 1988 Olympics in Seoul, South Korea.

Attitudes concerning the effectiveness of drug testing remain mixed among competitive athletes. A 2010 survey reveals that more than half (58.1%) of track and field throwers either agreed or strongly agreed that drug testing remains the most effective way of preventing or controlling drug use in sports. (See Figure 9.1.) At the same time, virtually all track and field throwers remain skeptical about the efficacy of current testing measures to deter the use of performance-enhancing drugs in athletic competition. (See Figure 9.2.)

FIGURE 9.1

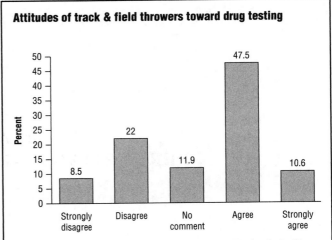

Attitudes of track & field throwers toward drug testing

SOURCE: Lawrence W. Judge et al., "Figure 1. Drug Testing Is the Most Effective Method of Preventing/Controlling Performance Enhancing Drugs in Sport," in "The Attitudes of Track and Field Throwers toward Performance Enhancing Drug Use and Drug Testing," *SD Journal of Research in Health, Physical Education, Recreation, Sport & Dance,* fall/winter 2010

FIGURE 9.2

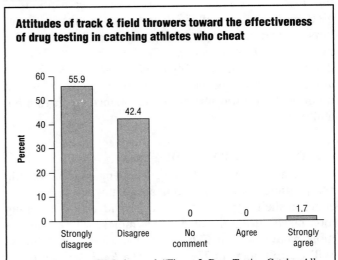

Attitudes of track & field throwers toward the effectiveness of drug testing in catching athletes who cheat

SOURCE: Lawrence W. Judge et al, "Figure 2. Drug Testing Catches All Athletes Who Cheat," in "The Attitudes of Track and Field Throwers toward Performance Enhancing Drug Use and Drug Testing," *SD Journal of Research in Health, Physical Education, Recreation, Sport & Dance,* Fall/Winter 2010

WHAT ARE PERFORMANCE-ENHANCING DRUGS?

Anabolic Steroids

When people speak of performance-enhancing drugs, more often than not they are referring to anabolic steroids. In *Steroid Abuse in Today's Society* (March 2004, http://www.deadiversion.usdoj.gov/pubs/brochures/steroids/professionals/), the U.S. Drug Enforcement Administration (DEA) defines anabolic steroids as "synthetically produced variants of the naturally occurring male hormone testosterone."

The full name of this class of drugs is androgenic anabolic steroids. The word *androgenic* means the drugs promote masculine physical characteristics, and *anabolic* means tissue building. According to the DEA, the list of commonly abused steroids that are commercially available in the United States includes:

- Fluoxymesterone
- Methyltestosterone
- Nandrolone
- Oxandrolone
- Oxymetholone
- Stanozolol
- Boldenone

Others that are not approved for use in the United States include ethylestrenol, methandriol, methenolone, and methandrostenolone.

The main users of anabolic steroids are athletes seeking to add bulk and strength to their bodies. Besides building lean body mass, another way steroids are purported to help athletes get stronger is by reducing the amount of recovery time that is needed between workouts, allowing them to train harder. Anabolic steroids are currently banned by most sports organizations, including the IOC, the National Football League (NFL), the National Basketball Association (NBA), the National Collegiate Athletic Association (NCAA), the National Hockey League (NHL), and Major League Baseball (MLB). Bob Harig reports in "Several PGA Tour Players Leery of Accidental Positives with New Doping Policy" (ESPN, June 30, 2008) that during the summer of 2008 the Professional Golf Association (PGA) initiated its own antidoping program, which included random drug testing during the PGA Tour.

There are a number of legitimate medical uses for which a doctor might prescribe steroids, including growth deficiencies, muscle-wasting diseases, loss of testicular function, breast cancer, low red blood cell count, or debilitated states resulting from surgery or illness. Steroids are also widely used in veterinary medicine to promote weight gain, treat anemia, or counteract tissue breakdown caused by illness or trauma.

Most illicit steroids come from one of two sources. Some are diverted from the legal U.S. market, often through stolen or fraudulent prescriptions. The largest share, however, has been smuggled into the United States from other countries, largely from Mexico, from European countries where a prescription is not required to obtain steroids, or, more recently, from China. Shaun Assael reports in "'Raw Deal' Busts Labs across U.S., Many Supplied by China" (ESPN, September 24, 2007) that in 2007 DEA agents concluded an 18-month crackdown on the illegal manufacturing and selling of steroids, closing down 56 labs and making 124 arrests in 27 states in what DEA officials called "the largest performance-enhancing drug crackdown in U.S. history." Thirty-seven Chinese factories were identified as reported suppliers of the labs. "The crackdown . . . grew out of a 2005 operation targeting eight Mexican labs that were responsible for 80 percent of America's underground steroid trade," explains Assael. "Several large Chinese factories had been supplying the Mexican labs. When the Mexican labs were closed . . . , those Chinese factories redirected their pipeline to the U.S." Assael concludes that with China quickly becoming a major player in the underground market for steroids, "the World Anti-Doping [Agency] estimates that Chinese factories are responsible for as much as 70–80 percent, or up to $480 million worldwide, of an annual $600 million black market in human growth hormone."

Steroids are available in several forms, including tablets, liquids, gels, and creams. Typically, users ingest the drugs orally, inject them into muscle, or rub them on their skin. The doses taken by people who abuse steroids can be 10 to 100 times stronger than those recommended for medical conditions. Many steroid abusers engage in what is called stacking, which means mixing oral steroids with injectable ones, often taking multiple forms of the drug. Another common practice among steroid abusers is pyramiding, which involves administering doses in cycles of six to 12 weeks. In pyramiding, the dose is slowly increased to a peak midway through the cycle and then tapered back down toward the end.

Other Substances and Supplements

There are numerous other performance-enhancing substances, some of which have, until recently, escaped the scrutiny of regulators. As a result, many of these substances, which are often billed as dietary supplements, have been readily available at nutrition and vitamin stores.

ERYTHROPOIETIN. Erythropoietin (EPO) is a hormone that is produced naturally by the kidneys. It plays a role in regulating the number of red blood cells in the blood stream. A synthetic version of EPO was developed during the 1980s, and it quickly became popular as a performance-enhancing drug, particularly among athletes who were involved in endurance sports such as cycling. Excessive doses of EPO can increase the number of red blood cells to such a degree that the blood becomes too thick to flow properly, potentially leading to heart attacks and strokes. According to the 2007 *World Almanac and Book of Facts*, during the late 1980s, shortly after the appearance of synthetic EPO, 30 top endurance athletes (mainly cyclists) in Belgium, Denmark, the Netherlands, and Sweden died; the likely cause of their deaths was EPO. A variant of EPO known as continuous erythropoietin receptor activator (CERA) began to appear in 2008. Many of the athletes who were ejected from the

2008 Tour de France and the 2008 Beijing Olympics had tested positive for CERA.

CREATINE. One of the most popular supplements used by athletes at all levels is creatine. Creatine is available without a prescription and is reputed to improve performance in sports that require short bursts of power, such as weightlifting, wrestling, and sprinting. Even though research has not yet established a connection between creatine and serious health problems, there is some evidence that heavy use may cause kidney, liver, and heart damage. Known side effects of creatine include muscle cramps, stomach pain, diarrhea, and nausea. In "Performance-Enhancing Drugs: Know the Risks" (December 23, 2010, http://www.mayoclinic.com/health/performance-enhancing-drugs/HQ01105), the Mayo Clinic explains that creatine causes the muscles to draw water away from the rest of the body. As a result, increased body mass is most likely caused by excess water stored in the muscles.

ANDROSTENEDIONE. Androstenedione (or andro) enjoyed a huge burst of popularity during the late 1990s, after the MLB player Mark McGwire (1963–) shattered the single-season home run record in 1998. McGwire admittedly used andro, which was perfectly legal and within the rules of the MLB at the time. Countless younger hitters followed his lead. Whether andro really helped McGwire hit 70 home runs is not known.

Andro is a direct precursor to testosterone—meaning it turns into testosterone in the body—and is found naturally in humans. It is also found naturally in Scotch pine trees, which is why manufacturers were allowed to sell it as a dietary supplement. Andro was discovered during the 1930s, but it was not until the 1950s that scientists learned that it is a precursor to testosterone. Andro is widely believed to boost testosterone production, which in turn increases muscle mass, energy, and strength. The Mayo Clinic disputes these claims, though proponents of andro cite research supporting andro's effectiveness as a performance enhancer. The Anabolic Steroid Control Act of 2004 reclassified andro as an anabolic steroid, making it illegal for use as a performance enhancer.

Heavy use of andro can produce side effects that are similar to those associated with other anabolic steroids. In men, andro can decrease testosterone production while increasing production of the female hormone estrogen. It can also cause acne, shrinking of the testicles, and reduced sperm count. In women side effects of andro can include acne as well as the onset of masculine characteristics such as deepening of the voice and male-pattern baldness.

EPHEDRA. Ephedra is an herb that has been used in Chinese medicine for thousands of years. An American version widely used by early settlers in the Southwest was called Mormon or Squaw tea. The main chemical constituent in ephedra is ephedrine, a powerful stimulant that is similar to amphetamines. It also contains a chemical called pseudoephedrine, long used as a nasal decongestant, although it has recently come under tighter regulation because of its use in manufacturing illegal methamphetamine. Athletes primarily use ephedra as an energy booster.

Ephedra can cause elevated blood sugar levels and irregular heartbeats. It has also been linked to serious side effects such as strokes, seizures, and heart attacks. Many people have died as a direct result of its use. In February 2003 the Baltimore Orioles pitcher Steve Bechler (1979–2003) died of heatstroke after a spring training workout. Ephedra toxicity was identified as a contributing factor in his death. Bechler's death sparked renewed efforts by the U.S. Food and Drug Administration (FDA) to take action against ephedra. In December 2003 the FDA banned ephedra from being sold over the counter as a dietary supplement. However, in April 2005 a federal judge overturned the FDA's ban on procedural grounds. The Combat Methamphetamine Epidemic Act of 2005, which was signed into law in March 2006, placed strict regulations on the sale of ephedrine-containing products.

THE BALCO SCANDAL

The cat-and-mouse game of doping and detection methods has been going on among athletes and those officiating their sports since the late 1960s. A major breakthrough in the effort to detect doping came in June 2003, when the track and field coach Trevor Graham (1962?–) gave authorities a syringe containing what turned out to be tetrahydrogestrinone (THG), a previously unknown anabolic steroid. THG was considered a designer steroid, in that it was manufactured to be undetectable by the existing methods. Lab testing methods were quickly adjusted to detect THG. Investigators soon turned their attention to the Bay Area Laboratory Co-Operative (BALCO), the California-based distributor of the drug.

On September 3, 2003, agents of the Internal Revenue Service, the FDA, the San Mateo County Narcotics Task Force, and the U.S. Anti-Doping Agency raided BALCO facilities and seized containers of steroids, human growth hormone, and testosterone. Two days later officials searched the home of Greg Anderson (1964–), the personal weight trainer of the baseball star Barry Bonds (1964–), and seized more steroids, as well as documents and computer files thought to implicate a number of high-profile athletes. Over the next few months urine samples from the U.S. Track and Field Championships were retested for THG, and several came up positive. One of those athletes was Kelli White (1977–), who had won both the 100- and 200-meter world championships in 2003. White was stripped of her titles and banned from competition for two years.

Victor Conte Jr. (1951–), the BALCO founder and owner; James Valente, a BALCO executive; Anderson; and the track coach Remi Korchemny (1932–) were indicted in February 2004 for distributing steroids. In March 2005 a congressional committee held hearings on the issue of steroids in baseball. A number of legislators mocked MLB officials for the sport's weak policy and feeble efforts to deal with the problem. Many of those who testified came out looking bad, including McGwire, who was evasive when asked whether his power-hitting abilities were chemically aided. Other current and former baseball players who testified included Jose Canseco (1964–), Rafael Palmeiro (1964–), Curt Schilling (1966–), Sammy Sosa (1968–), and Frank Thomas (1968–).

In October 2005 Conte was sentenced to four months in prison and another four months of house arrest. Anderson received three months each of prison time and home confinement. Valente and Korchemny were given probation: Valente for three years and Korchemny for one year.

The BALCO scandal, however, continued to cast a shadow over the sports world. A year before he was convicted, Conte appeared on the December 3, 2004, broadcast of American Broadcasting Company's *20/20*. During his interview, Conte revealed that he had provided performance-enhancing drugs to other elite athletes, including the sprinters Tim Montgomery (1975–) and Marion Jones (1975–). As the controversy unfolded, Jones repeatedly proclaimed her innocence and eventually sued Conte for defamation of character. She settled the suit out of court in 2006; later that year she was cleared after her alternate blood sample tested negative for banned substances.

The case, however, was not over. On October 5, 2007, in the U.S. District Court for the Southern District of New York, Jones admitted to having used illegal performance-enhancing drugs during the period surrounding the 2000 Olympics in Sydney, Australia, and lying about it to two grand juries. She pleaded guilty to lying to federal agents about her use of steroids and making false statements in a check fraud case. Under pressure from the U.S. Olympic Committee, she surrendered her three gold and two bronze medals from the 2000 Olympics. She was suspended for two years from all track and field competitions, including the 2008 Summer Olympics, and was retroactively disqualified from all events dating back to September 1, 2000. Judge Kenneth Karas (1964–) of the U.S. District Court sentenced her in January 2008 to six months in prison, 200 hours of community service, and two years of probation. She began her prison sentence on March 7, 2008, and was released on September 5, 2008. Several other high-profile track and field athletes received bans in the wake of the BALCO scandal, including the sprinters White, Montgomery, and Chryste Gaines (1970–).

HEALTH RISKS OF STEROID USE

Steroid abuse has been linked to a wide range of health hazards, both physical and mental. Among the physical problems are liver and kidney tumors, high blood pressure, and elevated cholesterol levels. Some studies have associated steroid use with serious cardiovascular problems, including cardiomyopathies (inflammation of the heart muscle), irregular heart rhythm, development of embolisms (blockage of an artery by a clot or particle that is carried in the bloodstream), and heart failure. Men sometimes experience symptoms such as shrunken testicles, reduced sperm count, baldness, breast development, and increased risk of prostate cancer. Among women, growth of facial hair, male-pattern baldness, menstrual cycle disruptions, and deepening of the voice have been reported. Adolescents who use steroids run the risk of halting their growth prematurely, as their bones fuse ahead of schedule. Another problem for teenagers is that steroids cause muscles to grow, but do not strengthen the tendons that connect these muscles to bones, thereby increasing the risk of injury.

Emotional/psychological problems stemming from abuse of steroids include extreme mood swings, depression, paranoid jealousy, irritability, delusions, and impaired judgment. Sometimes these steroid-induced mood swings lead to violent behavior, a condition popularly referred to as "'roid rage."

STEROID USE AND YOUTH

Data from Lloyd D. Johnston et al.'s *Monitoring the Future, National Results on Adolescent Drug Use: Overview of Key Findings, 2010* (February 2011, http://www.monitoringthefuture.org/pubs/monographs/mtf-overview2010.pdf), an ongoing study of behavior among secondary school students, college students, and young adults, suggest that steroid use among young people peaked during the early part of the 21st century and has been tapering off since then. (See Figure 9.3.) Steroid use among teens is predominantly limited to boys. According to Johnston et al., 2.5% of 12th-grade males had used steroids in 2010, compared to only 0.3% of girls. As steroid use has declined, Johnston et al. also note a decline in the percentage of high school students who claim that the drug is "fairly easy" or "very easy" to obtain. (See Figure 9.4.) Meanwhile, as Figure 9.5 shows, the perception of risk that is associated with steroid use has increased very slightly among high school students since 2000.

PERFORMANCE-ENHANCING DRUGS IN COLLEGE SPORTS

The NCAA Committee on Competitive Safeguards and Medical Aspects of Sports regularly compiles the results of the association's drug-testing program. As of August 2011, the most recent comprehensive report appeared in *NCAA Drug-Testing Results 2004–05* (July 6, 2006, http://www.ncaa.org/). According to the NCAA, positive steroid tests among student-athletes declined steeply during the early part of the 21st century. Forty-nine student-athletes

FIGURE 9.3

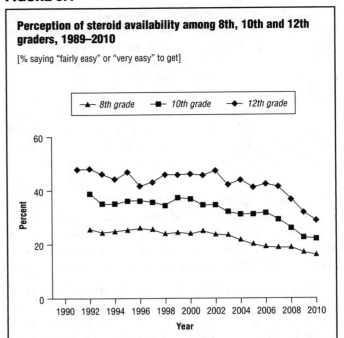

Steroid use trends among young people, 1989–2010

[Grades 8, 10, 12]

Note: Use = Used in last 12 months.

SOURCE: Adapted from Lloyd D. Johnston et al., "Steroids: Trends in Annual Use, Risk, Disapproval, and Availability, Grades 8, 10, 12—Use," in *Monitoring the Future, National Results on Adolescent Drug Use: Overview of Key Findings, 2010*, The University of Michigan, Institute for Social Research, February 2011, http://www.monitoringthefuture.org/pubs/monographs/mtf-overview2010.pdf (accessed May 31, 2011)

FIGURE 9.4

Perception of steroid availability among 8th, 10th and 12th graders, 1989–2010

[% saying "fairly easy" or "very easy" to get]

SOURCE: Adapted from Lloyd D. Johnston et al., "Steroids: Trends in Annual Use, Risk, Disapproval, and Availability, Grades 8, 10, 12—Availability," in *Monitoring the Future, National Results on Adolescent Drug Use: Overview of Key Findings, 2010*, The University of Michigan, Institute for Social Research, February 2011, http://www.monitoringthefuture.org/pubs/monographs/mtf-overview2010.pdf (accessed June 9, 2011)

FIGURE 9.5

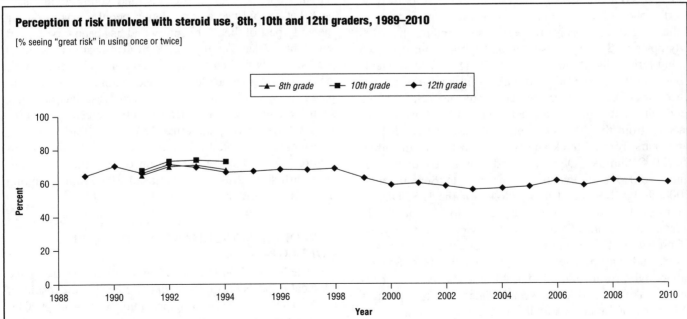

Perception of risk involved with steroid use, 8th, 10th and 12th graders, 1989–2010

[% seeing "great risk" in using once or twice]

Note: Question discontinued in 8th- and 10th-grade questionnaires in 1995.

SOURCE: Adapted from Lloyd D. Johnston et al., "Steroids: Trends in Annual Use, Risk, Disapproval, and Availability, Grades 8, 10, 12—Risk," in *Monitoring the Future, National Results on Adolescent Drug Use: Overview of Key Findings, 2010*, The University of Michigan, Institute for Social Research, February 2011, http://www.monitoringthefuture.org/pubs/monographs/mtf-overview2010.pdf (accessed June 9, 2011)

tested positive for steroids in year-round testing in 2004–05, compared to 93 positive tests in 2000–01. However, testing that was conducted in 2010 reveals that steroid use among student-athletes began to rise again toward the end of the decade. According to the NCAA, in "NCAA Drug-Testing Program Positive Results Summary, September 1, 2009–December 31, 2009 (Complete)" (November 24, 2010, http://www.ncaa.org/), 68 student-athletes tested positive for a banned substance in year-round testing during the first nine months of 2010. Of these, more than half (35) were Division I football players. The overall number of positive tests rose even higher in testing that was conducted at championships and bowl events, when 82 student-athletes tested positive for banned substances.

At the same time, the number of student-athletes testing positive for other banned substances, such as marijuana, has risen sharply. Jack Carey reports in "NCAA Drug Testing Shows Increase in Pot Use" (*USA Today*, June 22, 2011) that the number of positive tests for marijuana among NCAA athletes rose from 28 in 2008–09 to 71 in 2009–10, an increase of more than 153% in a single year.

STEROIDS IN PROFESSIONAL SPORTS

Every sport has its own way of testing for performance-enhancing drugs and its own policy for dealing with players who use them. The NFL requires its players to take year-round drug tests. The penalty for those caught using banned substances for the first time is a suspension that lasts four games, which amounts to a quarter of a season; a first offense also results in a loss of pay for missed games, as well as a prorated forfeiture of any signing bonuses. The second offense results in an eight-game suspension without pay, while a third results in a suspension of at least a year, and potentially longer, without pay. The MLB, which has the most widely publicized steroid problem among the major sports, implemented a new, much harsher drug policy in 2006. Under the new policy, an athlete's first positive test results in a 50-game suspension without pay. A second failed test brings a 100-game suspension without pay. A player who tests positive three times is banned for life. In the NBA first-time offenders are suspended for five games without pay, while second-time offenders are suspended for 10 games without pay. Three or more offenses result in a suspension of 25 games without pay. The NHL implemented random drug testing at the beginning of the 2005–06 season. According to the NHL's drug policy, a first positive drug test results in a 20-game suspension without pay, while a second offense carries a 60-game suspension without pay. A third offense results in a lifetime ban.

Football

Even though several players per year fail the NFL steroid test, there is reason to believe that many more steroid users are getting away with it. In "Steroids Prescribed to NFL Players" (February 11, 2009, http://www.cbsnews .com/stories/2005/03/29/60II/main683747.shtml), *60 Minutes Wednesday* reveals that three players on the Carolina Panthers had filled prescriptions for steroids before the 2004 Super Bowl. None of these players failed a drug test. Four years later it appeared that attempts to hide steroid use were still prevalent when Mark Maske reported in "Weight-Loss Pills Lead to Positive Banned Substances Tests in NFL" (*Washington Post*, October 25, 2008) that a "significant number" of NFL players had tested positive for the diuretic bumetanide (a drug that treats fluid retention). The drug is reportedly used to mask steroid use and is on the NFL's list of banned substances.

Over time, the NFL has begun to seek ways to test for other performance-enhancing drugs, notably human growth hormone (HGH). HGH is a protein-based hormone that occurs naturally in the body and that helps promote tissue growth. Because HGH is believed to increase muscle mass, reduce body fat, and help accelerate the healing process for injuries, it has become a popular substance among professional athletes in the 21st century. According to the article "Goodell: HGH Testing Critical to 'Credible' Drug Program" (NFL.com, June 18, 2011), in June 2011, as NFL owners and players worked to negotiate a new collective bargaining agreement, the league commissioner Roger Goodell (1959–) insisted that any deal between the two sides would need to include a comprehensive testing program for HGH. Nate Davis reports in "NFL, Players Announce New 10-Year Labor Agreement" (*USA Today*, July 25, 2011) that even though the two sides agreed to a new collective bargaining agreement in July, details surrounding HGH and other drug-testing policies would not become finalized until the player's union had officially recertified. Davis notes, however, that both players and owners seemed confident that drug testing would not become a "stumbling block" to completing the deal. In August 2011 the players agreed to allow testing for HGH.

Baseball

During the first decade of the 21st century the MLB suffered from a serious steroid-induced public relations problem. Baseball had no official steroid policy before 2002. That year, as part of the collective bargaining agreement between players and owners, a plan was put in place to hold survey testing in 2003; if more than 5% of players came up positive in anonymous tests, a formal testing policy, with accompanying penalties, would be implemented the following year. When the results of the survey showed a positive rate of between 5% and 7%, the policy development process was triggered. Beginning in 2004 every player was to be tested once per year during the season. The first time a player tested positive, he was to be placed in treatment; a second positive test would result in a 15-day suspension. A fifth positive test could result in a suspension lasting up to a year.

Under the policy, not a single player was suspended. However, it was clear that performance-enhancing drugs were still being used on a large scale, and pressure mounted to toughen the policy. The 2005 season brought a new policy in which steroids, steroid precursors (such as andro), designer steroids, masking agents, and diuretics were banned. All players would be subject to unannounced mandatory testing during the season. In addition, there would be testing of randomly selected players, with no maximum number, and random testing during the off-season. The penalties for a positive result were a 10-day suspension for the first offense, 30 days for the second, 60 days for the third, and one year for the fourth. All these suspensions were without pay. The following season the penalties were stiffened to those noted earlier.

The question of steroid use in baseball began to arise more frequently as long-standing home run records began to topple in quick succession. In 1998 McGwire and Sosa both passed the single-season home run record of 61 set by Roger Maris (1934–1985) in 1961, hitting 70 and 66, respectively. Both players were dogged by rumors that they were assisted by performance-enhancing drugs. In 2001 Bonds extended the record to 73. In 2005 Canseco published *Juiced: Wild Times, Rampant 'Roids, Smash Hits, and How Baseball Got Big*. In it, Canseco paints a lurid picture of rampant steroid use throughout the sport and names a number of players as steroid users.

Amid the furor that was created by Canseco's book, Congress convened in March 2005 a series of hearings on steroid use in baseball. Several prominent players were called to testify, including Canseco, McGwire, Palmeiro, Sosa, and Schilling. Canseco reiterated his claims before the congressional panel. McGwire was elusive, saying, "I'm not here to talk about the past," whereas Palmeiro denied all wrongdoing. Palmeiro, after testifying under oath that he had "never used steroids," tested positive for steroids in July 2005. Palmeiro was suspended for 10 games and fined $164,000.

Palmeiro was not the first high-profile baseball player to get caught using steroids. As the BALCO scandal continued to unfold, Bonds admitted during grand jury testimony in 2004 to having used steroids, though he claimed that he had done so unknowingly via an arthritis cream he thought was steroid-free. Baseball players test positive regularly, but most of them are lesser known, and their stories do not make the headlines. In 2009 it was revealed that 104 players had tested positive for performance-enhancing drugs in the league's 2003 drug testing survey, even though the 2003 tests were supposed to remain confidential. Among the elite players whose names appeared on the list were David Ortiz (1975–), Manny Ramirez (1972–), and Alex Rodriguez (1975–). Rodriguez publicly admitted having used banned drugs between 2001 and 2003, when he was playing for the Texas Rangers, but

speculation arose—notably in the 2009 book *A-Rod: The Many Lives of Alex Rodriguez* by Selena Roberts—that he used steroids as far back as high school and as recently as playing for the New York Yankees beginning in 2004. Ramirez later twice tested positive under the new testing policy, once in 2009 and a second time in 2011.

In *Game of Shadows: Barry Bonds, BALCO, and the Steroids Scandal That Rocked Professional Sports* (2006), Mark Fainaru-Wada and Lance Williams outlined a series of damaging accusations that were associated with the BALCO affair. Fainaru-Wada and Williams focused most of their attention on Bonds, but they also implicated several other athletes, including Jones and Montgomery. Shortly after the book came out, it was announced that Bud Selig (1934–), the baseball commissioner, had engaged the former U.S. senator George J. Mitchell (1933–) to head an independent investigation into steroid use in baseball, in an effort to stave off further intervention by Congress. As Bonds was surpassing Hank Aaron's (1934–) all-time home run record during the summer of 2007, a feat he accomplished on August 7, Mitchell announced that his investigation was in its final phase. Released at the end of 2007, the report (*Report to the Commissioner of Baseball of an Independent Investigation into the Illegal Use of Steroids and Other Performance Enhancing Substances by Players in Major League Baseball*, December 13, 2007, http://files .mlb.com/mitchrpt.pdf) documented the widespread use of steroids in baseball beginning in the 1980s, which involved players on every team. Mitchell noted that honest athletes were placed at a disadvantage in competing with those who were on steroids and that many records from the period could be invalid.

Mitchell recommended that the MLB create a Department of Investigations, work more closely with law enforcement authorities, establish an education program to explain the health risks of steroids and how to achieve some of the same results through training and nutrition, and institute mandatory, unannounced drug testing. Mitchell caused a furor by naming many players who were reported to have used performance-enhancing drugs, as well as by suggesting that these players should not be punished. "I urge the Commissioner to forgo imposing discipline on players for past violations of baseball's rules on performance enhancing substances, including the players named in this report, except in those cases where he determines that the conduct is so serious that discipline is necessary to maintain the integrity of the game." In the aftermath of Mitchell's findings, the link between steroids and professional baseball had become firmly entrenched in the public's mind. Indeed, by 2011 ESPN (May 20, 2011, http://espn.go.com/mlb/ topics/_/page/the-steroids-era) was referring to the period from the 1980s through the first decade of the 21st century as the "steroids era" of the MLB.

Steroid use in baseball appears to be particularly widespread among players from Latin American countries. Joseph Contreras notes in "Too Intense?" (*Newsweek*, May 27, 2006) that a majority of players who tested positive during the MLB's first year of mandatory testing were from Latin America. Contreras quotes some insiders as pointing to the increased pressure on young players from poor countries to do well, because baseball presents one of the few potential paths out of poverty for these individuals. In "Caught Looking" (ESPN, April 15, 2009), Ian Gordon points to a language barrier as part of the problem, suggesting that some Spanish-speaking players may not be getting the message about banned substances in spite of the league's best outreach efforts. Players from the Dominican Republic appear to be particularly susceptible to the lure of performance-enhancing drugs. Mike Fish indicates in "Steroid Problem Reaches Critical Mass in the D.R." (ESPN, March 2, 2009) that according to MLB data, more than half of the major and minor league baseball players who tested positive between 2005 and 2009 hailed from that country.

Basketball

Rookie NBA players are tested up to four times per season, and veterans are subject to one random test during training camp. Prohibited substances include amphetamines, cocaine, opiates, marijuana, and steroids. Penalties range from suspensions for a number of games to a lifetime ban. As of August 2011, basketball had largely avoided the kind of scandals involving performance-enhancing drugs that plagued the baseball world.

Hockey

In the wake of the drug scandals that dogged the other major leagues, the NHL unveiled its first antidoping policy in September 2005, at a congressional hearing on drug use in professional sports. Under the new policy, NHL players are subject to a maximum of two random tests with no advance notice during the NHL season for the performance-enhancing drugs that are designated on the World Anti-Doping Agency's (WADA) "Prohibited List" (2011, http://www.wada-ama.org/en/World-Anti-Doping-Program/ Sports-and-Anti-Doping-Organizations/International-Standards/ Prohibited-List/). A first-time positive test results in a 20-game suspension. The ban increases to 60 games for a second offense and a third positive test can result in permanent suspension.

Cycling

Perhaps no other sport has been tainted by doping scandals more than professional bicycle racing, particularly the sport's most illustrious event, the Tour de France. The first major drug scandal in cycling took place in 1998, when the Festina cycling team was thrown out of the competition after the team masseur, Willy Voet (1945–), was caught in possession of several banned substances, including EPO, growth hormones, testosterone, and amphetamines. In 2004 David Millar (1977–), a time-trial world champion, was banned from the tour following the discovery of banned drugs at the offices of his cycling team, Cofidis. Doping allegations have plagued the career of the American cyclist Lance Armstrong (1971–), who won his seventh consecutive Tour de France in 2005. In 2002 Armstrong was linked to the sports physician Michele Ferrari (1953–), who was reputed to have developed a system for taking EPO without detection. In 2005 EPO was found in Armstrong's old laboratory samples from the 1999 Tour de France. Armstrong vehemently denied ever using banned drugs. In 2006 investigators cleared him of all charges, while criticizing antidoping authorities for mishandling evidence.

Armstrong's exoneration notwithstanding, the situation only became worse for the Tour de France. On the eve of the 2006 race, several top riders, including the contenders Jan Ullrich (1973–) and Ivan Basso (1977–), were banned from competing as a result of accusations made by Spanish police after a long investigation called Operacion Puerto. The 2006 Tour was won by the American cyclist Floyd Landis (1975–). However, shortly after the conclusion of the race, it was revealed that Landis had failed a drug test at the 17th stage of the tour, with tests showing an abnormally high level of testosterone in his blood. Landis maintained his innocence, but he was nevertheless stripped of his title and fired from his racing team. He appealed the decision to strip his title, but the appeal was denied.

The doping situation for the Tour de France continued its downward spiral in 2007. Several prominent riders either tested positive for banned substances before or during the race, or were punished for avoiding testing. They included the German cyclist Patrik Sinkewitz (1980–), who tested positive at a pre-tour training camp; Alexander Vinokourov (1973–) of Russia, who was pulled after the 15th stage for receiving an illicit blood transfusion; and the Danish racer Michael Rasmussen (1974–), who was ejected from the tour for intentionally avoiding a required blood test. The 2008 and 2009 Tours were relatively free of doping controversy, even though Alberto Contador (1982–), the winner in 2007 and 2009, remained the subject of ongoing doping rumors. Meanwhile, a new investigation alleging Armstrong's involvement in an international doping ring surfaced in 2011, once again calling his record-setting run of tour victories into question.

STEROIDS AND THE LAW

Anabolic steroids are Schedule III–controlled substances in the United States. In October 2004 the federal Anabolic Steroid Control Act was signed into law. The act updated the Anabolic Steroid Control Act of 1990 in a number of ways. It amended the definition of anabolic steroids by adding THG, andro, and certain related chemicals to the list of substances that the law covered. The act also directed the U.S. Sentencing Commission to review federal sentencing guidelines for offenses related to steroids and provided for increased penalties for committing these offenses. It authorized the U.S. attorney general to exempt from regulation steroid-containing drugs that do not pose a drug abuse threat. Finally, the law directed the U.S. secretary of health and human services to provide grants for the development of science-based educational programs for elementary and secondary schools on the hazards of anabolic steroid use. A number of states have passed their own laws that are aimed at curbing steroid use among youths.

Antidoping Agencies

By the end of the 20th century the global sports community recognized that it would take a coordinated international effort to bring the problem of performance-enhancing drugs under control. WADA was created in 1999 as a collaborative initiative between sports agencies and governments across the globe. WADA's role is to lead international efforts against doping in sports through public education, advocacy, research, and drug testing and to provide leadership for the efforts of agencies working against doping in individual countries. The U.S. Anti-Doping Agency, an independent nonprofit organization, was launched in October 2000 to lead this work at the national level.

CHAPTER 10
SPORTS AND GAMBLING

The drive in humans to gamble on sports seems to be almost as strong as the drive to participate in them. People have been betting on the outcome of sporting events since ancient times. In ancient Rome the wealthy class wagered on chariot races, animal fights, and gladiator battles. The Romans spread their penchant for gambling across the breadth of their empire, including Britain. During the 16th and 17th centuries people throughout Europe enjoyed betting on cockfights, wrestling, and footraces. During the 18th century horse racing and boxing rose to prominence as spectator sports on which the public enjoyed gambling. The 19th and 20th centuries brought a new emphasis on team sports, and Europeans began risking their wages on rugby, soccer, and cricket games.

Colonists brought their yen for gambling on sports with them to North America. Horse racing was a particularly popular sport among those inclined toward gambling. Most forms of gambling, including sports gambling, became illegal in the United States during the 19th century. Nevertheless, it remained legal to bet on horse racing, and other sports gambling continued to flourish underground. The state of Nevada legalized gambling in 1931, although it eventually became so tainted by organized crime and other scandals that during the 1950s it became the subject of government crackdowns. A new, tightly regulated version of sports betting returned to Nevada in 1975, and continues to thrive in the 21st century.

Modern sports gambling in the United States can be roughly divided into three categories: pari-mutuel gambling on horse racing, greyhound racing, and jai alai games; legal sports betting through a licensed bookmaker; and illegal sports gambling. The third category makes up the biggest portion of sports gambling in the nation.

PARI-MUTUEL GAMBLING

Pari-mutuel betting was invented in late 19th-century France by Pierre Oller. *Pari-mutuel* is a French term that means "mutual stake." In this kind of betting all the money bet on an event is combined into a single pool, which is then split among the winning bettors, with management taking some share, called a takeout, off the top. The takeout rate, which in the United States is set by state law, is usually about 20% of the total betting pool. Unlike many other forms of sports wagering, an individual betting on a pari-mutuel event is betting against other gamblers rather than against the house. The house keeps the same percentage of the total bets regardless of the outcome of the event. Another source of revenue from pari-mutuel betting is breakage. Winning bettors are not usually paid out to the exact penny; rather, payouts are rounded down. The leftover money, or breakage, is usually only a few cents per bet, but it adds up to a substantial sum over the course of thousands of transactions. Breakage may be split in various ways. For example, breakage generated by California horse tracks is split among the state, the track operators, and the horse owners.

In pari-mutuel betting the total pool in a race depends on how much is bet on that race. Every bet that is placed on a particular horse or player affects the odds; as a result, the more people who bet on a particular outcome, the lower the payout is for those who bet on that outcome. Betting on a long shot offers a lower likelihood of winning, but a potentially larger payout.

The pari-mutuel system has been used in horse racing since about 1875, but it did not become widespread until the 1920s and 1930s, with the introduction of the totalizor, a special calculator that could automatically calculate the odds for each horse in a race based on the bets that had been placed. Before the 1930s most betting on horse races was done through bookmakers. In 1933 California, Michigan, Ohio, and New Hampshire legalized pari-mutuel gambling on horse racing mainly as a way to regulate the industry, decrease corruption, and generate revenue for the state. Many other states followed their lead over the next several years.

Historically, most pari-mutuel betting has taken place in person at the location where the event is happening. However, in recent years bets have been placed at off-track betting facilities, which were first approved by the New York legislature in 1970. Wagering via telephone or the Internet is also available in some states. Many races are simulcast (short for "simultaneous broadcast,' programs that are broadcast across more than one medium, or more than one service on the same medium, at the same time) to in-state and out-of-state locations, including off-track betting sites. This allows bettors to engage in intertrack wagering, which means one can bet on a race at one track while watching live races at another.

An increasing share of pari-mutuel wagering has been taking place at racinos. Racinos, a growing phenomenon in the gaming industry, are horse or greyhound racetracks that also offer casino gaming on site. According to the article "Racinos' Revenue" (*Arizona Republic* [Phoenix, AZ], January 19, 2011), as of January 2011 there were 44 racinos in 12 states. Taken together, these racinos generate more than $2.6 billion in tax revenues per year.

Thoroughbred Horse Racing

People have been betting on horse races for thousands of years. Horse racing was a popular spectator sport among wealthy Greeks and Romans. Later, knights returning to western Europe from the Crusades brought with them speedy Arabian stallions, which were bred with English mares to create the line now called Thoroughbred. Thoroughbreds are fast, graceful runners and are identified by their height and long, slim legs. Thoroughbred racing quickly caught on among the British aristocracy, and it was soon dubbed the "Sport of Kings." The sport came to North America with the colonists; there are records of horse racing taking place in the New York area as early as 1665.

Thoroughbred racing remained popular in the United States throughout the 18th and 19th centuries. The sport was scaled back significantly during World War II (1939–1945), and after the war it remained in steep decline. However, even though attendance at horse races has decreased substantially, the money continues to flow and has actually increased since the 1990s. Gary Rotstein reports in "How Slot Machines Have Saved Racetracks" (*Pittsburgh [PA] Post-Gazette*, February 25, 2007) that in 1990 the total amount bet (handle) on Thoroughbred races in the United States was $9.4 billion. In "Pari-Mutuels as a Source for Purses Trending Down" (May 27, 2010, http://www.tra-online.com/press.html), the Thoroughbred Racing Associations indicates that the annual handle for Thoroughbred racing peaked at $15.2 billion in 2003, before shrinking back to $12.3 billion in 2009.

The National Thoroughbred Racing Association (2011, http://www.ntra.com/) indicates that in 2011 there

were 39 major Thoroughbred racetracks in the United States and Canada. The racetracks that are located in the warm parts of the country are open throughout the year, whereas others are active only during those locations' warm months. Some are government owned, whereas others are privately held. The Thoroughbred gambling business is dominated by a handful of companies, the largest being two publicly traded firms: Churchill Downs and Magna Entertainment.

The three most prestigious Thoroughbred races together make up the Triple Crown of horse racing. These races, which take place over a five-week period during May and June each year, are the Kentucky Derby at Churchill Downs in Louisville, Kentucky; the Preakness Stakes at Pimlico in Baltimore, Maryland; and the Belmont Stakes at Belmont Park in Elmont, New York. According to the article "Kentucky Derby 137 Breaks Long-Time Attendance Record as 164,858 Watch Animal Kingdom Rule the 'Run for the Roses'" (Globe-Newswire, May 7, 2011), a record crowd of 164,858 spectators watched Animal Kingdom win the 137th annual Kentucky Derby in 2011. Globally, gamblers wagered a total of $165.2 million on the race, an increase of 1.5% over the $162.7 million that was wagered in 2010, and the third-highest amount all time. On-track betting for the 2011 derby topped $11.5 million, which was 4.2% higher than the 2010 total of $11.1 million. Stephen Whyno reports in "Partyers Reach Finish Line Unscathed" (*Washington Times*, May 23, 2011) that overall betting for the 2011 Preakness was $76.4 million, the seventh highest in race history. According to Kevin Van Valkenburg, in "Notebook: Monzon's Run to Ninth Was Memorable" (*Baltimore Sun*, June 11, 2011), betting at the 2011 Belmont Stakes was significantly lower. For the day, the total on-track handle, including bets that were placed via simulcast, came to roughly $11.6 million.

Non-Thoroughbred Horse Racing

Even though Thoroughbreds dominate the horse racing scene in the United States, pari-mutuel gambling is available for other types of horses as well. Harness racing, in which horses trot or pace rather than gallop and pull the jockey in a two-wheeled cart called a sulky, uses a horse called a Standardbred, which is typically shorter and more muscular than a Thoroughbred. The U.S. Trotting Association (USTA) notes in *Tracks* (March 2011, http://www.ustrotting.com/trackside/tpg/pdf/T&PGuide 2011_Tracks_6-62.pdf) that in 2010 there were 37 pari-mutuel USTA tracks in the United States, in addition to another 207 USTA-sanctioned "Fair Tracks." Another type of horse commonly raced is the quarter horse, which gets its name from the fact that it excels at sprinting distances under a quarter of a mile. Finally, the Arabian Jockey Club (2011, http://www.arabianracing.org/) is the governing body for races that feature Arabian horses, the only true purebred horses on the circuit, throughout the United States and Canada.

Greyhound Racing

Like horses, greyhounds have been raced for amusement and gambling purposes for centuries. Greyhound racing has been called the "Sport of Queens," probably because it was Queen Elizabeth I (1533–1603) of England who first standardized the rules for greyhound coursing (a sport in which greyhounds are used to hunt rabbits) during the 16th century. Greyhound racing was brought to the United States during the late 19th century, and the first circular greyhound track was opened in California in 1919.

According to the Greyhound Racing Association of America (GRA-America), in "The Most Exciting Dogs in the World" (2011, http://www.gra-america.org/the _sport/history.html), the sport reached its peak of popularity in 1992, when nearly 3.5 million people attended the 16,827 races that took place at more than 50 tracks. Nearly $3.5 billion was bet on greyhound races that year. Since then, revenue has dropped by more than 50%, as a number of states began to ban greyhound racing amid allegations that the dogs were routinely mistreated. The GRA-America indicates in "Racing in America" (2011, http://www.gra-america.org/the_sport/tracks.php) that in 2011 there were 40 greyhound tracks operating in 12 states, with gamblers betting roughly $2 billion annually on races.

Jai Alai

Jai alai is played on a court and involves bouncing a ball against a wall. In jai alai the ball is caught using a long, curved basket called a cesta, while a jai alai court is called a fronton. According to the National Jai-Alai Association (NJAA), in "History of Jai-Alai" (2011, http://www.national-jai-alai.com/history_of_jai-alai/index.php), professional jai alai in the United States originated in Miami, Florida, in 1926. After peaking during the 1970s and 1980s, jai alai slipped into a precipitous decline. Hal Habib reports in "Jai-Alai, a Sport with a South Florida Flair" (*Palm Beach [FL] Post*, May 30, 2009) that $68.7 million was bet on jai alai during fiscal year 2007–08; 20 years earlier this figure was $430.3 million. In the United States jai alai is confined almost entirely to Florida, where the sport retains a sizable, if shrinking, following. Most of the frontons in Florida, however, rely on revenue from other forms of gambling, such as poker, to stay in business.

LEGAL SPORTS GAMBLING

As of 2011 unlimited gambling on multiple sports was legal in only one state: Nevada. In Nevada legal sports gambling takes place through licensed establishments (books) that accept and pay out bets on sporting events. Sports books are legal only in Nevada. Betting on sports such as professional football, basketball, or baseball is prohibited elsewhere in the United States, although Delaware, Oregon, and Montana allow limited forms of sports gambling. These limitations were reinforced with the passage of the Professional and Amateur Sports Protection Act of 1992.

In May 2009 the Delaware legislature voted to legalize certain kinds of betting on various big-time sports. The four major professional sports leagues, as well as the National Collegiate Athletic Association (NCAA), filed a lawsuit against Delaware, claiming the state was in violation of the 1992 ban because it had not previously allowed that specific type of wagering. A federal court of appeals eventually ruled that sports betting in Delaware would be limited to parlay wagers—where the bettor must choose the winners of at least three separate games in one bet—on professional football games. In 2010 the New Jersey state senate's Economic Growth Committee approved a measure to amend the state constitution to legalize sports wagering. In "State Senate Committee Approves Sports Betting in N.J." (NewJersey NewsRoom.com, November 22, 2010), Tom Hester Sr. reports that the amendment would be subject to approval by New Jersey voters. At the same time, New Jersey state Senator Raymond J. Lesniak (1946–) filed a lawsuit in federal court questioning the constitutionality of the federal ban on sports betting. Hester notes in "N.J. Sports Betting Lawsuit Dismissed" (NewJerseyNews Room .com, March 8, 2011) that the lawsuit was dismissed by a U.S. District Court judge, who stated that the referendum would first need to go before New Jersey voters. The referendum was scheduled to appear on the November 2011 ballot.

Bookmaking

Bookmaking is the term that is used for determining gambling odds and handling bets and payouts. The person doing the bookmaking is called a bookmaker or bookie. Bookmakers make their money by charging a commission on each bet; the commission is usually between 4% and 5%.

Most sports bets are based on a point spread, which is set by the bookmaker. A point spread is how much a favored team must win a game by for those betting on that team to collect. For example, if Team A is a 10-point favorite to defeat Team B, the bettor is actually betting on whether Team A will beat Team B by at least this margin. If Team A wins by nine points, then those betting on Team B are the winners and those picking team A are the losers. In this example, Team B has lost the game, but has "beat the spread." The point spread concept was introduced during the 1940s by the bookmaker Charles K. McNeil (1903–1981) as a way of encouraging people to bet on underdogs. Before the point spread system, bookmakers risked losing large sums on lopsided games in which everybody bet on the favorite to win.

Nevada: The Gambling Capital of the United States

Nevada legalized gambling in the 1930s as a way of generating revenue during the Great Depression (1929–1939). The state's legislature made off-track betting on horses legal during the 1940s. Betting on sports and horse racing was popular in Nevada's casinos throughout that decade. At the beginning of the 1950s, however, the Nevada gambling world came under the scrutiny of Congress for its ties to organized crime. Senator Estes Kefauver (1903–1963; D-TN) initiated hearings to investigate the matter. These nationally televised hearings drew attention to a culture of corruption and gangland activity that had settled in Las Vegas. The hearings resulted in the imposition of a 10% federal excise tax on sports betting. This tax effectively strangled casino-based sports bookmaking in Nevada.

In 1974 the federal excise tax on sports betting was reduced to 2%; by 1983 it had been reduced to 0.3%. Koleman S. Strumpf of the University of North Carolina, Chapel Hill, indicates in *Illegal Sports Bookmakers* (February 2003, http://www.unc.edu/~cigar/papers/Bookie4b .pdf) that by the 1980s sports and race bookmaking was again a booming industry. Between 1982 and 1987 Nevada sports book betting increased by 230%. Bookmakers

such as Jimmy Snyder (1919–1996) became national celebrities by appearing regularly on television. Even though the total amounts wagered on sports betting dropped slightly in 2008 and 2009, the betting volume grew in 2010. (See Table 10.1.)

Football is the biggest betting draw among the major sports. As Table 10.2 shows, gamblers wagered nearly $1.2 billion on football games in 2010, compared to $831.2 million on basketball and $529 million on baseball. The Super Bowl alone is a gigantic gambling event. Super Bowl betting peaked in 2006, when a total of $94.5 million was wagered on the title game between the Pittsburgh Steelers and the Seattle Seahawks. (See Table 10.3.) Even though Super Bowl betting dropped sharply over the next few years, it began to increase again toward the end of the decade, climbing from $81.5 million in 2009 to $87.5 million in 2011.

ATTITUDES TOWARD SPORTS GAMBLING

On the whole, a relatively small percentage of the American public engages in sports betting. In *U.S. Public: Keep Las Vegas in Las Vegas* (March 11, 2010, http://publicmind.fdu.edu/casino/final.pdf), Fairleigh Dickinson University notes that its PublicMind Poll found that in 2010 only one out of five (20%) people surveyed had participated in an office betting pool to wager on sporting events. (See Table 10.4.) Men (24%) were far more likely than women

TABLE 10.1

Percentage growth in amount wagered, amount won, and win percentage, by sport, 2005–10

	2005	2006	2007	2008	2009	2010
Total sports pool						
Drop*	8.19%	7.61%	6.91%	−0.72%	−0.99%	8.21%
Win	12.09%	51.80%	−12.08%	−18.98%	−0.05%	10.79%
Win %	0.19%	2.30%	−1.40%	−1.19%	0.05%	0.13%
Football						
Drop*	8.36%	8.19%	3.56%	−4.80%	−2.41%	8.52%
Win	−13.65%	125.78%	−19.32%	−46.80%	24.39%	15.95%
Win%	−0.98%	4.18%	−1.77%	−2.76%	0.96%	0.30%
Basketball						
Drop*	6.67%	9.60%	8.19%	7.58%	8.63%	3.51%
Win	25.89%	20.43%	−18.92%	16.52%	−12.35%	2.91%
Win%	1.01%	0.65%	−1.82%	0.45%	−1.14%	−0.03%
Baseball						
Drop*	8.76%	−1.32%	15.59%	−1.34%	−9.95%	12.49%
Win	187.62%	−15.24%	14.62%	−7.04%	−9.29%	5.72%
Win %	3.50%	−0.79%	−0.04%	−0.28%	0.03%	−0.27%
Sports parlay						
Drop*	4.90%	8.58%	0.53%	−5.66%	−8.90%	−3.86%
Win	−21.65%	34.93%	−3.81%	−0.10%	−5.20%	−1.11%
Win %	−8.43%	6.03%	−1.33%	1.74%	1.27%	0.93%
Other sports pool						
Drop*	15.39%	30.82%	2.82%	−2.42%	−3.58%	25.03%
Win	−9.82%	92.62%	7.10%	−16.46%	−9.85%	54.54%
Win %	−1.59%	2.69%	0.35%	−1.25%	−0.49%	1.65%

*"Drop" refers to total money wagered.

SOURCE: "Table 2. Growth in Total Drop, Win, and Win%, by Type of Sports Pool," State of Nevada Gaming Control Board, 2011

TABLE 10.2

Amounts wagered and won on sports betting, with win percentage, by sport, 2005–10

	2005	2006	2007	2008	2009	2010
Total sports pool						
Drop*	2,256,439,996	2,428,220,051	2,596,104,723	2,577,506,769	2,551,938,106	2,761,382,680
Win	126,176,134	191,538,121	168,405,563	136,440,850	136,379,044	151,096,448
Win %	5.59%	7.89%	6.49%	5.29%	5.34%	5.47%
Football						
Drop*	1,049,835,382	1,135,808,903	1,176,259,413	1,119,822,033	1,092,848,755	1,185,947,696
Win	40,365,710	91,138,501	73,531,702	39,122,160	48,665,088	56,427,684
Win %	3.84%	8.02%	6.25%	3.49%	4.45%	4.76%
Basketball						
Drop*	579,531,095	635,186,480	687,190,254	739,244,997	803,067,804	831,240,858
Win	38,356,303	46,190,701	37,452,046	43,638,916	38,247,923	39,361,750
Win %	6.62%	7.27%	5.45%	5.90%	4.76%	4.74%
Baseball						
Drop*	463,993,512	457,870,371	529,246,155	522,179,222	470,238,543	528,953,126
Win	26,127,436	22,145,098	25,382,354	23,594,982	21,402,302	22,626,664
Win %	5.63%	4.84%	4.80%	4.52%	4.55%	4.28%
Sports parlay						
Drop*	62,871,466	68,263,935	68,625,700	64,738,954	58,975,130	56,698,552
Win	15,627,795	21,086,902	20,282,942	20,263,176	19,209,513	18,996,725
Win %	24.86%	30.89%	29.56%	31.30%	32.57%	33.50%
Other sports pool						
Drop*	100,208,541	131,090,362	134,783,201	131,521,563	126,807,874	158,542,448
Win	5,698,890	10,976,919	11,756,519	9,821,616	8,854,219	13,683,625
Win %	5.69%	8.37%	8.72%	7.47%	6.98%	8.63%

*"Drop" refers to total money wagered.

SOURCE: "Table 1. Total Drop, Win, and Win% by Sports Pool," State of Nevada Gaming Control Board, 2011

TABLE 10.3

Super Bowl betting history, 2002–11

Year	Wagers	Win/(Loss)	Win%	Game results
2011	$87,491,098	$724,176	0.83%	Green Bay 31, Pittsburgh 25
2010	$82,726,367	$6,857,101	8.30%	New Orleans 31, Indianapolis 17
2009	$81,514,748	$6,678,044	8.20%	Pittsburgh 27, Arizona 23
2008	$92,055,833	$(2,573,103)	−2.80%	N.Y. Giants 17, New England 14
2007	$93,067,358	$12,930,175	13.90%	Indianapolis 29, Chicago 17
2006	$94,534,372	$8,828,431	9.30%	Pittsburgh 21, Seattle 10
2005	$90,759,236	$15,430,138	17.00%	New England 24, Philadelphia 21
2004	$81,242,191	$12,440,698	15.30%	New England 32, Carolina 29
2003	$71,693,032	$5,264,963	7.30%	Tampa Bay 48, Oakland 21
2002	$71,513,304	$2,331,607	3.30%	New England 20, St. Louis 17

SOURCE: Adapted from "Summary of Nevada Sports Book Performance for the Last Ten Super Bowls," State of Nevada Gaming Control Board, February 8, 2011

(14%) to place bets in an office sports pool. At the same time, 53% of Americans opposed making sports betting legal outside of Nevada in 2010. (See Table 10.5.) Even though 57% of people between the ages of 18 and 29 years support the idea of legalizing sports gambling nationwide, this percentage dropped steadily among older Americans.

The potential for government revenue generated by legal sports gambling is the strongest argument for proponents of legalizing betting on professional and college sports in states where it is currently banned. Ari Weinberg estimates in "The Case for Legal Sports Gambling" (*Forbes*, January 27, 2003) that the 1992 law that locks

all states except Nevada out of the sports gambling market deprives other states of taxes on perhaps hundreds of billions of dollars in illegal sports bets each year.

ILLEGAL SPORTS GAMBLING

Even though legal sports betting is a multibillion dollar industry in the United States, the amount of money involved is dwarfed by the sums that are wagered illegally each year. The American Gaming Association (AGA) reveals in the fact sheet "Sports Wagering" (2011, http://www.americangaming.org/industry-resources/research/fact-sheets/sports-wagering) that a total of $2.8 billion in sports

TABLE 10.4

Participation in office sports betting pools, by gender, political orientation, and age, 2010

QUESTION: IN THE PAST 12 MONTHS HAS ANYONE IN YOUR HOUSEHOLD PARTICIPATED IN AN OFFICE BETTING POOL SUCH AS FOR THE WORLD SERIES, THE SUPERBOWL OR ANOTHER GAME?

| | All | Men | Women | Ideology | | | Age | | | |
				Liberal	Moderate	Conservative	18–29	30–44	45–59	60+
Yes, total	**20%**	**24**	**14**	**21**	**23**	**17**	**11**	**26**	**24**	**12**
Yes, respondent	11%	17	5	11	11	11	4	17	13	6
Yes, household	6%	4	7	8	8	4	7	6	7	4
Yes, both	3%	3	2	2	4	2	0	3	4	2
No	80%	75	84	78	76	83	87	73	74	87
DK	1%	1	1	1	1	1	2	2	1	1

DK = Don't know.

SOURCE: Adapted from "Question: G8. In the past 12 months has in your household participated in an office betting pool such as for the World Series, the Superbowl or another game?" in *U.S. Public: Keep Las Vegas in Las Vegas*, Farleigh Dickinson University's PublicMind Poll, March 11, 2010, http://publicmind.fdu.edu/casino/final.pdf (accessed June 9, 2011).

TABLE 10.5

Attitudes toward legalizing sports betting, by gender, political orientation, and age, 2010

QUESTION: CURRENTLY, BETTING ON SPORTS—LIKE FOOTBALL GAMES AND BASKETBALL GAMES—IS LEGAL ONLY IN LAS VEGAS AND ON A LIMITED BASIS IN DELAWARE. DO YOU SUPPORT OR OPPOSE CHANGING THE LAW TO ALLOW PEOPLE TO PLACE BETS ON SPORTS IN ALL STATES?

| | All | Men | Women | Ideology | | | Age | | | |
				Liberal	Moderate	Conservative	18–29	30–44	45–59	60+
Support	39%	45	34	44	44	46	57	40	39	27
Oppose	53%	50	55	49	47	66	37	53	52	63
D/K	8%	6	11	8	8	6	6	6	9	10

D/K = Don't know.

SOURCE: "Question: G3. Currently, betting on sports—like football games and basketball games—is legal only in Las Vegas and on a limited basis in Delaware. Do you support or oppose changing the law to allow people to place bets on sports in all states?" in *U.S. Public: Keep Las Vegas in Las Vegas*, Farleigh Dickinson University's PublicMind Poll, March 11, 2010, http://publicmind.fdu.edu/casino/final.pdf (accessed June 9, 2011).

wagers were placed legally in Nevada in 2010. According to estimates provided by the National Gambling Impact Study Commission, the amount spent on illegal sports betting comes to approximately $380 billion per year. Nevertheless, data concerning illegal sports wagering can vary widely. For example, the AGA notes that according to Federal Bureau of Investigation estimates, roughly $2.5 billion in illegal wagers are placed on the March Madness NCAA basketball tournament each year. In "Top Sports for Illegal Wagering" (2011, http://www.cnbc.com/id/34312813/Top_Sports_for_Illegal_Wagers), CNBC estimates that this amount is actually substantially higher, and ranges from $6 billion to $12 billion annually. (See Table 10.6.)

FIXING, SHAVING, AND TAMPERING: SPORTS GAMBLING SCANDALS

In the 21st century a large portion of illegal sports gambling is still believed to be controlled by organized crime. Shady characters, including prominent organized crime figures, have always gravitated toward sports, sometimes as a means of laundering money obtained illicitly in other business activities. The history of sports

TABLE 10.6

Illegal betting, by sport and sporting event

Sport	Amount wagered illegally, per year
National Football League (NFL)	$80–$100 billion
Super Bowl	$6–10 billion
College football	$60–$70 billion
College basketball	$50 billion
National Collegiate Athletic Association (NCAA) basketball tournament (March Madness)	$6–12 billion
National Basketball Association (NBA)	$35–40 billion
Major League Baseball (MLB)	$30–40 billion
Hockey, golf, National Association for Stock Car Auto Racing (NASCAR), other sports	$1–3 billion

SOURCE: Adapted from "Top Sports for Illegal Wagering," CNBC, 2011, http://www.cnbc.com/id/34312813/Top Sports for Illegal Wagers (accessed July 18, 2011)

is rife with tales of gamblers paying off athletes to "take a dive" or miss the crucial shot. Major professional sports leagues and the NCAA have taken measures to distance themselves from sports gambling, but their efforts have not prevented a long list of sports gambling scandals from taking place in the last several decades.

Perhaps the most notorious sports gambling scandal in history was the so-called Black Sox Scandal of 1919, in which gamblers bribed several members of the Chicago White Sox to intentionally throw the World Series. A huge point-shaving scandal encompassing seven schools and 32 players rocked college basketball in 1951. Point shaving is a type of game fixing in which players, who are usually bribed by gamblers, conspire to avoid beating a published point spread. In 1978 associates of the Lucchese organized crime family orchestrated a point-shaving scheme with key members of the Boston College basketball team. Another point-shaving scheme involving college basketball was uncovered at Arizona State University in 1994.

Many high-profile professional athletes have gotten in trouble over the years for gambling on the sport in which they participate, which inevitably creates suspicion about game fixing. In 1963 the National Football League (NFL) players Alexander R. Karras (1935–) of the Detroit Lions and Paul Hornung (1935–) of the Green Bay Packers were suspended for betting on their own teams' games. Denny McLain (1944–) of the Detroit Tigers, the last pitcher to win 30 or more games in a season, was suspended for most of the 1970 season for associating with gamblers. In 1989 the baseball player Pete Rose (1941–), who holds the record for the most career hits, was kicked out of baseball for gambling on Major League Baseball games. He denied doing so at the time but has since admitted to betting on baseball games while serving as manager of the Cincinnati Reds. Rose's lifetime suspension has kept him out of the Baseball Hall of Fame.

The National Basketball Association (NBA) was rocked during the summer of 2007 by revelations that the veteran referee Tim Donaghy (1967–) had been involved in gambling on NBA games, including games in which he had officiated. The NBA immediately took the position that Donaghy's activities represented an isolated case and that gambling among referees was extremely rare. In August 2007 Donaghy pleaded guilty to two felony charges that he had provided betting recommendations to gamblers based on inside information about games.

Since the 1990s college sports have been at the center of some of the most visible gambling scandals. During the 1994–95 season two Northwestern University basketball players were caught shaving points. Two years later, 13 football players at Boston College were suspended for gambling on college football games. Other cases have involved the University of Florida basketball player Teddy Dupay (1979–), the Florida State University quar-

terback Adrian McPherson (1983–), and the University of Michigan basketball player Chris Webber (1973–).

After decades of seeking to avoid the appearance of impropriety by distancing themselves from gambling entirely, people associated with the major sports leagues have recently established cozier relationships with the gambling industry. A prime example are the Maloof brothers—Joseph (1955–), Gavin (1956–), and George Jr. (1964–)—who together own both the NBA's Sacramento Kings and the Palms Casino in Las Vegas. When the Maloofs sought to buy the Kings in 1998, the NBA was willing to give its blessing provided the Maloofs stopped accepting bets on NBA games in their casino's legal bookmaking operation. In 2005 and 2006 the National Hockey League's Pittsburgh Penguins attempted to obtain a license for a slot machine casino to raise funds for a new arena. In December 2006 the Pennsylvania gaming board awarded the only available license to another group, which included the Pittsburgh Steelers running back Jerome Bettis (1972–). Bettis's participation in a proposal to open a horse track/casino/hotel complex raised some concern around the NFL, but not as much as might have been raised a few years earlier. Of course, Bettis had a good role model: the Rooney family, the owners of the Steelers, also own two horse racing facilities.

GAMBLING IN COLLEGE SPORTS

Gambling on sports has become increasingly common among college athletes, even though it represents a direct violation of NCAA rules regarding sports wagering. The NCAA notes in *Results from the 2008 NCAA Study on Collegiate Wagering* (November 13, 2009, http://www .ncaa.org/) that 29.5% of male college athletes wagered on sporting events in 2008, compared to 23.5% who did so in 2004. The highest proportion of sports gambling occurred at Division III schools, where over one-third (36.9%) of male athletes wagered on sports. In comparison, sports betting among female college athletes saw a slight dip between 2004, when 6.7% gambled on sporting events, and 2008, when the percentage dropped to 6.6%.

The NCAA has long supported a complete ban on college sports gambling. Naturally, Nevada-based gambling interests strongly oppose such a measure. The gaming industry points out that the problems associated with gambling on college sports are mostly related to illegal gambling, not legitimate wagering that takes place through licensed bookmakers. For example, the AGA notes in "Sports Wagering" that the $80 million to $90 million that is bet legally on the NCAA basketball tournament each year is equal to only about 4% of the sum that is bet illegally.

Since 2000 some members of Congress have advocated banning college sports betting, but they have met with little success. Among the biggest proponents of banning all gambling on college sports has been Senator

John McCain (1936–; R-AZ), the unsuccessful 2008 Republican nominee for president, who first introduced the Amateur Sports Integrity Act in 2000. Initially, the bill had Nevada gambling businesses worried, but in the end it made little progress in the face of heavy lobbying on the part of the gaming industry and a lack of public support. McCain reintroduced the bill during the next two congressional sessions, but it met the same fate. Representative Tom Osborne (1937–; R-NE), the U.S. House of Representatives sponsor of the bill, reintroduced a version in March 2005 (though McCain opted not to do so in the U.S. Senate at the time). Gaming industry representatives working against the bill claimed that it would have a devastating effect on their business, noting that college sports gambling accounts for a sizable share—as much as one-third at some bookmaking establishments—of the total bets placed with licensed Nevada bookmakers. Tony Batt reports in "McCain Joins in on NCAA Contest Fun" (*Las Vegas Review-Journal*, March 15, 2007) that by March 2007 McCain himself had apparently softened his stance on betting on college sports; indeed, his presidential campaign website invited visitors to join him in picking winners in the NCAA men's basketball tournament. In August 2009, as reported by the article "NCAA Bans Events in Some States" (Associated Press, August 7, 2009), the NCAA approved a new policy banning championship tournaments from taking place in the few states that allow betting on individual games.

ONLINE GAMBLING

The new frontier of sports gambling is the Internet. Online gambling first became available during the late 1990s, and the Nevada sports books quickly sensed that it presented a serious challenge. Many authorities argued that, based on the federal Wire Act of 1961, which was originally enacted to get organized crime out of sports betting, online sports gambling is technically illegal in the United States; however, not everybody agreed with this analysis. Moreover, most Internet gambling operations are based offshore, which complicates legal issues. The Internet knows no geographic boundaries—an online gambling operation based in Antigua can be accessed as easily from Riyadh, Saudi Arabia, as it can from Dubuque, Iowa. The U.S. government has attempted to take measures to curb online gambling, both sports betting and other types, but because these businesses are not based in the United States, enforcement is problematic. After all, these businesses are legal in the countries in which they are based.

Nobody knows exactly how much money is bet online, and the legal status of some aspects of online gambling remains ambiguous. In 2006 Congress passed the Unlawful Internet Gambling Enforcement Act (UIGEA), a provision of the Security and Accountability for Every Port Act that prohibited the transfer of wagering money over the Internet. In *Online Gambling Five Years after UIGEA* (2011, http://www.americangaming.org/files/aga/uploads/docs/whitepapers/final_online_gambling_white_paper_5-18-11.pdf), David O. Stewart of Ropes & Gray, LLP, estimates that Americans still bet roughly $4 billion per year over the Internet, although this sum represents a small proportion of the $30 billion in annual online gambling revenues that are generated worldwide. In spite of the passage of the UIGEA, Internet gambling among student-athletes actually rose between 2004 and 2008. The NCAA reports in *Results from the 2008 NCAA Study on Collegiate Wagering* that 18.8% of male college athletes reported placing sports bets online in 2008, up from only 10.9% in 2004.

The World Trade Organization has urged the United States to give up its attempts to ban Internet betting, but some members of Congress continue to champion legislation banning online gambling. The most active proponent of banning Internet gambling has been Senator Jon Kyl (1942–; R-AZ), who first introduced the Internet Gambling Prohibition Act in 1997. Others in Congress argued that rather than trying to prohibit online gambling, it should instead be regulated and taxed, generating substantial revenue for state and federal governments. Even though the UIGEA does not outlaw Internet gambling, it does prohibit U.S. financial institutions from transferring funds to and from online gambling operations. The first significant criminal case involving violations of the UIGEA occurred in April 2011, when federal authorities issued an indictment against three online poker companies on charges of engaging in illegal money transfers worth several billion dollars. The article "3 Major Online Poker Companies Targeted in Federal Crackdown" (Associated Press, April 15, 2011) indicates that all three entities—Full Tilt Poker, Absolute Poker, and PokerStars—were based outside of the United States.

The impact of the UIGEA on online sports gambling was still being assessed as of August 2011, although one immediate result was that a number of prominent online gaming establishments stopped accepting bets from U.S. customers, even though the act did not directly require them to do so. Representative Barney Frank (1940–; D-MA), backed primarily by the online poker industry, championed legislation to repeal the UIGEA, but as of August 2011 the law remained on the books.

IMPORTANT NAMES
AND ADDRESSES

Amateur Athletic Union
1910 Hotel Plaza Blvd.
Lake Buena Vista, FL 32830
(407) 934-7200
FAX: (407) 934-7242
URL: http://www.aausports.org/

American Gaming Association
1299 Pennsylvania Ave. NW, Ste. 1175
Washington, DC 20004
(202) 552-2675
FAX: (202) 552-2676
E-mail: info@americangaming.org
URL: http://www.americangaming.org/

**Association of Tennis Professionals
Tour**
201 ATP Tour Blvd.
Ponte Vedra Beach, FL 32082
(904) 285-8000
FAX: (904) 285-5966
URL: http://www.atpworldtour.com/

**Bowling Proprietors' Association of
America**
621 Six Flags Dr.
Arlington, TX 76011
1-800-343-1329
FAX: (817) 633-2940
URL: http://www.bpaa.com/

Indy Racing League
4565 W. 16th St.
Indianapolis, IN 46222
(317) 492-6526
E-mail: indycar@indycar.com
URL: http://www.indycar.com/

**International Boxing
Federation**
899 Mountain Ave., Ste. 2C
Springfield, NJ 07081
(973) 564-8046
FAX: (973) 564-8751
URL: http://www.ibf-usba-boxing.com/

International Olympic Committee
Château de Vidy, C.P. 356
CH-1007 Lausanne, Switzerland
(011-41-21) 621-6111
FAX: (011-41-21) 621-6351
URL: http://www.olympic.org/

Ladies Professional Golf Association Tour
100 International Golf Dr.
Daytona Beach, FL 32124-1092
(386) 274-6200
FAX: (386) 274-1099
URL: http://www.lpga.com/

Major League Baseball
Office of the Commissioner
245 Park Ave., 31st Floor
New York, NY 10167-0002
(212) 931-7800
FAX: (212) 949-5654
URL: http://mlb.mlb.com/index.jsp

Major League Baseball Players Association
12 E. 49th St., 24th Floor
New York, NY 10017
(212) 826-0808
FAX: (212) 752-4378
E-mail: feedback@mlbpa.org
URL: http://mlbplayers.mlb.com/pa/index.jsp

Major League Soccer
420 Fifth Ave., Seventh Floor
New York, NY 10018
(212) 450-1200
FAX: (212) 450-1302
E-mail: feedback@mlssoccer.org
URL: http://www.mlssoccer.com/

National Alliance for Youth Sports
2050 Vista Pkwy.
West Palm Beach, FL 33411
(561) 684-1141
1-800-729-2057
FAX: (561) 684-2546
E-mail: nays@nays.org
URL: http://www.nays.org/

**National Association for Stock Car Auto
Racing**
1801 W. International Speedway Blvd.
Daytona Beach, FL 32114
URL: http://www.nascar.com/

National Basketball Association
Olympic Tower
645 Fifth Ave.
New York, NY 10022
(212) 407-8000
FAX: (212) 832-3861
URL: http://www.nba.com/

National Basketball Players Association
310 Lenox Ave.
New York, NY 10027
(212) 655-0880
1-800-955-6272
FAX: (212) 655-0881
E-mail: info@nbpa.com
URL: http://www.nbpa.com/

National Collegiate Athletic Association
700 W. Washington St.
PO Box 6222
Indianapolis, IN 46206-6222
(317) 917-6222
FAX: (317) 917-6888
URL: http://www.ncaa.org/

National Football League
280 Park Ave., 15th Floor
New York, NY 10017
(212) 450-2000
FAX: (212) 681-7573
URL: http://www.nfl.com/

**National Football League Players
Association**
1133 20th St. NW
Washington, DC 20036
(202) 756-9100
1-800-372-2000
FAX: (202) 756-9320
URL: http://www.nflplayers.com/

National Hockey League
1185 Avenue of the Americas, 12th Floor
New York, NY 10036
(212) 789-2000
FAX: (212) 789-2020
URL: http://www.nhl.com/

National Hockey League Players Association
20 Bay St., Ste. 1700
Toronto, ON M5J 2N8 Canada
(416) 313-2300
FAX: (416) 313-2301
URL: http://www.nhlpa.com/

National Sporting Goods Association
1601 Feehanville Dr., Ste. 300
Mt. Prospect, IL 60056-6035
(847) 296-6742
FAX: (847) 391-9829
E-mail: info@nsga.org
URL: http://www.nsga.org/

National Thoroughbred Racing Association
2525 Harrodsburg Rd.
Lexington, KY 40504
(859) 245-6872
1-800-792-6872
FAX: (859) 223-3945
E-mail: ntra@ntra.com
URL: http://www.ntra.com/

Nevada Gaming Commission and State Gaming Control Board
1919 College Pkwy.
Carson City, NV 89706
(775) 684-7750
FAX: (775) 687-5817
URL: http://gaming.nv.gov/

Professional Bowlers Association
719 Second Ave., Ste. 701
Seattle, WA 98104
(206) 332-9688
FAX: (206) 332-9722
URL: http://www.pba.com/

Professional Golfers' Association of America
100 Avenue of the Champions
Palm Beach Gardens, FL 33410
(561) 624-8400
URL: http://www.pga.com/

Special Olympics
1133 19th St. NW
Washington, DC 20036-3604
(202) 628-3630
1-800-700-8585
FAX: (202) 824-0200
URL: http://www.specialolympics.org/

Sporting Goods Manufacturers Association
8505 Fenton St., Ste. 211
Silver Spring, MD 20910
(301) 495-6321
FAX: (301) 495-6322
E-mail: info@sgma.com
URL: http://www.sgma.com/

U.S. Anti-Doping Agency
5555 Tech Center Dr., Ste. 200
Colorado Springs, CO 80919-2372
(719) 785-2000
1-866-601-2632
FAX: (719) 785-2001
URL: http://www.usantidoping.org/

U.S. Bowling Congress
621 Six Flags Dr.
Arlington, TX 76011
1-800-514-2695
E-mail: bowlinfo@bowl.com
URL: http://www.bowl.com/

U.S. Golf Association
PO Box 708
Far Hills, NJ 07931
(908) 234-2300
FAX: (908) 234-9687
URL: http://www.usga.org/

U.S. Olympic Committee
27 South Tejon
Colorado Springs, CO 80903
1-888-222-2313
URL: http://www.teamusa.org/

U.S. Tennis Association
70 W. Red Oak Ln.
White Plains, NY 10604
(914) 696-7000
URL: http://www.usta.com/

Women's National Basketball Association
Olympic Tower
645 Fifth Ave.
New York, NY 10022

(212) 688-9622
FAX: (212) 750-9622
URL: http://www.wnba.com/

Women's Professional Soccer
1750 Montgomery St., First Floor
San Francisco, CA 94111
(415) 553-4467
FAX: (415) 553-4459
URL: http://www.womensprosoccer.com/

Women's Sports Foundation
Eisenhower Park, 1899 Hempstead Turnpike, Ste. 400
East Meadow, NY 11554
(516) 542-4700
1-800-227-3988
URL: http://www.womenssportsfoundation.org/

Women's Tennis Association
One Progress Plaza, Ste. 1500
St. Petersburg, FL 33701
(727) 895-5000
FAX: (727) 894-1982
URL: http://www.wtatennis.com/

World Boxing Association
Avenue Aquilino de la Guardia & Calle 47
Ocean Business Plaza, 14th Floor, Office 14-05
Marbella, Panama, Panama
(507) 340-6425
E-mail: info@wbanews.com
URL: http://www.wbaonline.com/

World Boxing Council
Cuzco 87
Mexico City D.F., 07300 Mexico
(52 55) 5119-5274
FAX: (52 55) 5119-5293
E-mail: contact@wbcboxing.com
URL: http://www.wbcboxing.com/

World Boxing Organization
First Federal Bldg., Ste. 711-714
1056 Muñoz Rivera Ave.
San Juan 00927 Puerto Rico
(787) 765-4444
FAX: (787) 758-9053
E-mail: boxing@wbo-int.com
URL: http://www.wbo-int.com/

RESOURCES

Much of the information in this volume that pertains to sports participation originated in surveys conducted by two industry organizations: the Sporting Goods Manufacturers Association (SGMA), which is the trade association for sporting goods manufacturers, and the National Sporting Goods Association (NSGA), the trade group for sporting goods retailers. The SGMA releases the annual *Topline Participation Report*, as well as other reports on specific aspects of sports participation. The NSGA conducts its own survey research on participation, as well as industry research on nationwide sales of sporting goods.

The U.S. Census Bureau's *Statistical Abstract of the United States: 2011* (2010) includes information on attendance at sporting events. The Census Bureau obtains these data from a variety of sources, including the major sports leagues and private market research companies.

Polling data provided by Harris Interactive were key in assembling information on the preferences of sports fans, including trends that are related to race, gender, age, and geography.

"Sports and Television" (2011) by the Museum of Broadcast Communications provided information on the history of sports on television. Another key source on this topic, as well as other aspects of sports media, was *The Business of Sports* (2004), edited by Scott R. Rosner and Kenneth L. Shropshire. *The Business of Sports* provides comprehensive coverage of all economic aspects of the sports industry. Besides sports media, the book includes essential information on the financial structure of professional team sports, college sports, and the Olympics. Also, the *SportsBusiness Journal* provided valuable information on the way that Americans use social media to engage with sports.

Nonprofit advocacy and public education groups provided substantial information for this volume. Child Trends provided data on exercise and fitness trends among young people. The Women's Sports Foundation offered research on gender equity in sports. Another key source of information on gender equity was *Women in Intercollegiate Sport: A Longitudinal, National Study—Thirty-Three Year Update, 1977–2010* (2010) by R. Vivian Acosta and Linda Jean Carpenter.

The National Collegiate Athletic Association (NCAA) provided a wealth of data on many aspects of college sports. Key NCAA publications that contributed information include *1981–82–2009–10 NCAA Sports Sponsorship and Participation Rates Report* (Erin Zgonc, November 2010), *1999–2000–2009–10 NCAA Student-Athlete Ethnicity Report* (Erin Zgonc, September 2010), *2004–10 Revenues and Expenses of NCAA Division I Intercollegiate Athletics Programs Report* (Daniel L. Fulks, August 2011), and *Academics and Athletes: Education and Research* (2010). Information on eligibility rules for college athletes was found in the NCAA's *2011–12 Guide for the College-Bound Student-Athlete* (2011).

The Nielsen Company offered a range of data on national sports viewing trends. Team-by-team revenue and valuation figures were provided by *Forbes*, and *SportsBusiness Journal* provided data on sports media contracts. Most of the information about the structure and workings of the major sports leagues came from the leagues themselves. Likewise, information about the PGA Tour, the Association of Tennis Professionals Tour, the National Association for Stock Car Auto Racing, the various boxing organizations, and other nonteam sports was obtained from the websites of these organizations. Revenues from Sports Venues, a company specializing in directories and other publications about the sports venue industry, also provided helpful information.

The International Olympic Committee (IOC) provided helpful information about the structure and workings of the Olympic movement. Two important IOC factsheets, "Olympic Summer Games" (January 2010) and "Olympic Winter

Games" (December 2010), offered detailed information on diverse Olympics sites throughout history.

The Healthy People 2020 website, which is managed by the U.S. Department of Health and Human Services (HHS), provided valuable information about government-sponsored fitness and healthy living initiatives. The HHS publication *2008 Physical Activity Guidelines for Americans* (October 2008) also offered insights into various health benefits that are associated with physical exercise.

The American Gaming Association and the Nevada Gaming Commission and State Gaming Control Board were useful sources of information on legal sports gambling. Fairleigh Dickinson University's PublicMind Poll provided information about the prevalence of and attitudes toward gambling among the American public.

INDEX

National Collegiate Athletic Association (NCAA)

O